Mike Mignola's
HELLBOY ™

WEIRD TALES
Volume Two

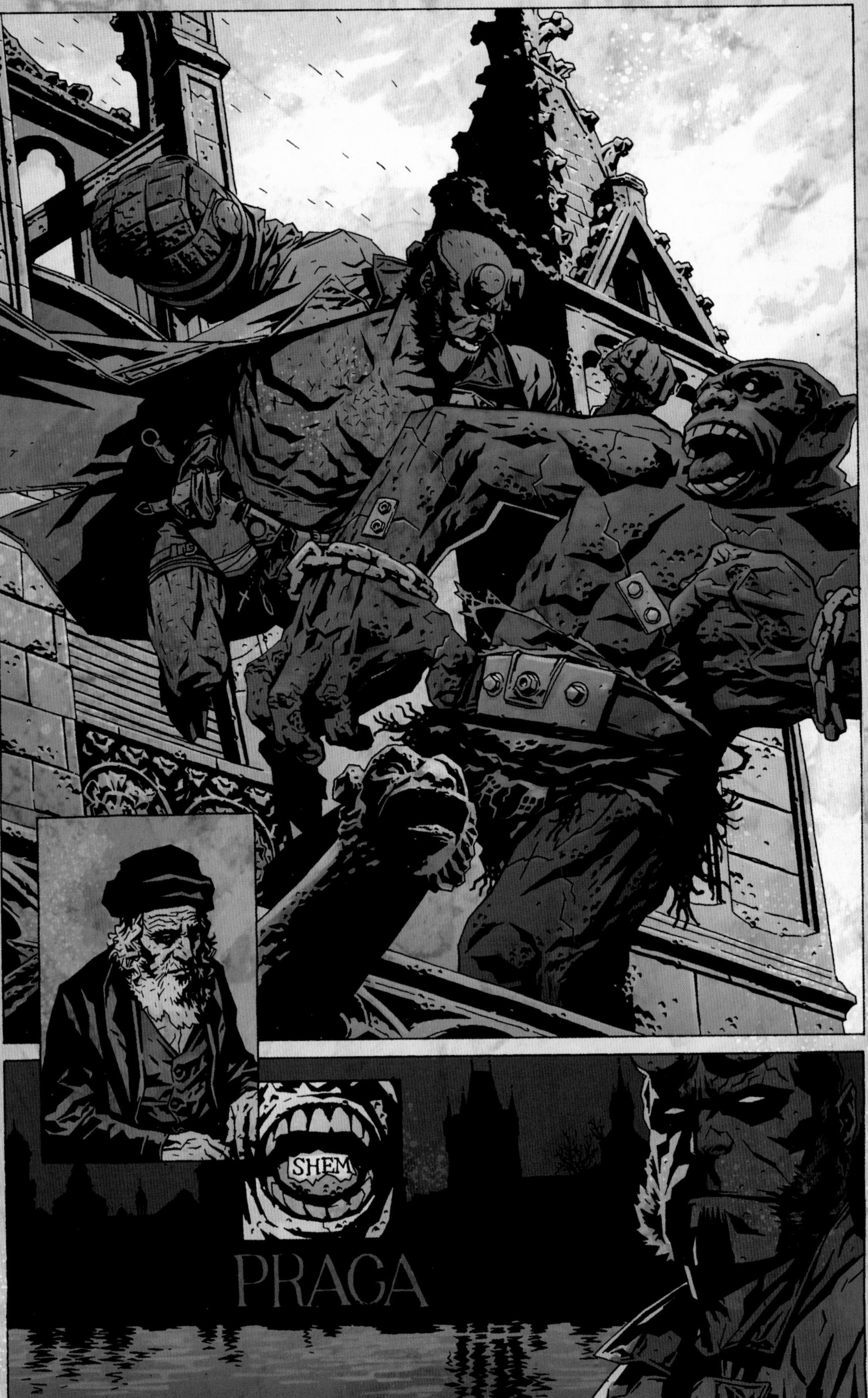
SHEM
PRAGA

MIKE MIGNOLA'S

HELLBOY ™

WEIRD TALES
Volume Two

KIA ASAMIYA, LEE BERMEJO, HADEN BLACKMAN

JOHN CASSADAY, FRANK CHO, GENE COLAN, EVAN DORKIN

TOMMY LEE EDWARDS, TOM FASSBENDER, GARY FIELDS

MICHAEL WM. KALUTA, RON MARZ, SCOTT MORSE

PHIL NOTO, JIM PASCOE, DOUG PETRIE, WILL PFEIFER

STEVE PURCELL, P. CRAIG RUSSELL, JIM STARLIN, DAVE STEVENS

CAMERON STEWART, BEN TEMPLESMITH, CRAIG THOMPSON

JILL THOMPSON, KEV WALKER, SIMEON WILKINS

J.H. WILLAMS III & AKIRA YOSHIDA

✠

Cover art by MIKE MIGNOLA

Cover colors by DAVE STEWART

Edited by SCOTT ALLIE *with* MATT DRYER

Collection designed by RICHARD E. JONES

Published by MIKE RICHARDSON

DARK HORSE BOOKS™

Published by Dark Horse Books
a division of Dark Horse Comics, Inc.
10956 SE Main Street
Milwaukie, OR 97222
www.darkhorse.com

First edition: October 2004
ISBN: 1-56971-953-5

This volume collects issues five through eight and the "Lobster Johnson" strips serialized
in issues one through eight of the Dark Horse comic-book series, *Hellboy: Weird Tales*.

1 3 5 7 9 10 8 6 4 2

Printed in China

INTRODUCTION

by SCOTT ALLIE

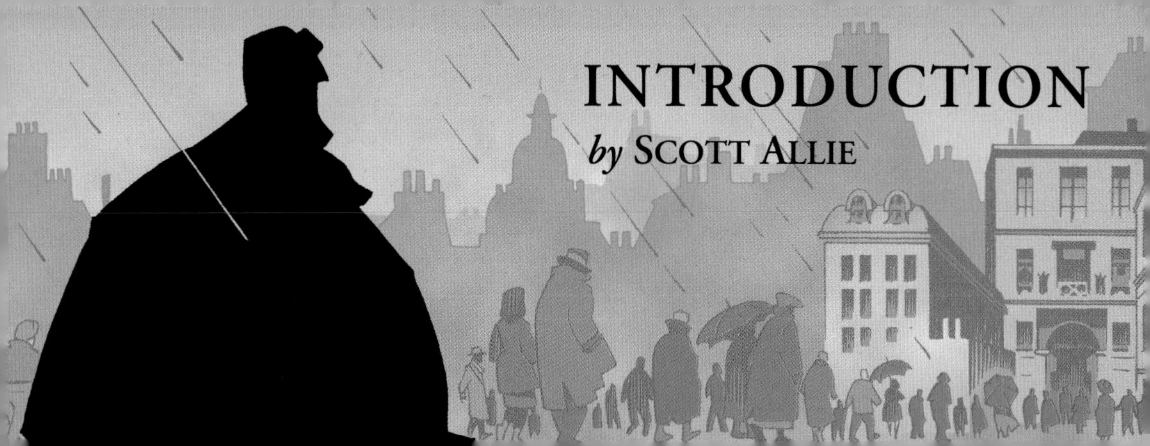

CONTENTS

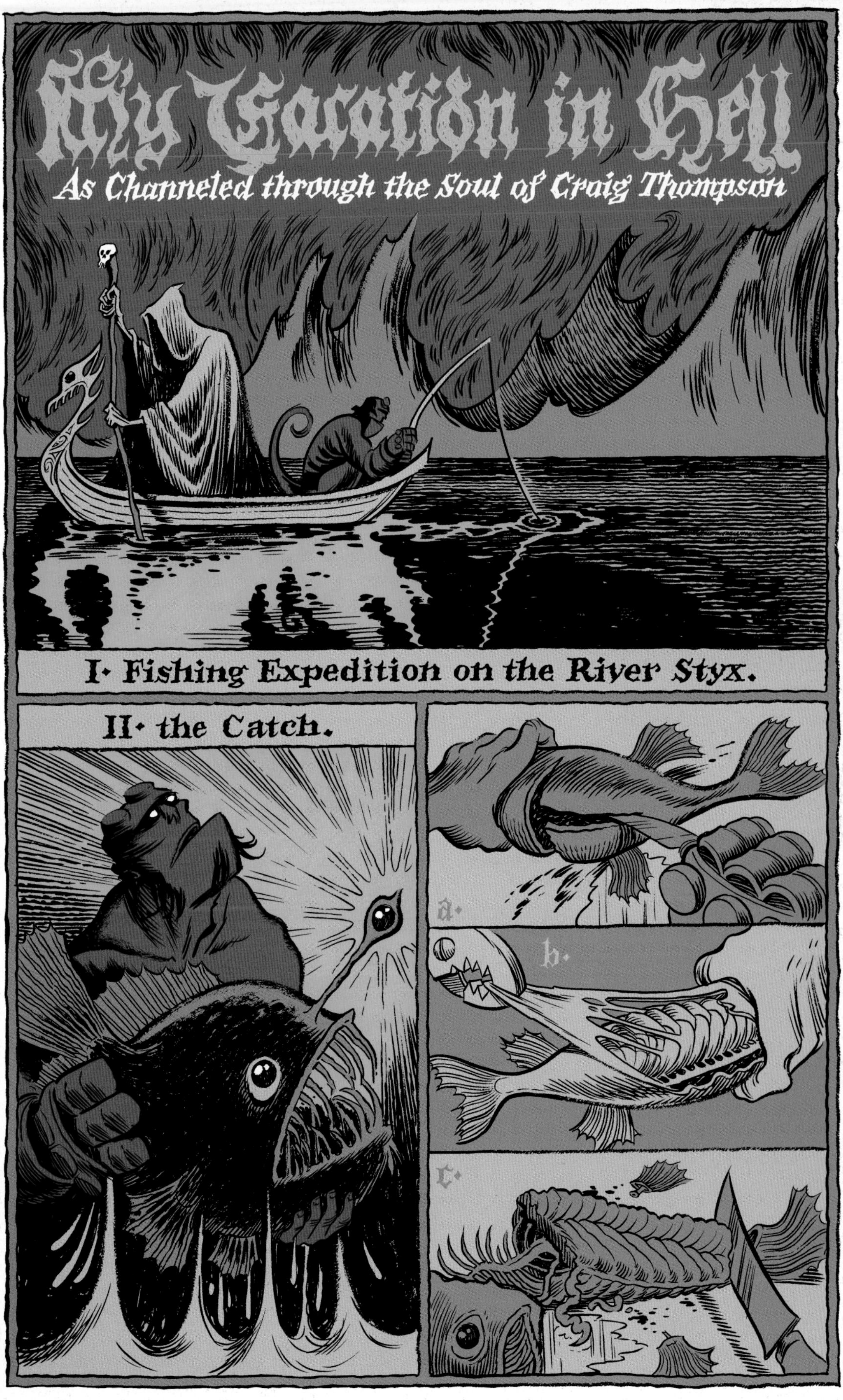

My Vacation in Hell
As Channeled through the Soul of Craig Thompson
I· Fishing Expedition on the River Styx.
II· the Catch.
a·
b·
c·

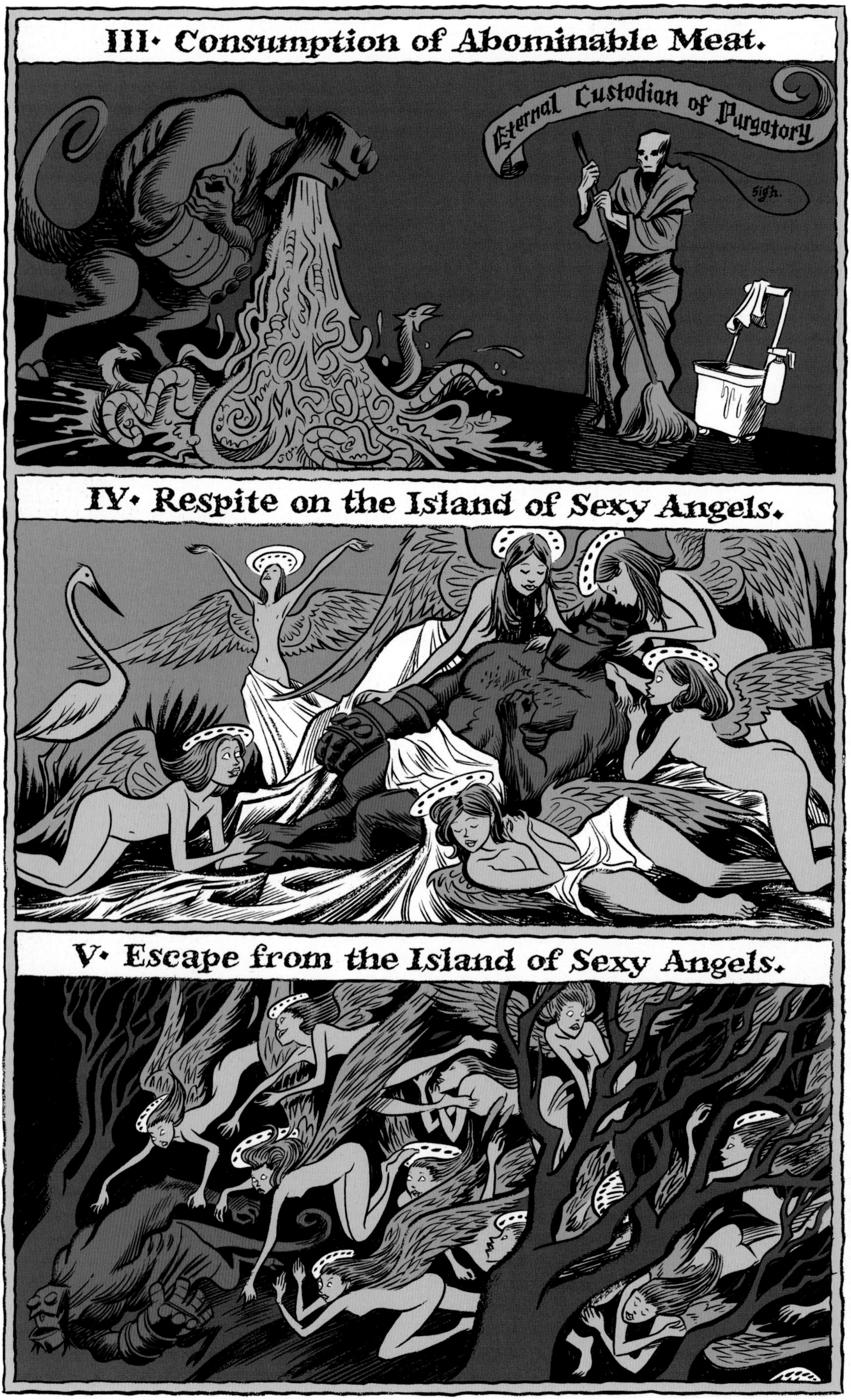
III· Consumption of Abominable Meat.
Eternal Custodian of Purgatory
sigh.
IV· Respite on the Island of Sexy Angels.
V· Escape from the Island of Sexy Angels.

VI· Beneath the Island of Sexy Angels.

VII· Evening with the Lake of Fire Symphony.

VIII· Butt-Trumpet Induced Headache.

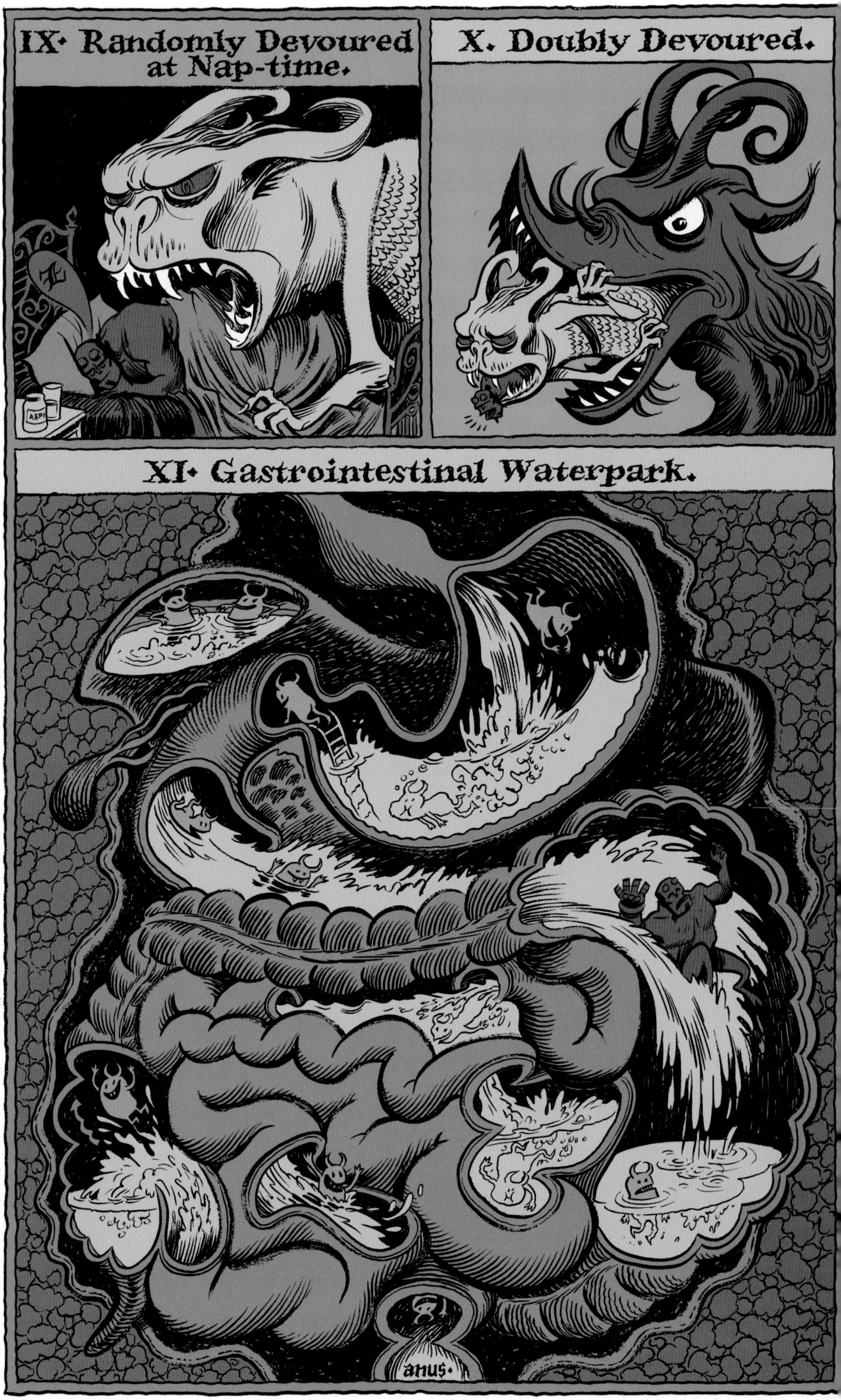
IX• Randomly Devoured at Nap-time.
ASPI
X. Doubly Devoured.
XI• Gastrointestinal Waterpark.
anus.

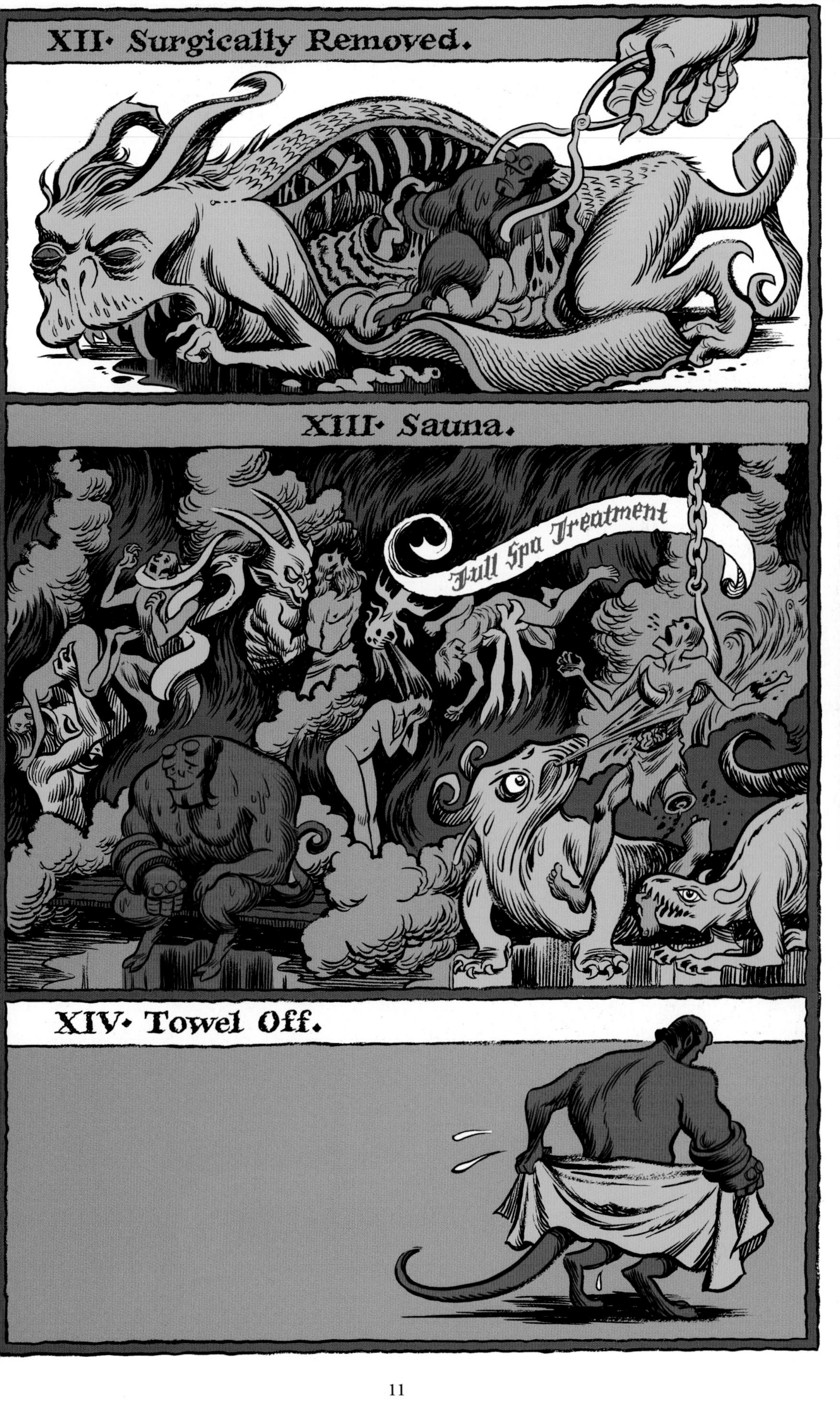
XII· Surgically Removed.
XIII· Sauna.
Full Spa Treatment
XIV· Towel Off.

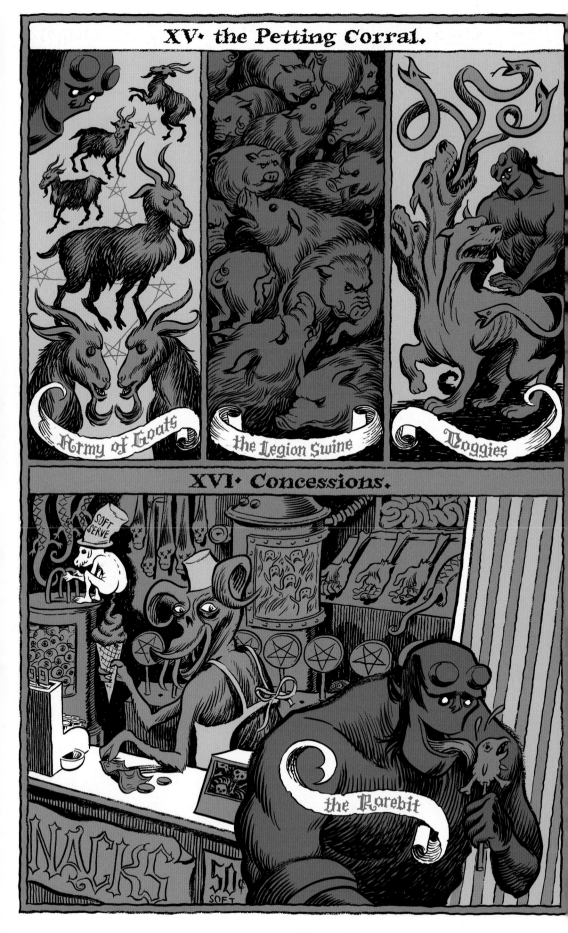

XV· the Petting Corral.

Army of Goats

the Legion Swine

Doggies

XVI· Concessions·

the Rarebit

12

XVII. the Bad Dream.

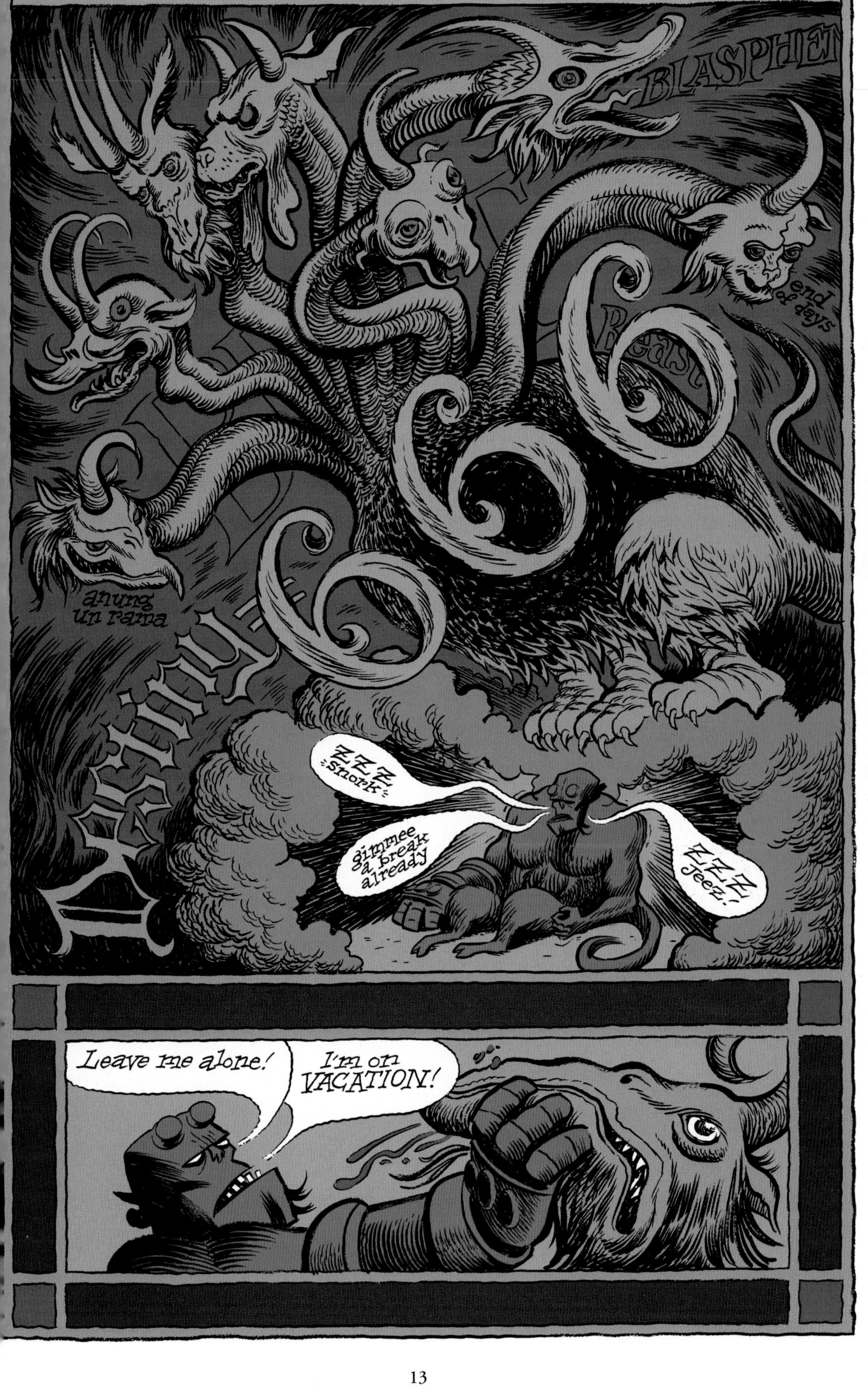

end of days
Beast
anung un rama
ZZZ snork
gimmee a break already
ZZZ Jeez!
Leave me alone!
I'm on VACATION!

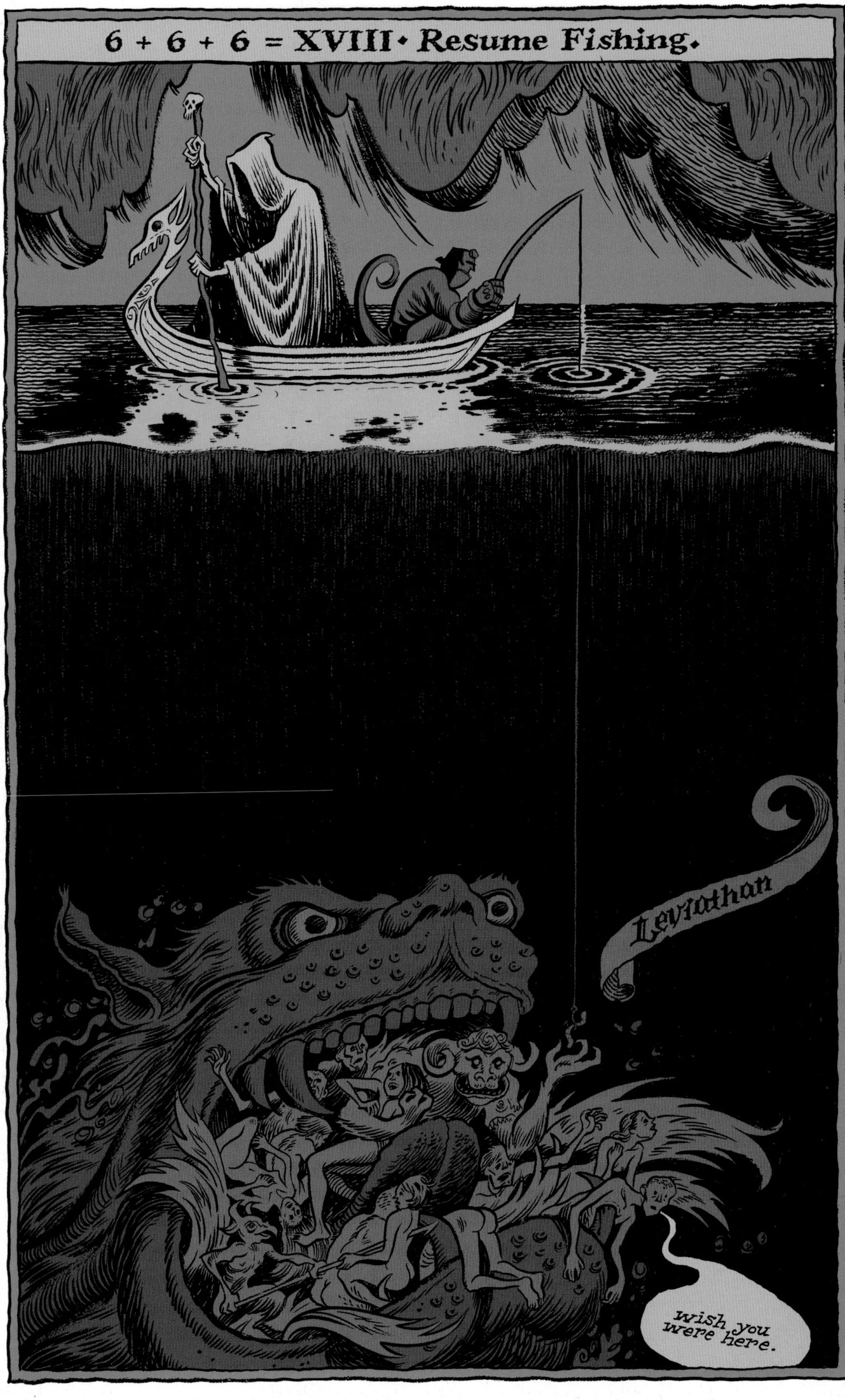
6 + 6 + 6 = XVIII • Resume Fishing.
Leviathan
wish you were here.

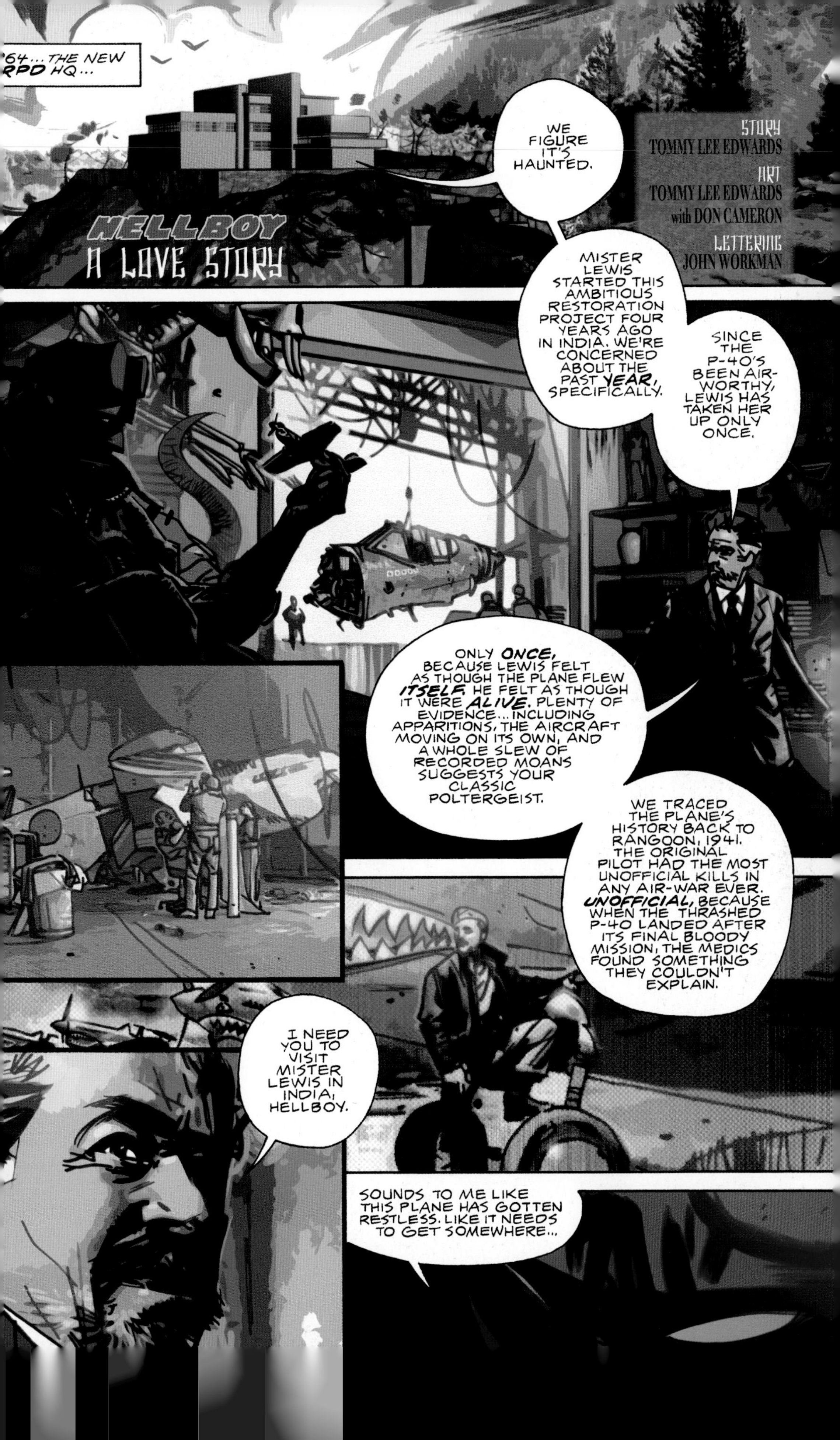
'64... THE NEW
RPD HQ...
WE FIGURE IT'S HAUNTED.
STORY TOMMY LEE EDWARDS
ART TOMMY LEE EDWARDS with DON CAMERON
LETTERING JOHN WORKMAN
HELLBOY
A LOVE STORY
MISTER LEWIS STARTED THIS AMBITIOUS RESTORATION PROJECT FOUR YEARS AGO IN INDIA. WE'RE CONCERNED ABOUT THE PAST YEAR, SPECIFICALLY.
SINCE THE P-40'S BEEN AIR-WORTHY, LEWIS HAS TAKEN HER UP ONLY ONCE.
ONLY ONCE, BECAUSE LEWIS FELT AS THOUGH THE PLANE FLEW ITSELF. HE FELT AS THOUGH IT WERE ALIVE. PLENTY OF EVIDENCE... INCLUDING APPARITIONS, THE AIRCRAFT MOVING ON ITS OWN, AND A WHOLE SLEW OF RECORDED MOANS SUGGESTS YOUR CLASSIC POLTERGEIST.
WE TRACED THE PLANE'S HISTORY BACK TO RANGOON, 1941. THE ORIGINAL PILOT HAD THE MOST UNOFFICIAL KILLS IN ANY AIR-WAR EVER. UNOFFICIAL, BECAUSE WHEN THE THRASHED P-40 LANDED AFTER ITS FINAL BLOODY MISSION, THE MEDICS FOUND SOMETHING THEY COULDN'T EXPLAIN.
I NEED YOU TO VISIT MISTER LEWIS IN INDIA, HELLBOY.
SOUNDS TO ME LIKE THIS PLANE HAS GOTTEN RESTLESS. LIKE IT NEEDS TO GET SOMEWHERE...

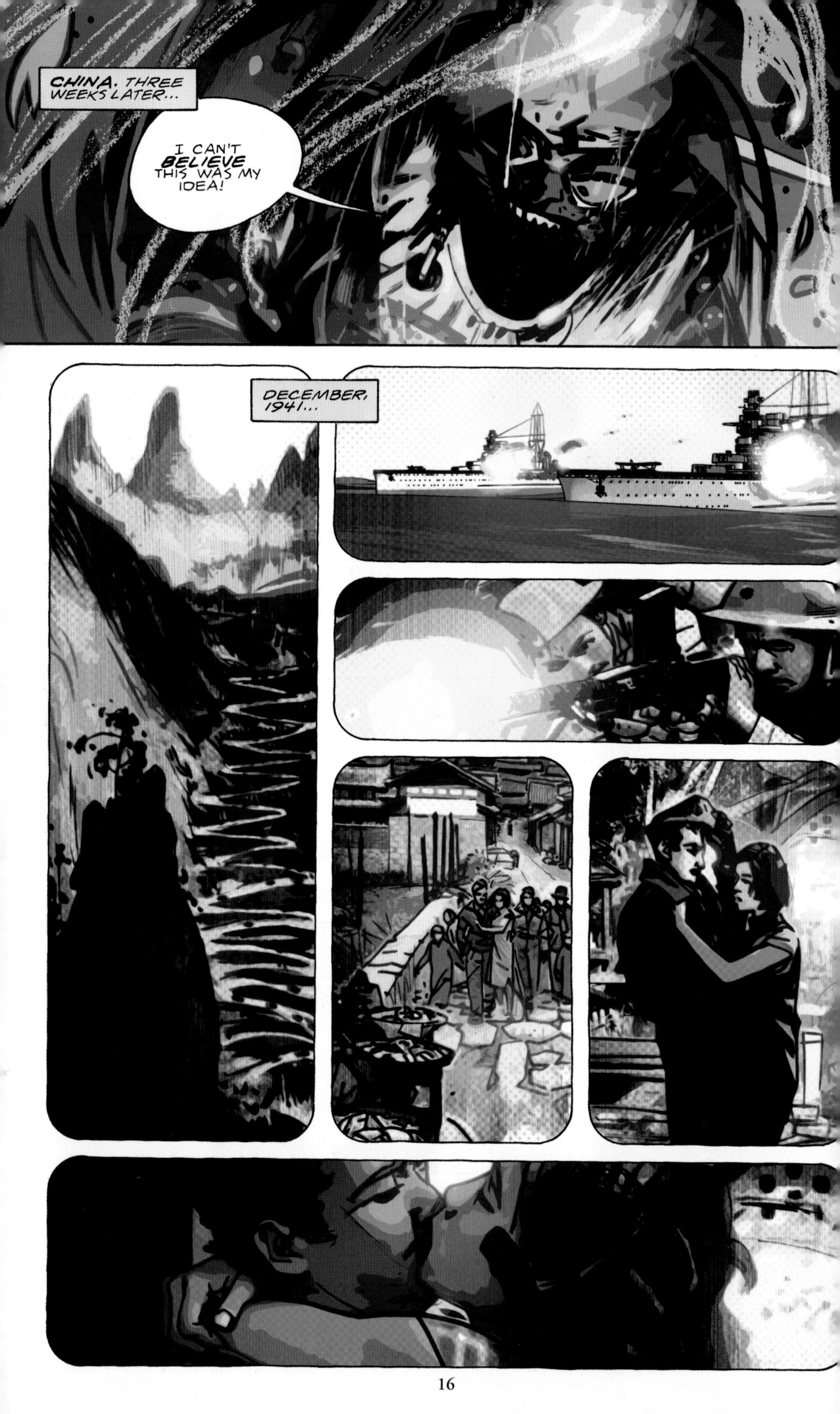
CHINA. THREE WEEKS LATER...
I CAN'T BELIEVE THIS WAS MY IDEA!
DECEMBER, 1941...

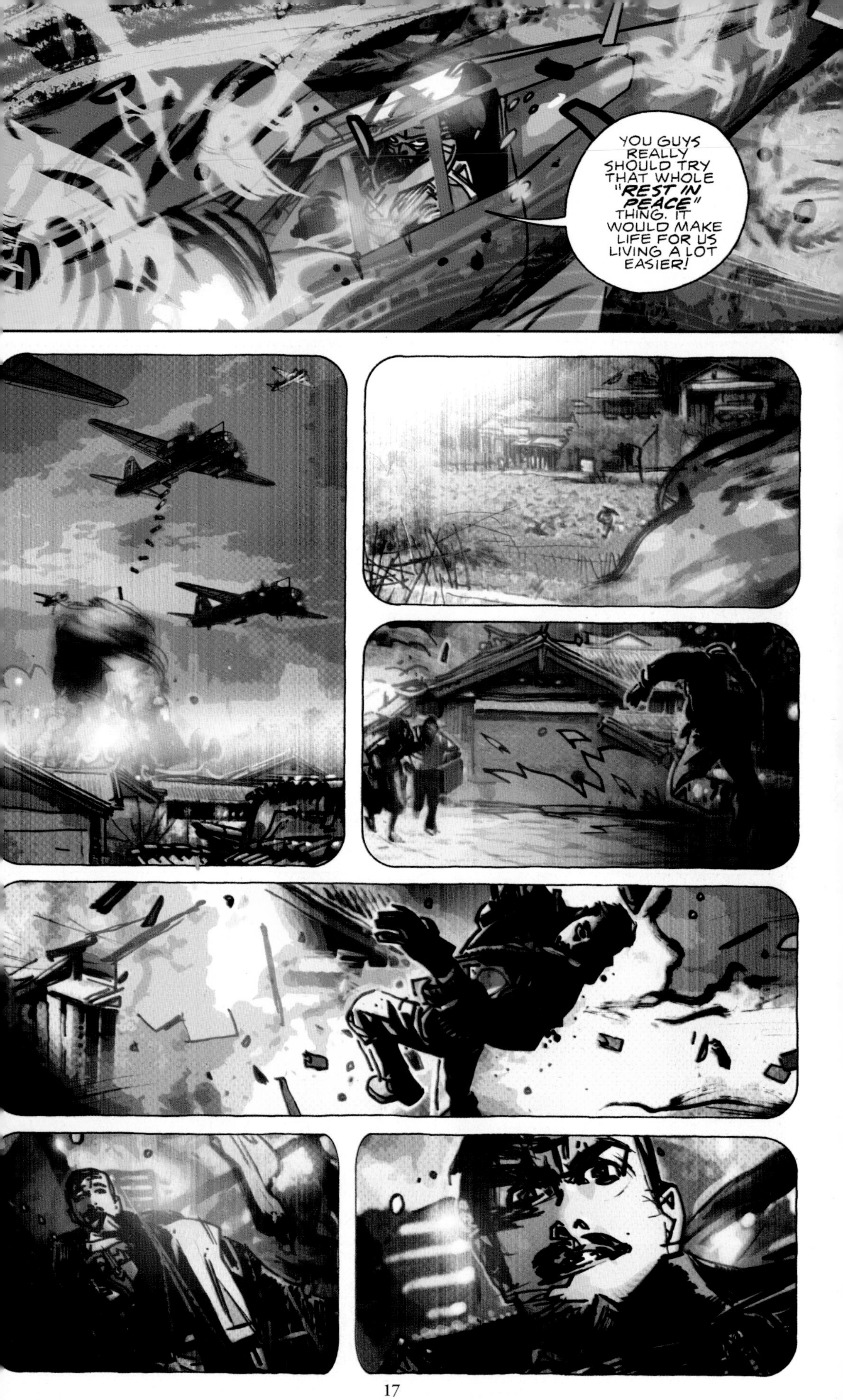
YOU GUYS REALLY SHOULD TRY THAT WHOLE "REST IN PEACE" THING. IT WOULD MAKE LIFE FOR US LIVING A LOT EASIER!

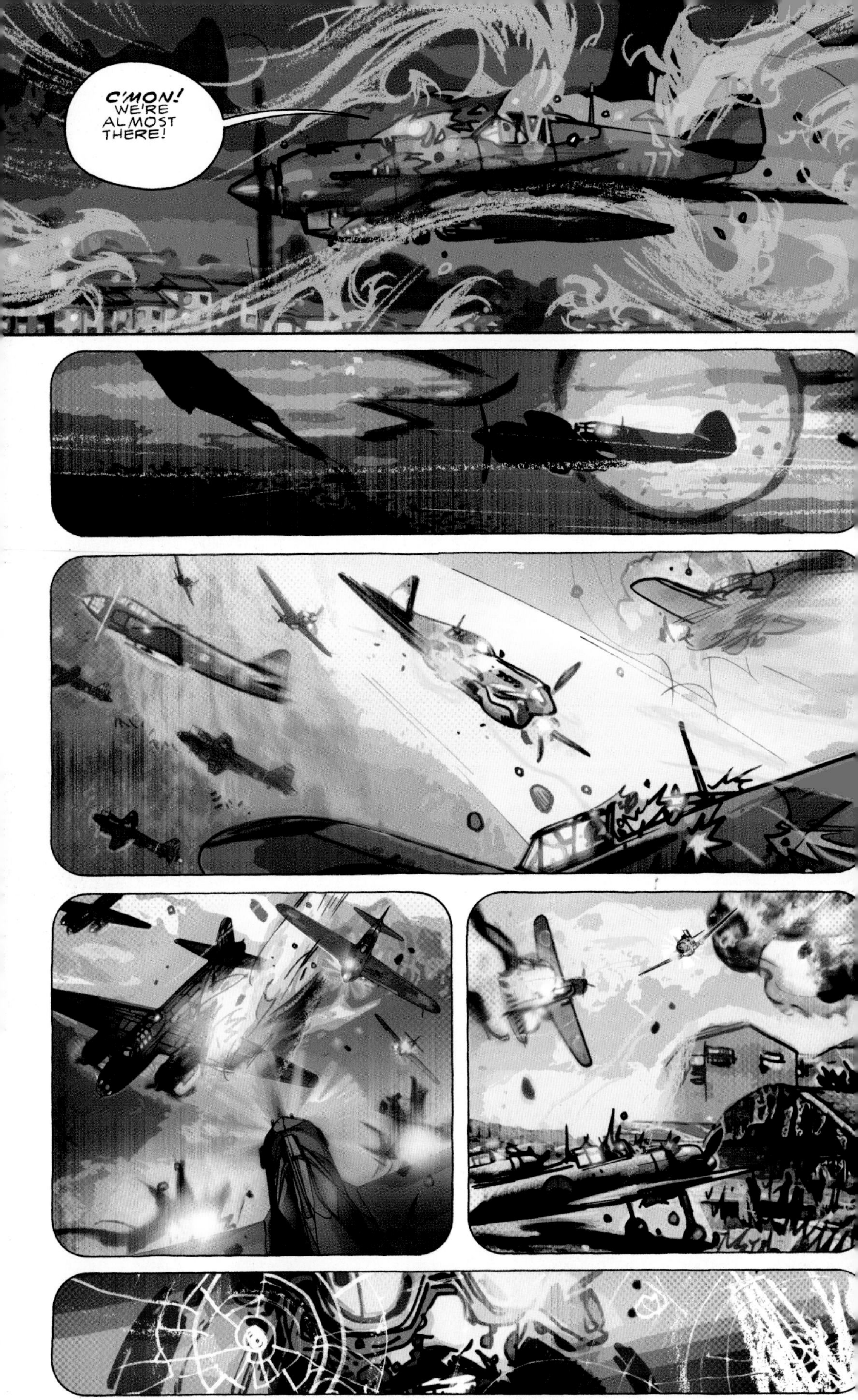
C'MON! WE'RE ALMOST THERE!

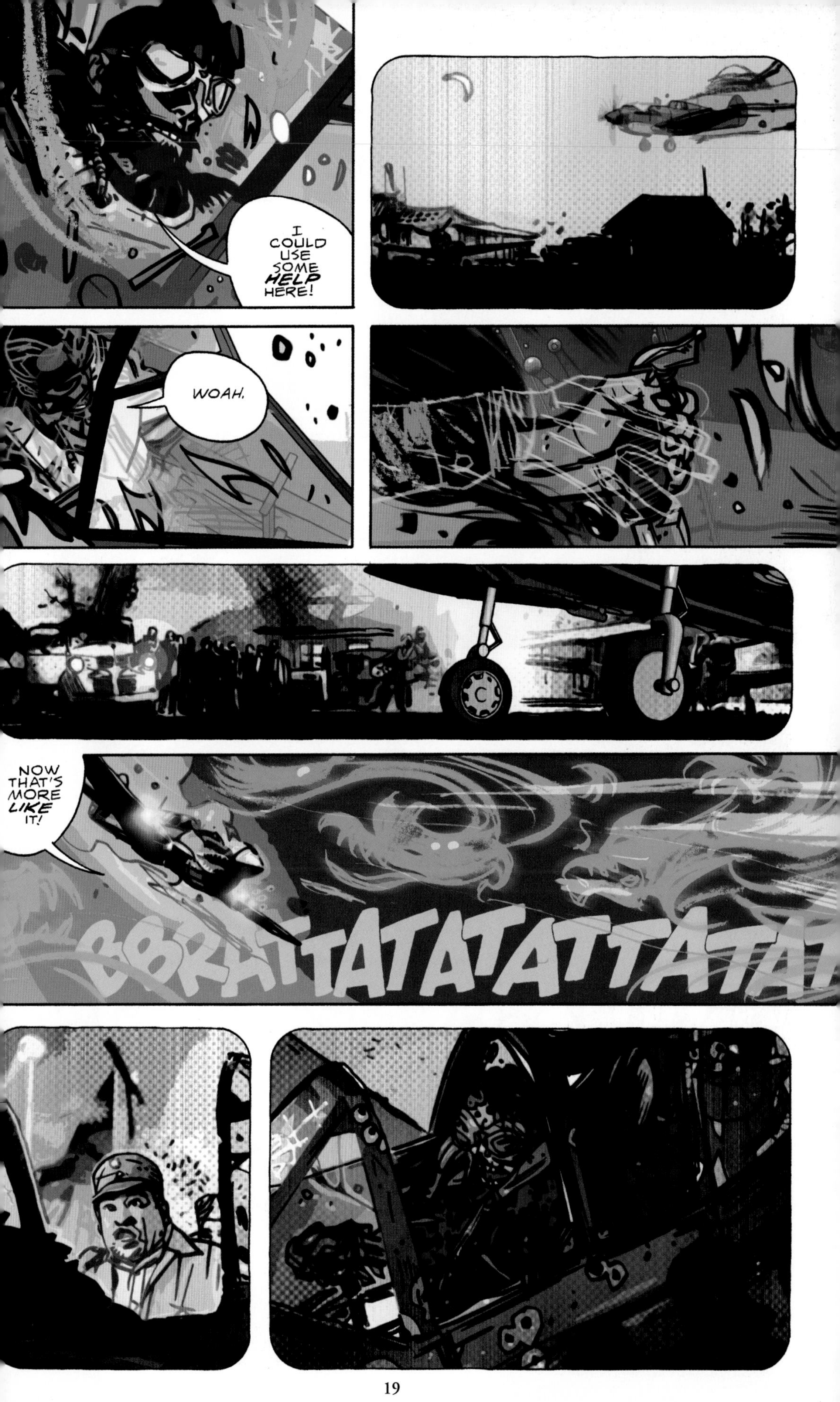
I COULD USE SOME HELP HERE!
WOAH.
NOW THAT'S MORE LIKE IT!
BBRATTATATATTATAT

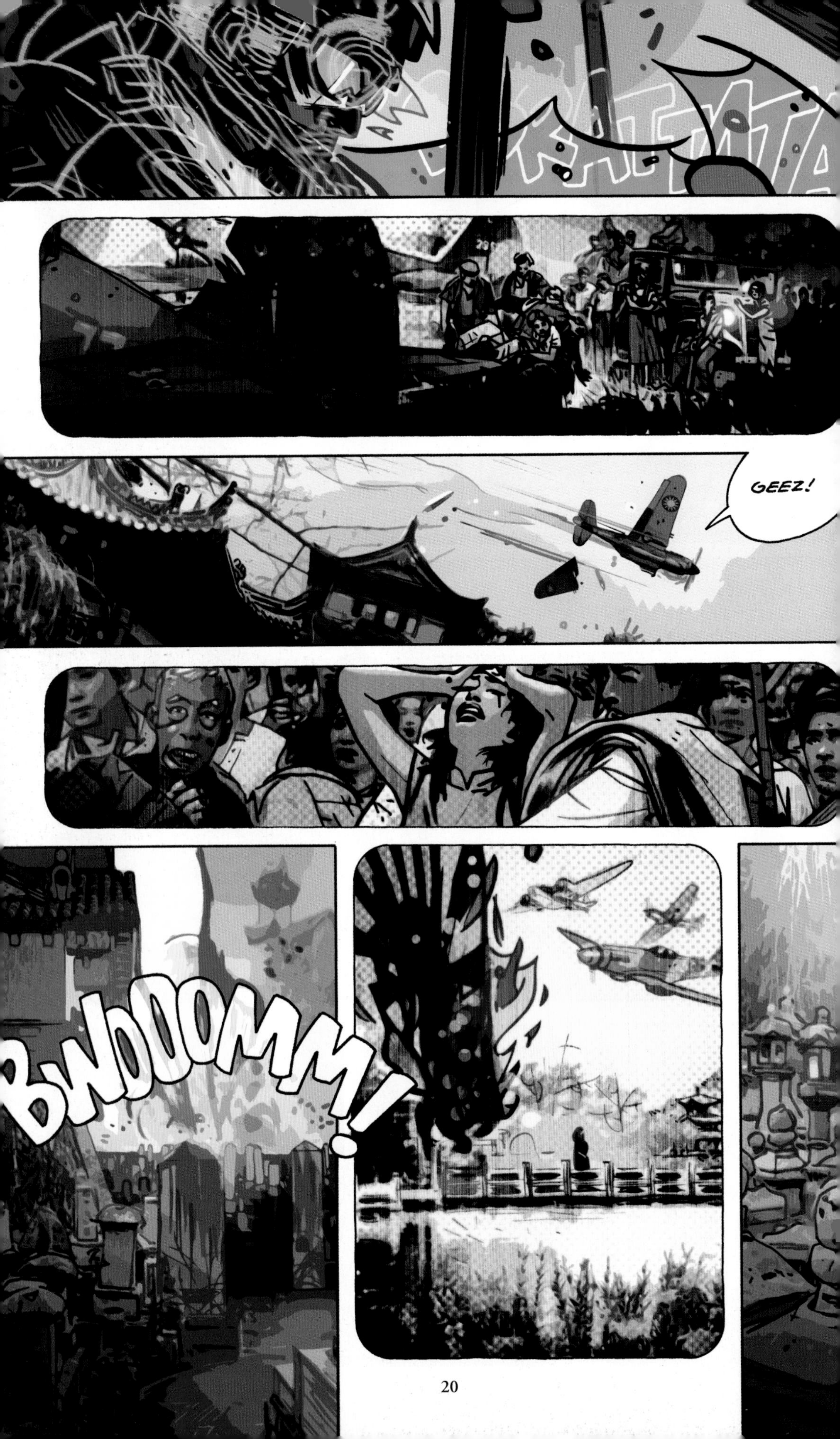
GEEZ!
BWOOOMM!

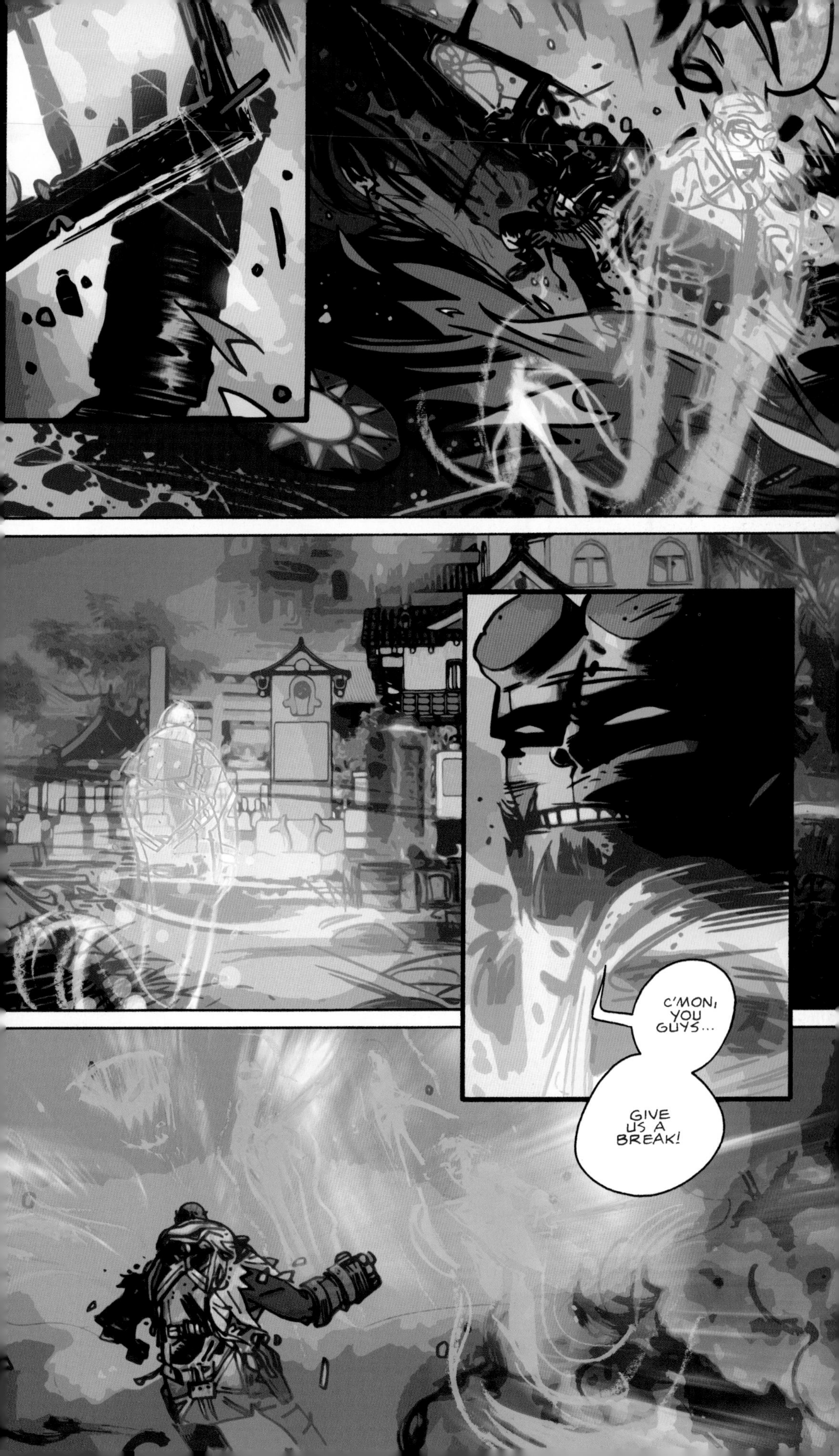
C'MON, YOU GUYS...
GIVE US A BREAK!

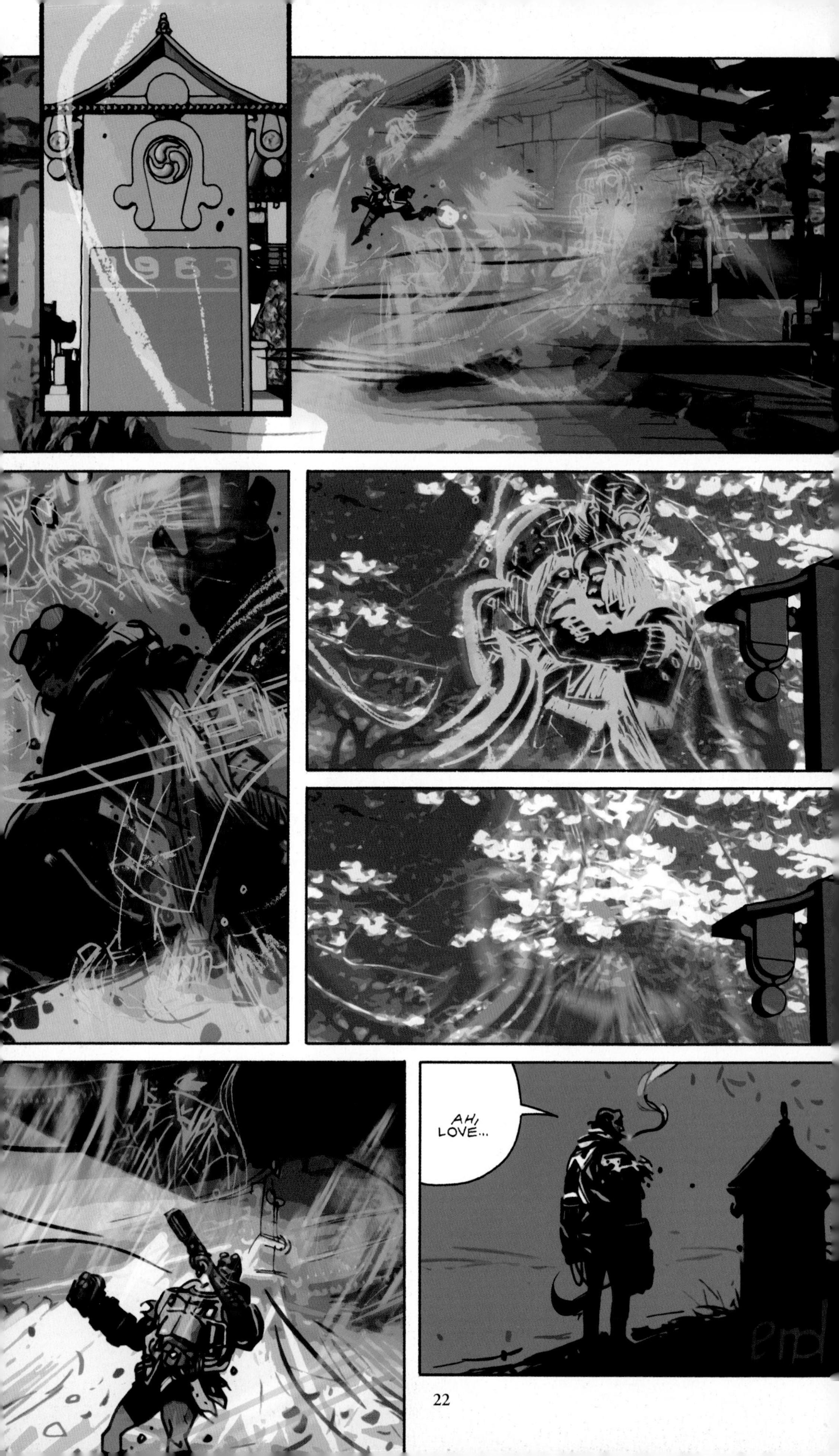
1963
AH, LOVE...
end

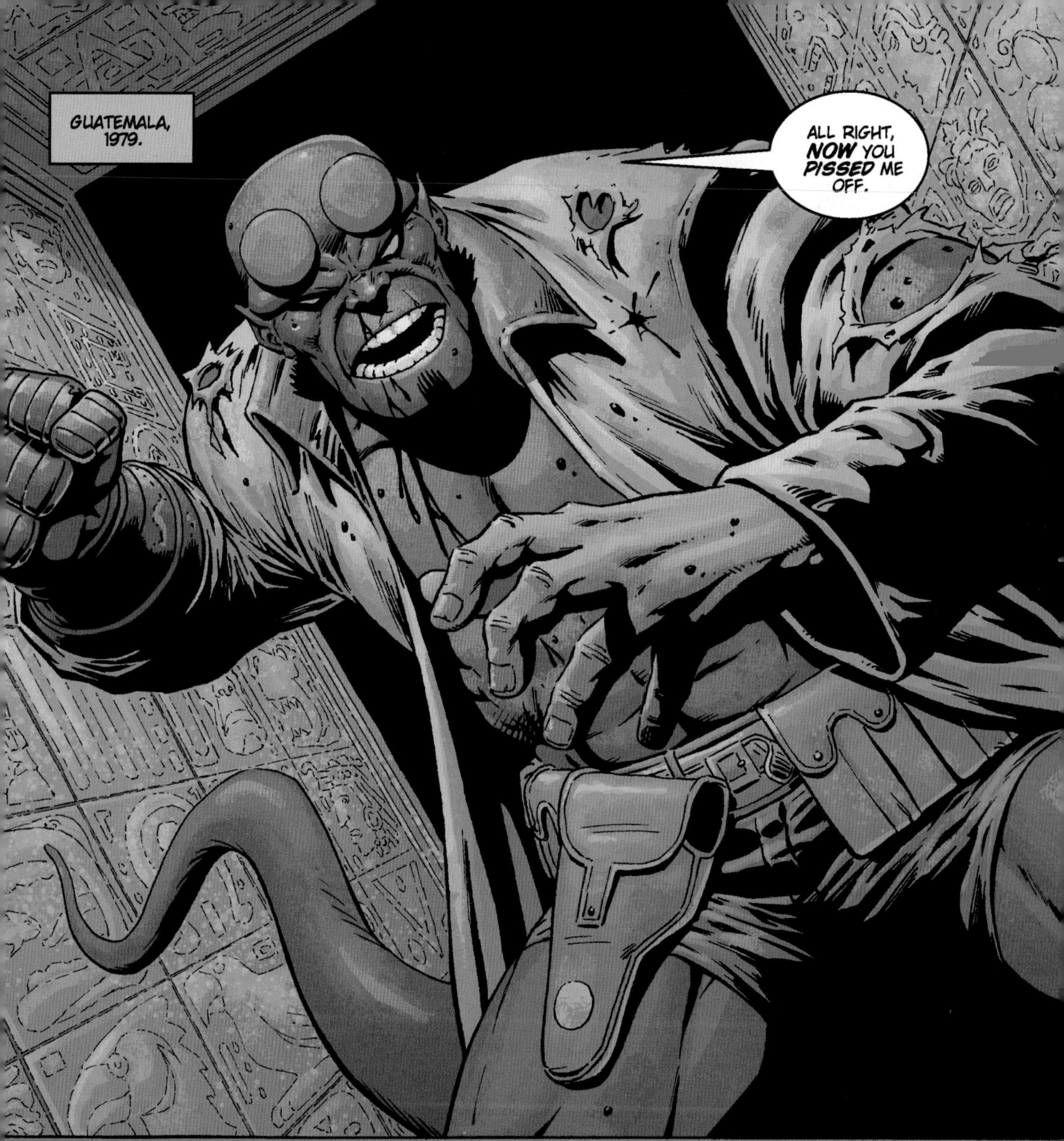
GUATEMALA, 1979.
ALL RIGHT, **NOW** YOU ***PISSED*** ME OFF.

SHATTERED

MARZ STARLIN STEWART MADSEN

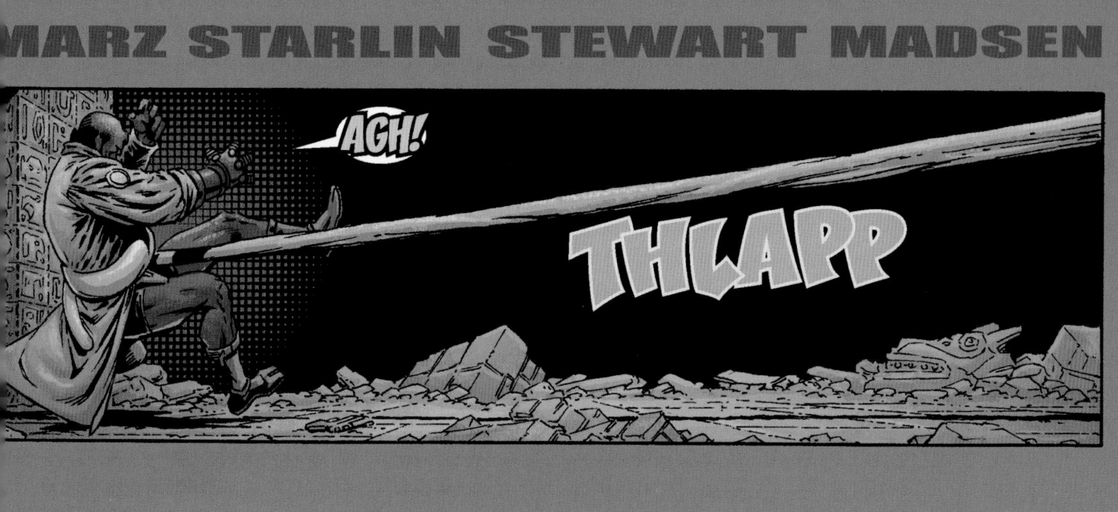
AGH!
THLAPP

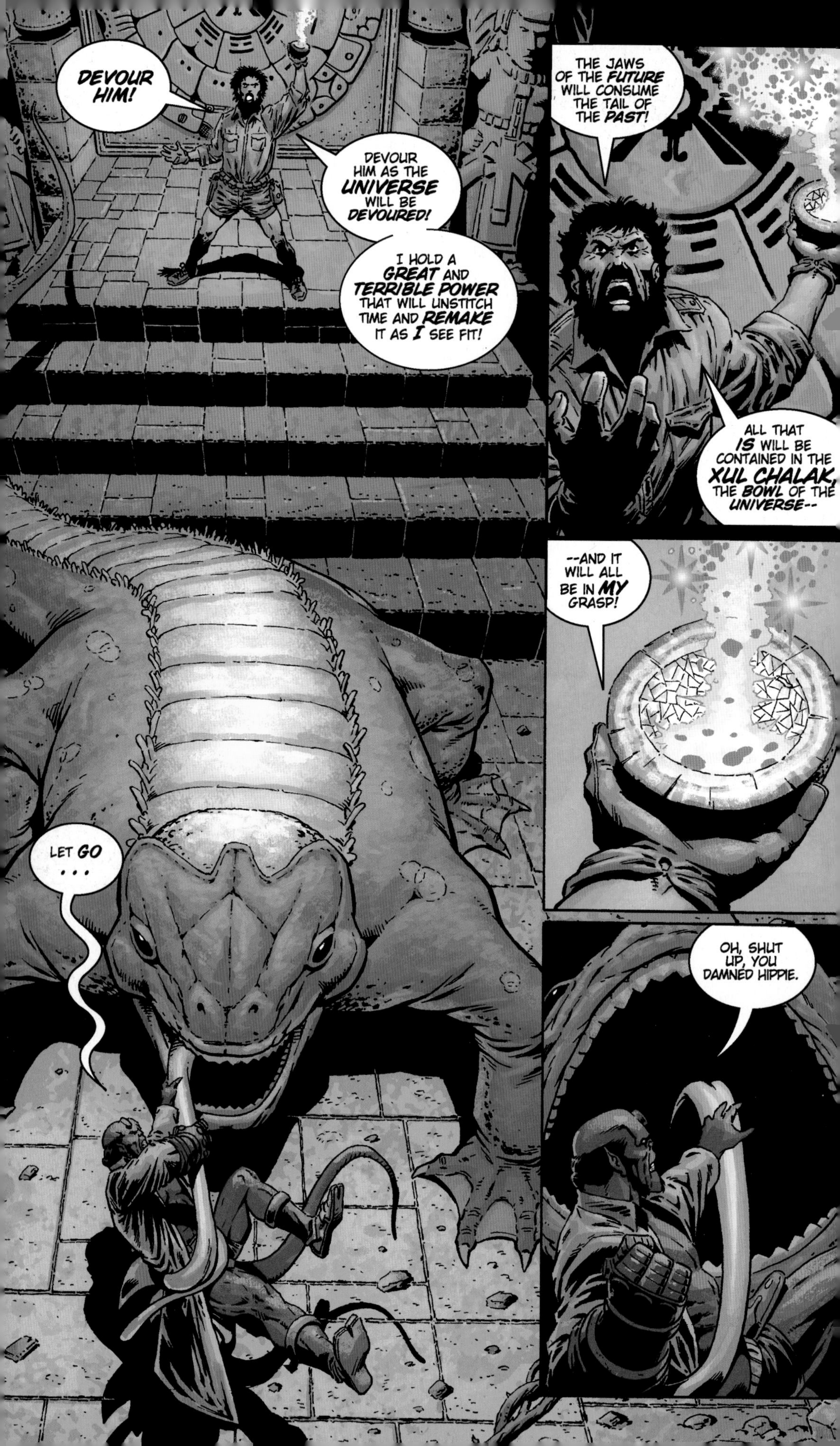
DEVOUR HIM!
DEVOUR HIM AS THE UNIVERSE WILL BE DEVOURED!
I HOLD A GREAT AND TERRIBLE POWER THAT WILL UNSTITCH TIME AND REMAKE IT AS I SEE FIT!
THE JAWS OF THE FUTURE WILL CONSUME THE TAIL OF THE PAST!
ALL THAT IS WILL BE CONTAINED IN THE XUL CHALAK, THE BOWL OF THE UNIVERSE--
--AND IT WILL ALL BE IN MY GRASP!
LET GO . . .
OH, SHUT UP, YOU DAMNED HIPPIE.

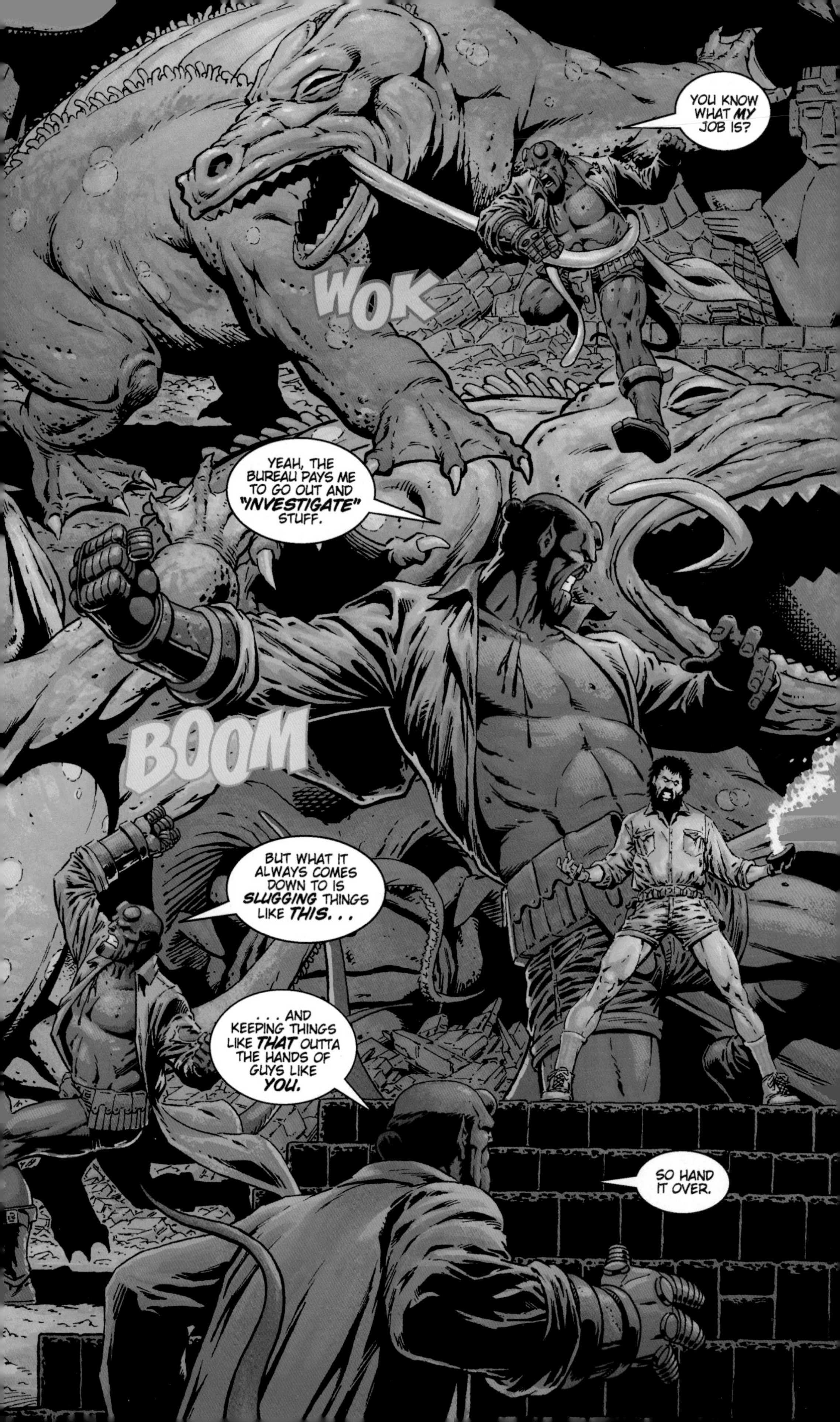
YOU KNOW WHAT MY JOB IS?
WOK
YEAH, THE BUREAU PAYS ME TO GO OUT AND "INVESTIGATE" STUFF.
BOOM
BUT WHAT IT ALWAYS COMES DOWN TO IS SLUGGING THINGS LIKE THIS. . .
. . . AND KEEPING THINGS LIKE THAT OUTTA THE HANDS OF GUYS LIKE YOU.
SO HAND IT OVER.

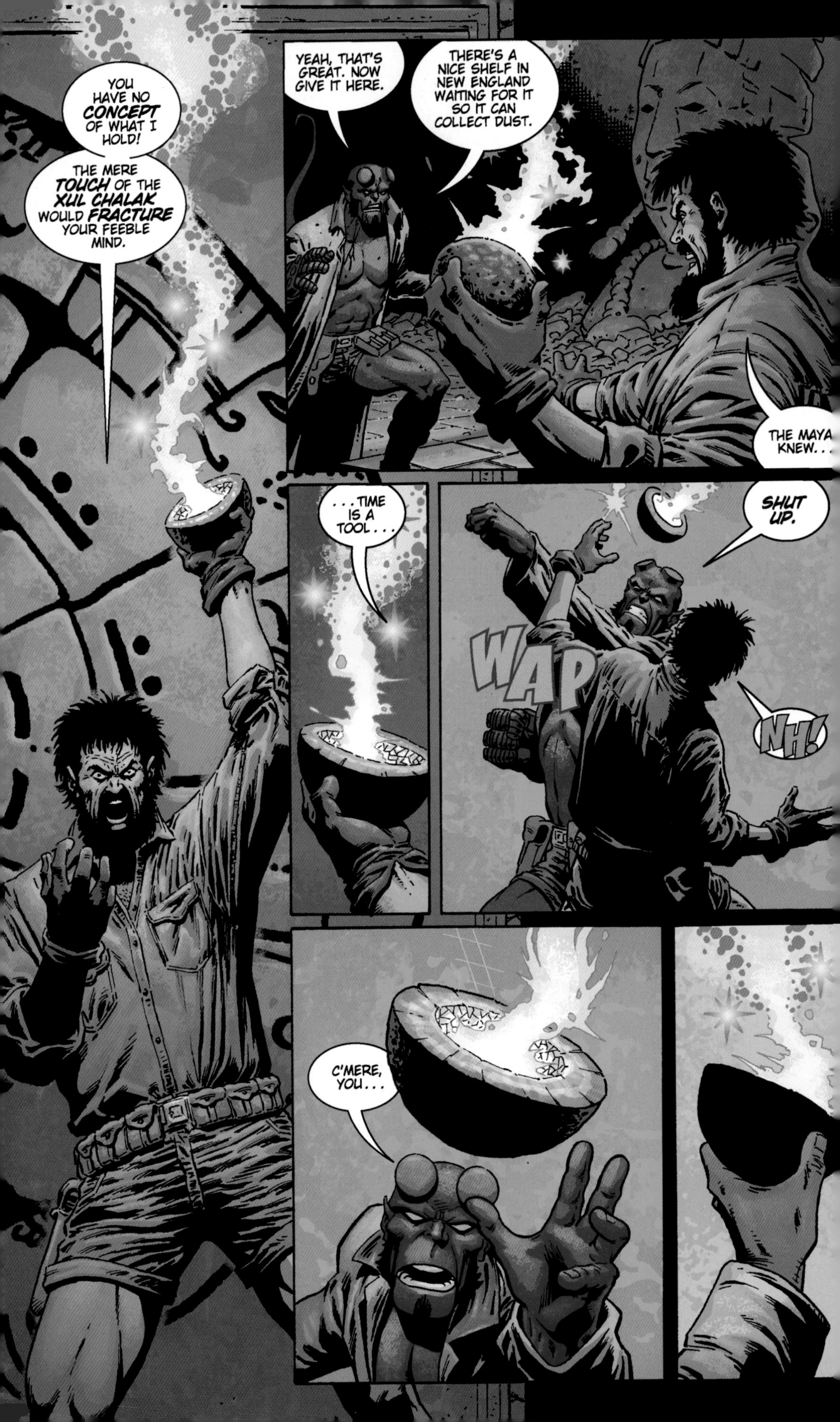
YOU HAVE NO CONCEPT OF WHAT I HOLD!
THE MERE TOUCH OF THE XUL CHALAK WOULD FRACTURE YOUR FEEBLE MIND.
YEAH, THAT'S GREAT. NOW GIVE IT HERE.
THERE'S A NICE SHELF IN NEW ENGLAND WAITING FOR IT SO IT CAN COLLECT DUST.
THE MAYA KNEW...
...TIME IS A TOOL...
SHUT UP.
WAP
NH!
C'MERE, YOU...

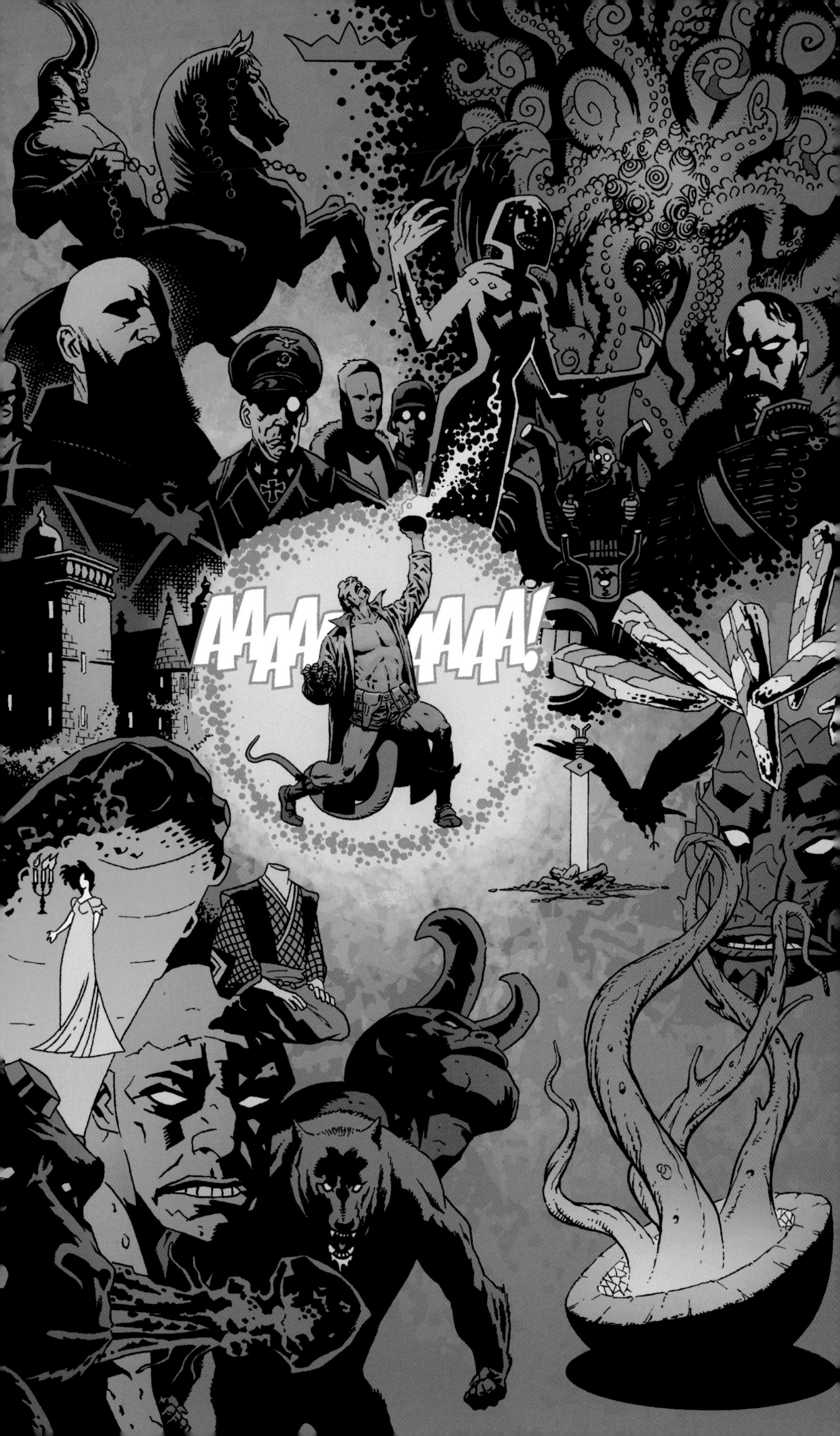
AAAA AAAA!

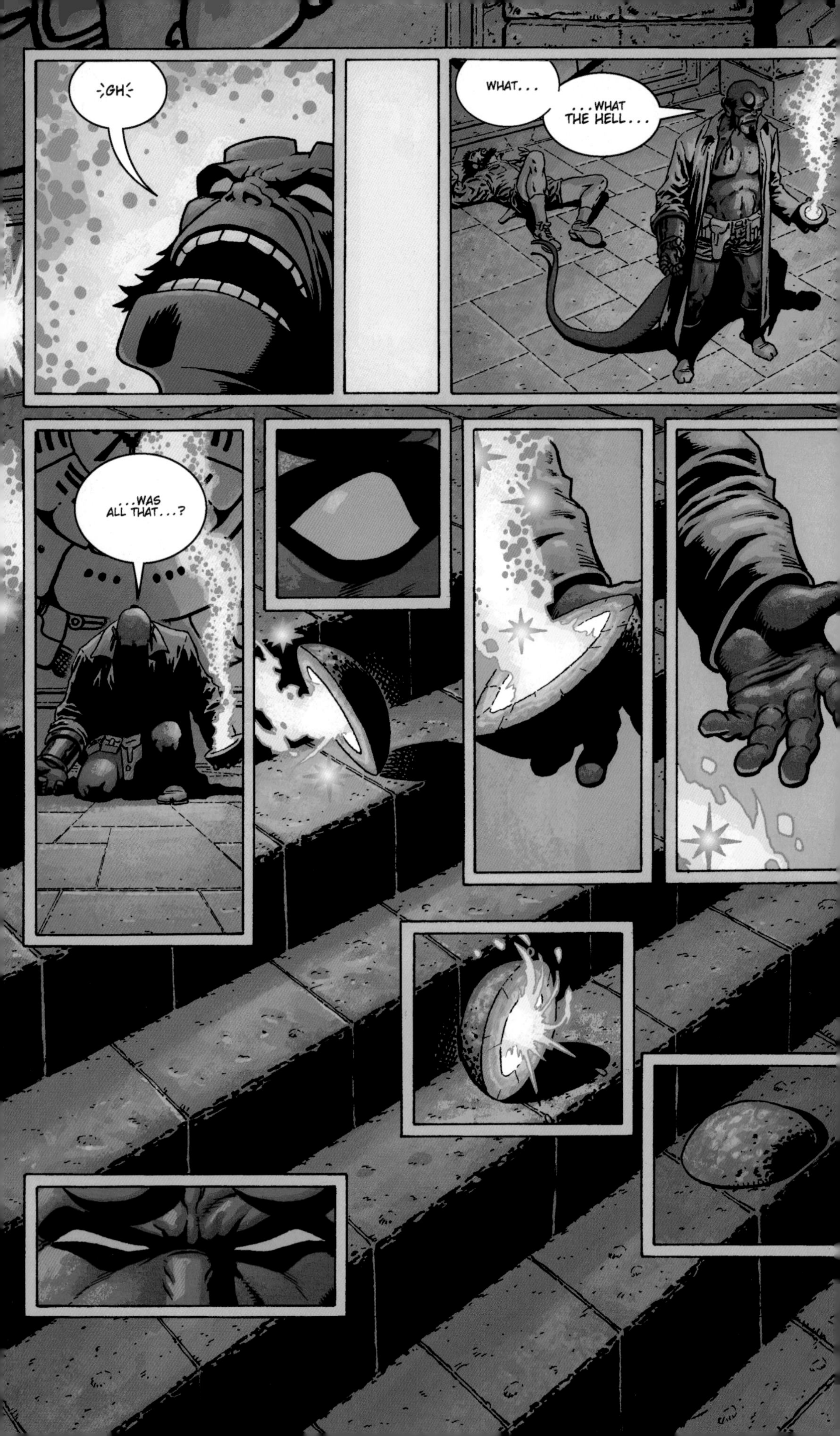

GH
WHAT...
...WHAT THE HELL...
...WAS ALL THAT...?

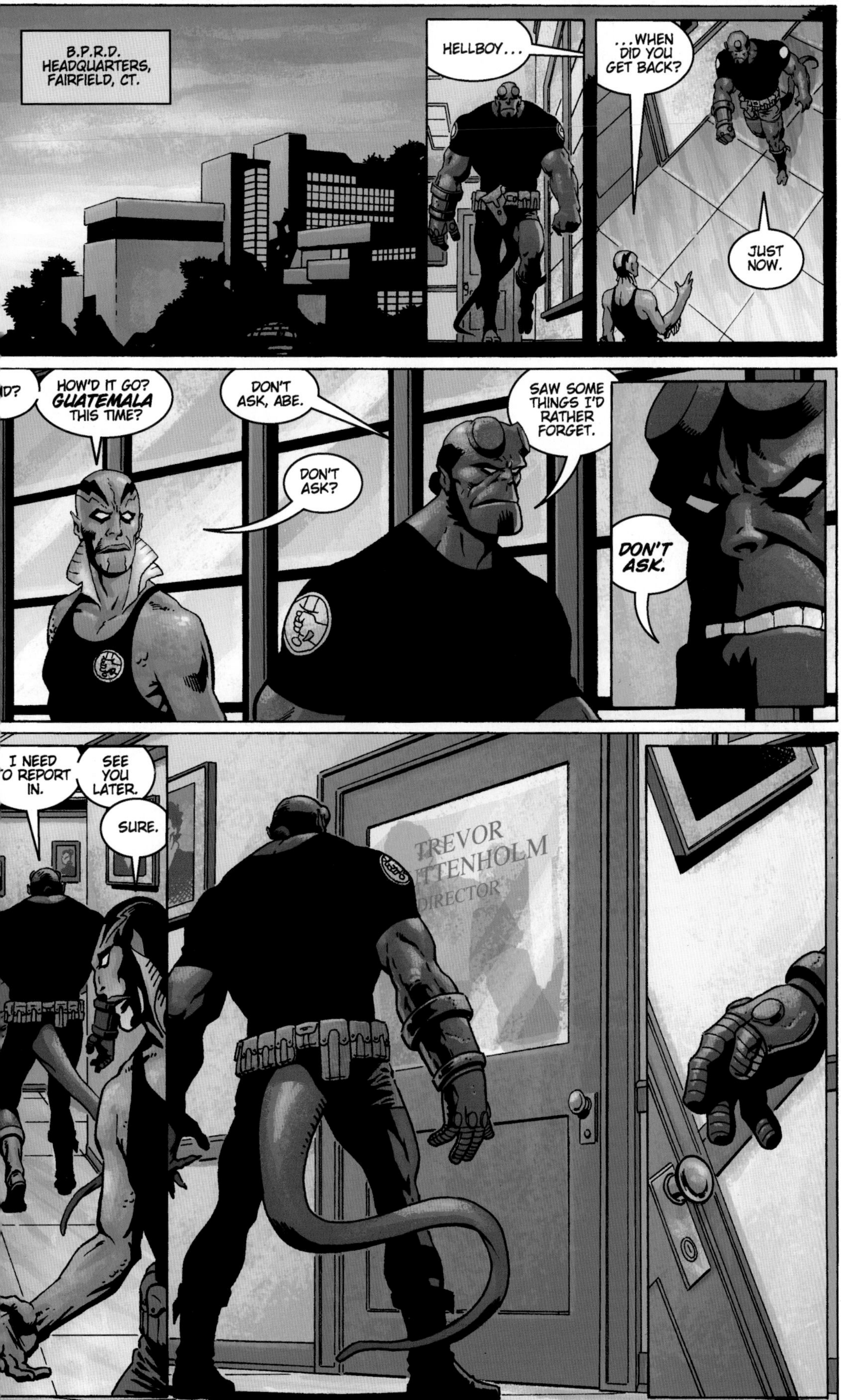
B.P.R.D. HEADQUARTERS, FAIRFIELD, CT.
HELLBOY...
...WHEN DID YOU GET BACK?
JUST NOW.
D?
HOW'D IT GO? **GUATEMALA** THIS TIME?
DON'T ASK, ABE.
DON'T ASK?
SAW SOME THINGS I'D RATHER FORGET.
DON'T ASK.
I NEED O REPORT IN.
SEE YOU LATER.
SURE.
TREVOR
TTENHOLM
DIRECTOR

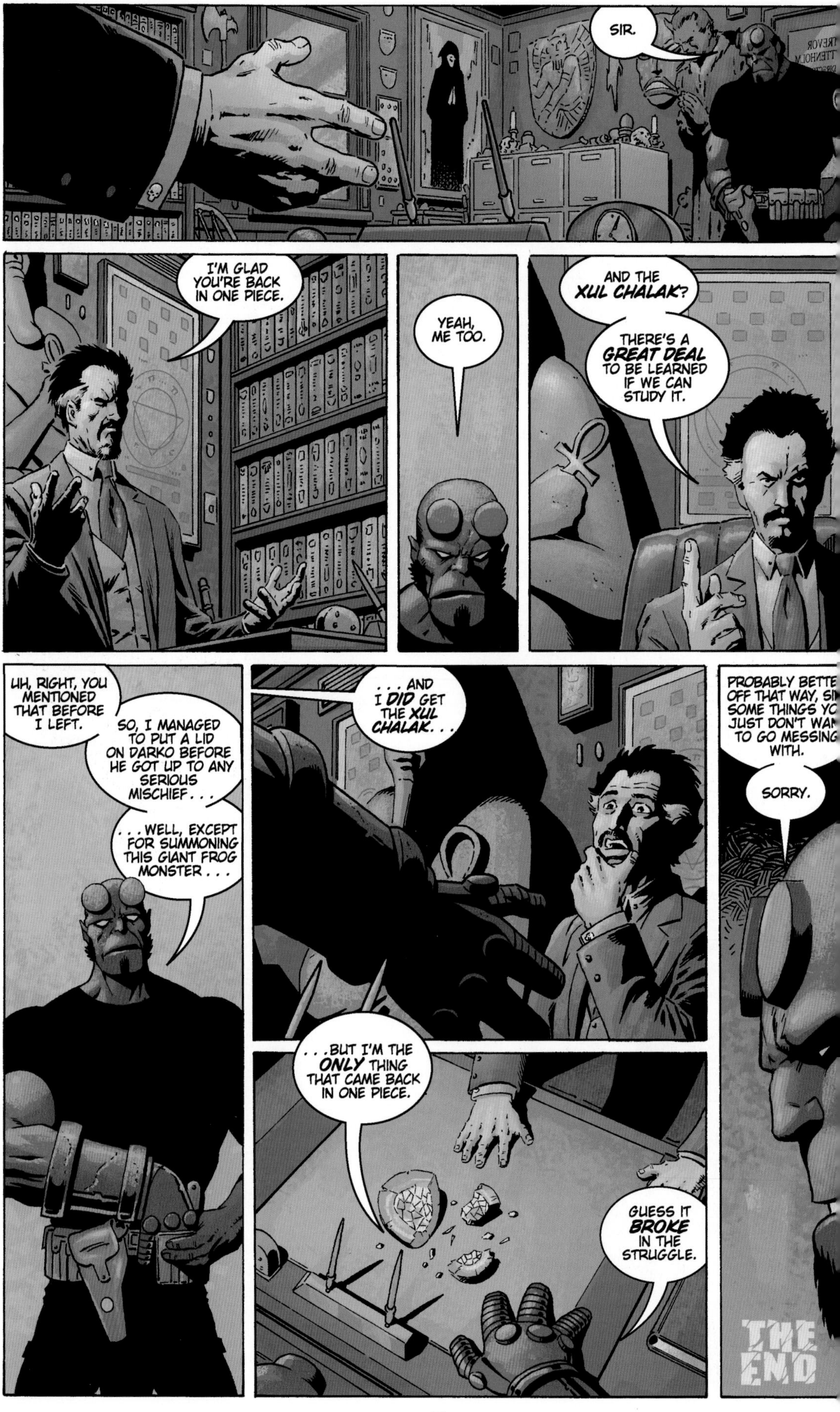
SIR.
I'M GLAD YOU'RE BACK IN ONE PIECE.
YEAH, ME TOO.
AND THE XUL CHALAK?
THERE'S A GREAT DEAL TO BE LEARNED IF WE CAN STUDY IT.
UH, RIGHT, YOU MENTIONED THAT BEFORE I LEFT.
SO, I MANAGED TO PUT A LID ON DARKO BEFORE HE GOT UP TO ANY SERIOUS MISCHIEF . . .
. . . WELL, EXCEPT FOR SUMMONING THIS GIANT FROG MONSTER . . .
. . . AND I DID GET THE XUL CHALAK . . .
. . . BUT I'M THE ONLY THING THAT CAME BACK IN ONE PIECE.
GUESS IT BROKE IN THE STRUGGLE.
PROBABLY BETTE OFF THAT WAY, SI SOME THINGS YO JUST DON'T WA TO GO MESSING WITH.
SORRY.
THE END

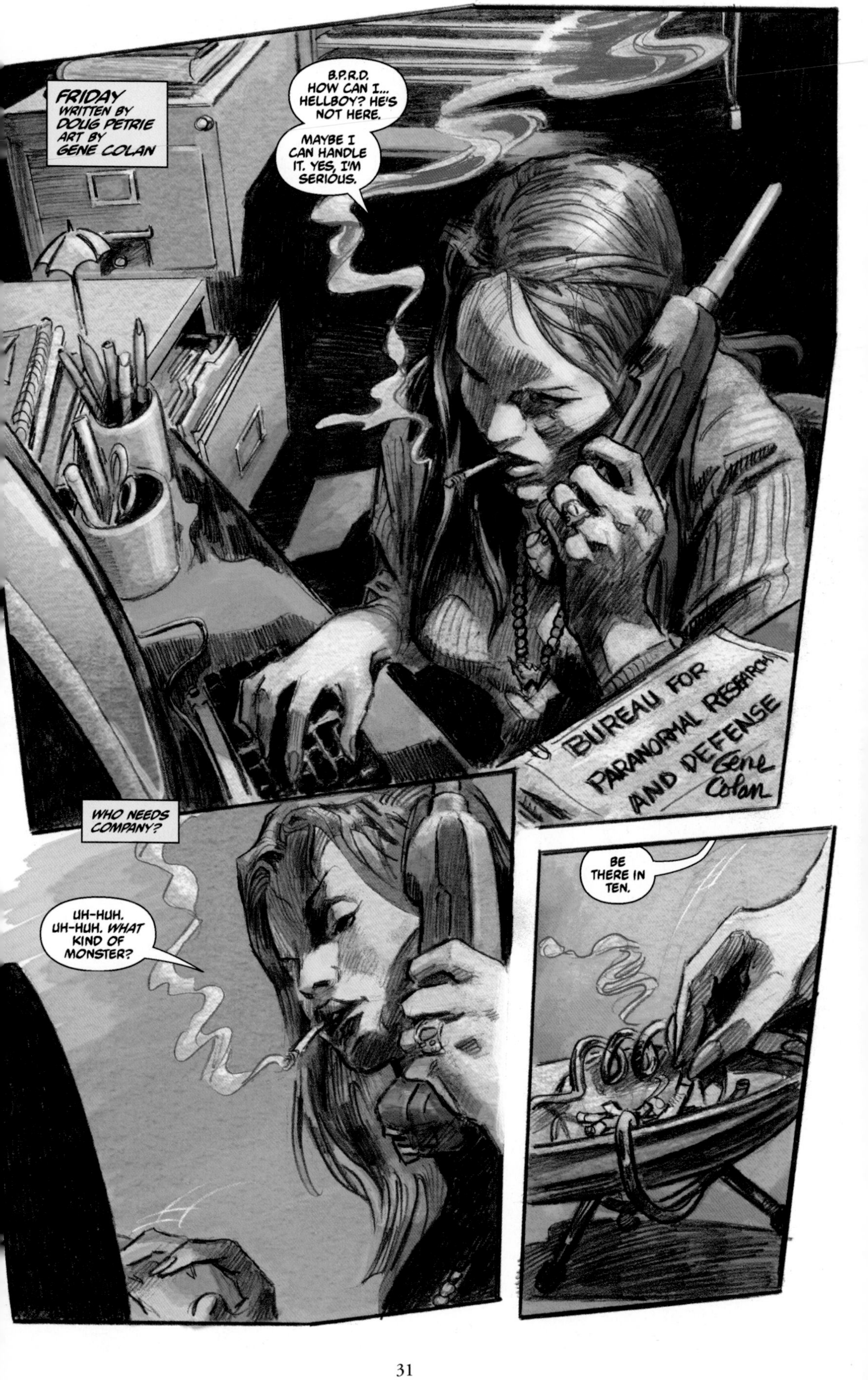
FRIDAY
WRITTEN BY
DOUG PETRIE
ART BY
GENE COLAN
B.P.R.D. HOW CAN I... HELLBOY? HE'S NOT HERE.
MAYBE I CAN HANDLE IT. YES, I'M SERIOUS.
BUREAU FOR PARANORMAL RESEARCH AND DEFENSE
Gene Colan
WHO NEEDS COMPANY?
UH-HUH. UH-HUH. WHAT KIND OF MONSTER?
BE THERE IN TEN.

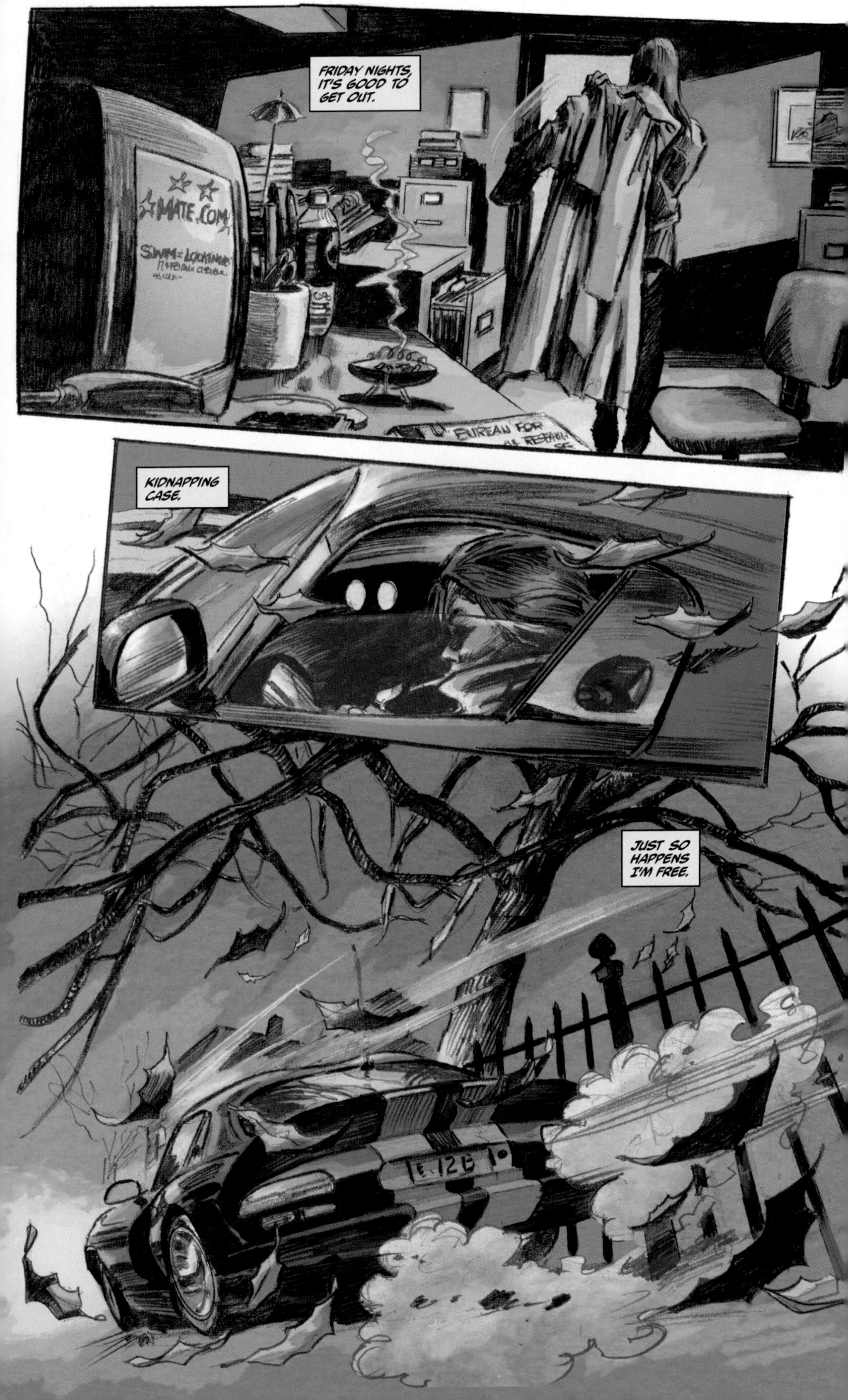
FRIDAY NIGHTS, IT'S GOOD TO GET OUT.
MATE.COM
BUREAU FOR
KIDNAPPING CASE.
JUST SO HAPPENS I'M FREE.

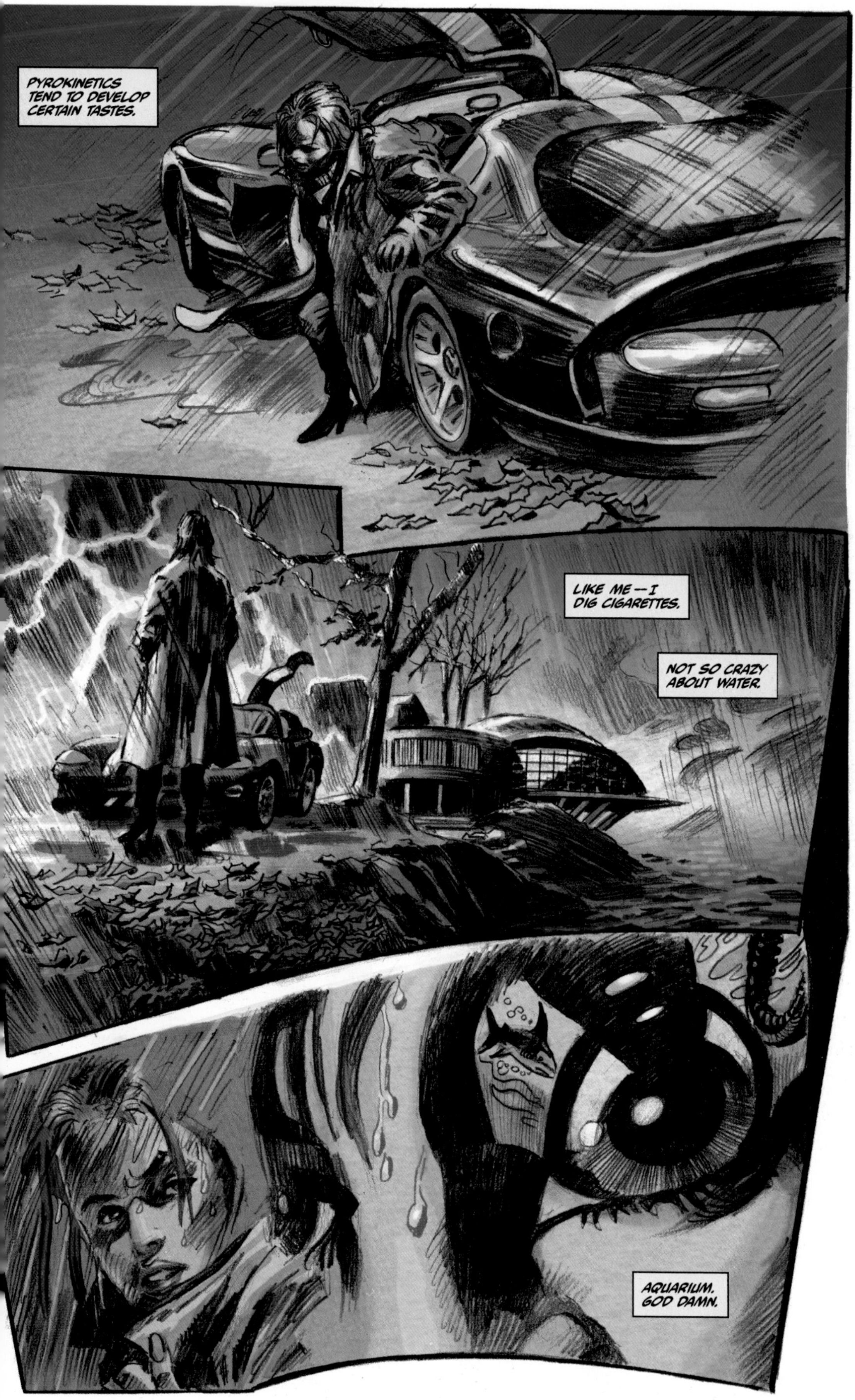
PYROKINETICS TEND TO DEVELOP CERTAIN TASTES.
LIKE ME -- I DIG CIGARETTES.
NOT SO CRAZY ABOUT WATER.
AQUARIUM. GOD DAMN.

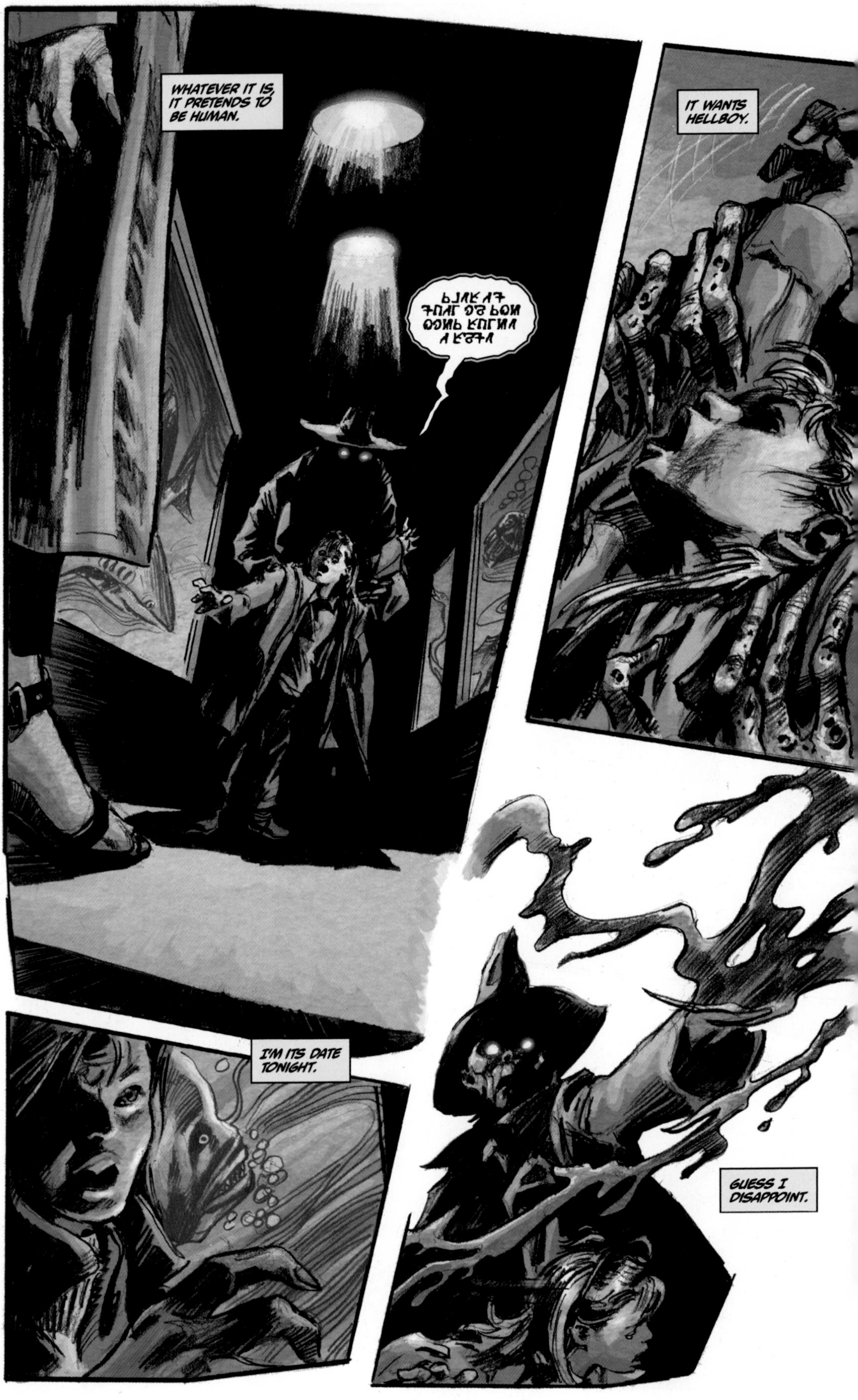
WHATEVER IT IS, IT PRETENDS TO BE HUMAN.
IT WANTS HELLBOY.
I'M ITS DATE TONIGHT.
GUESS I DISAPPOINT.

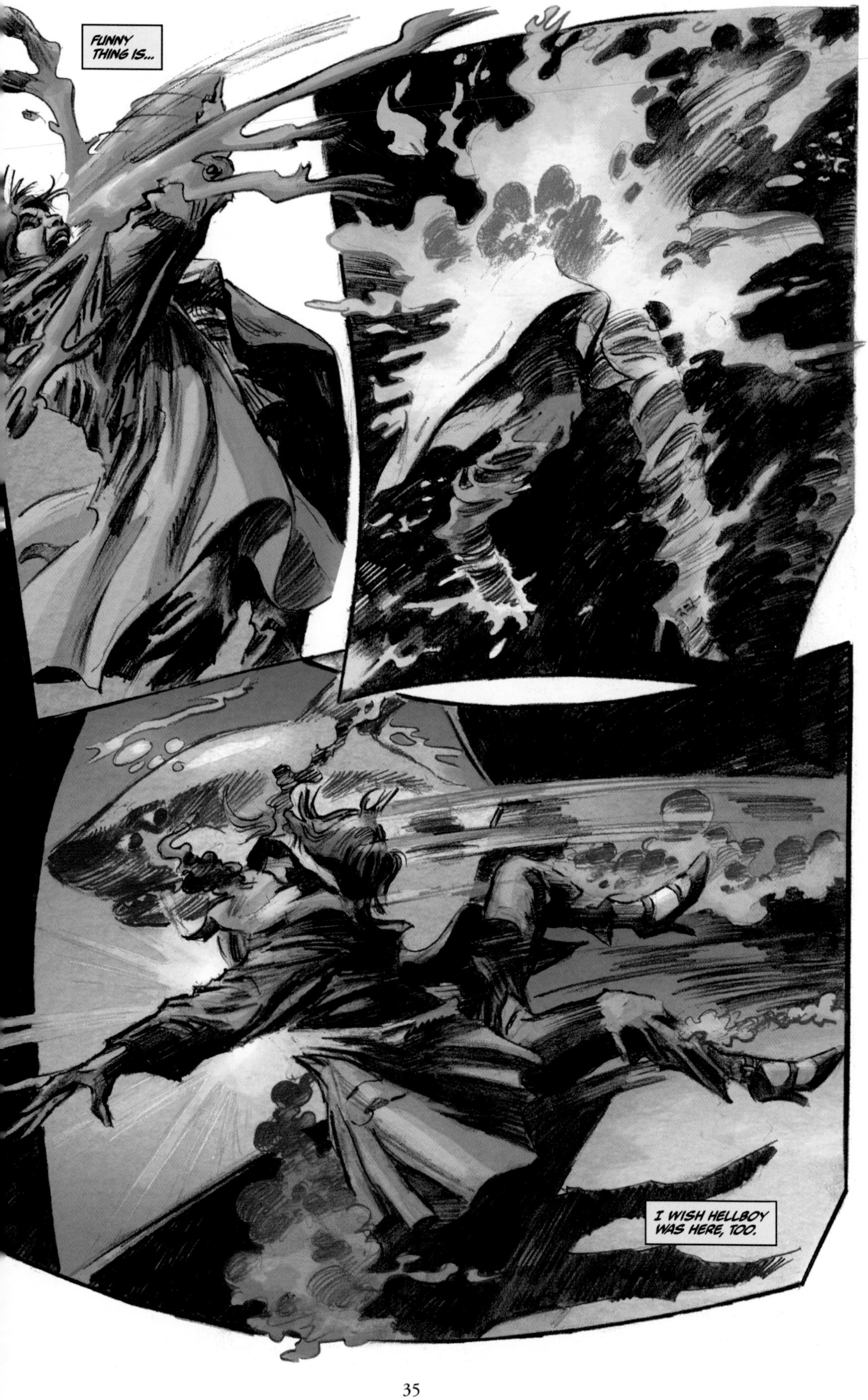
FUNNY THING IS...
I WISH HELLBOY WAS HERE, TOO.

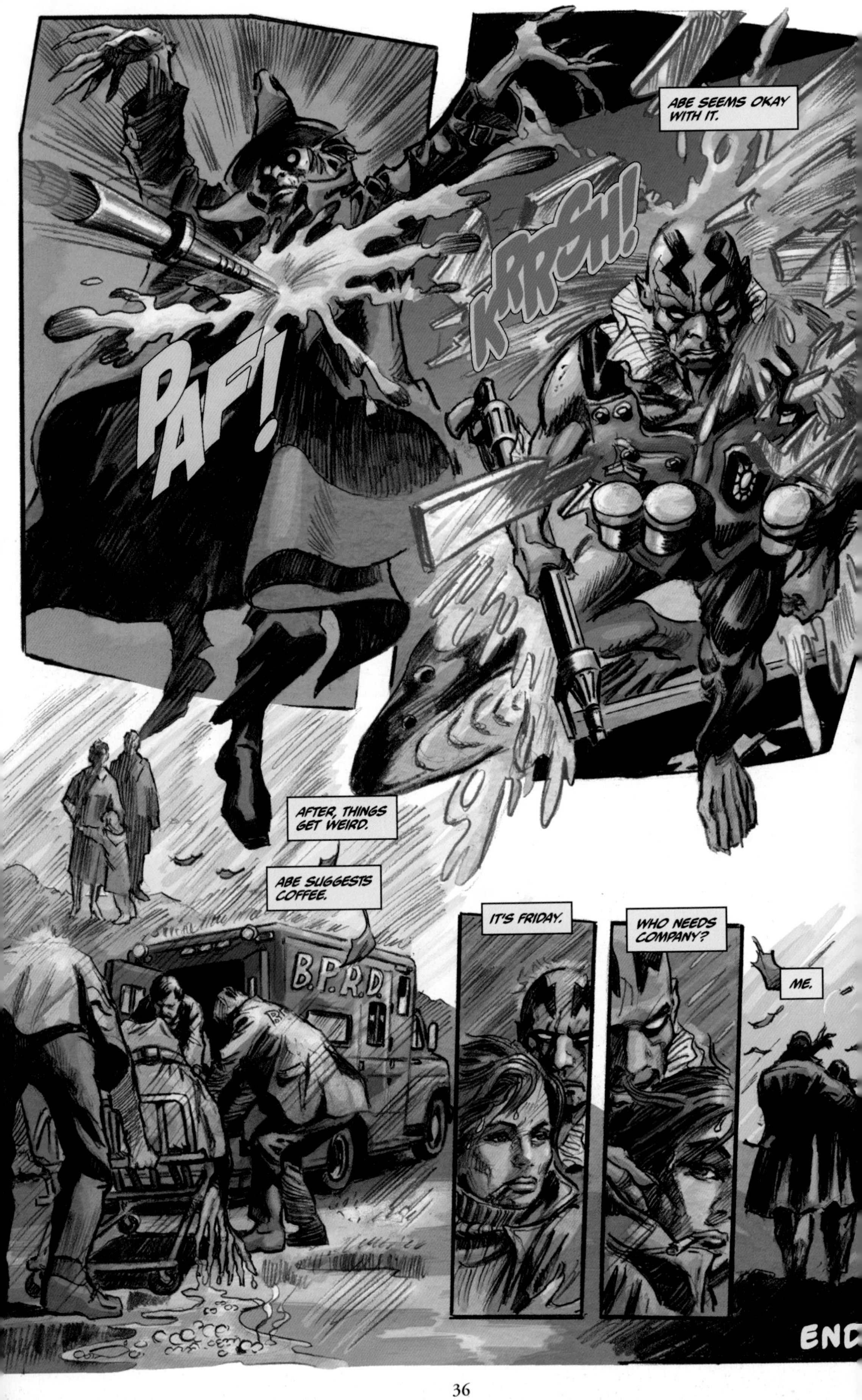
ABE SEEMS OKAY WITH IT.
KRRSH!
PAF!
AFTER, THINGS GET WEIRD.
ABE SUGGESTS COFFEE.
B.P.R.D.
IT'S FRIDAY.
WHO NEEDS COMPANY?
ME.
END

THIS IS A BAD ONE . . .

"MURDERS—*NASTY* MURDERS— GOING BACK ALMOST *100 YEARS.*

"*BERLIN, 1910:* FAMILY OF ARISTOCRATS."

"*LONDON, 1936:* DUKE OF SOMETHING OR OTHER, PLUS HIS WIFE."

"*VIENNA, 1955:* DRAMA CRITIC, HIS WIFE, *AND* HIS MISTRESS."

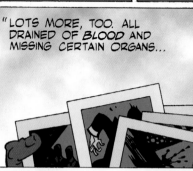

"LOTS MORE, TOO. ALL DRAINED OF *BLOOD* AND MISSING CERTAIN ORGANS..."

"...PLUS *PARTS* OF ORGANS."

PARIS, 1991.

GRAND GUIGNOL

"FOR DECADES, THE *GRAND GUIGNOL* THEATER TROUPE'S BEEN STAGING *GORY* PLAYS. AND, APPARENTLY, THEY'VE BEEN UP TO A LOT *MORE,* TOO. *THAT'S* WHY I'M IN PARIS. TIME TO *END* THIS RUN ONCE AND FOR *ALL.*"

COMMAND PERFORMANCE

WRITER
WILL PFEIFER

ARTIST
P. CRAIG RUSSELL

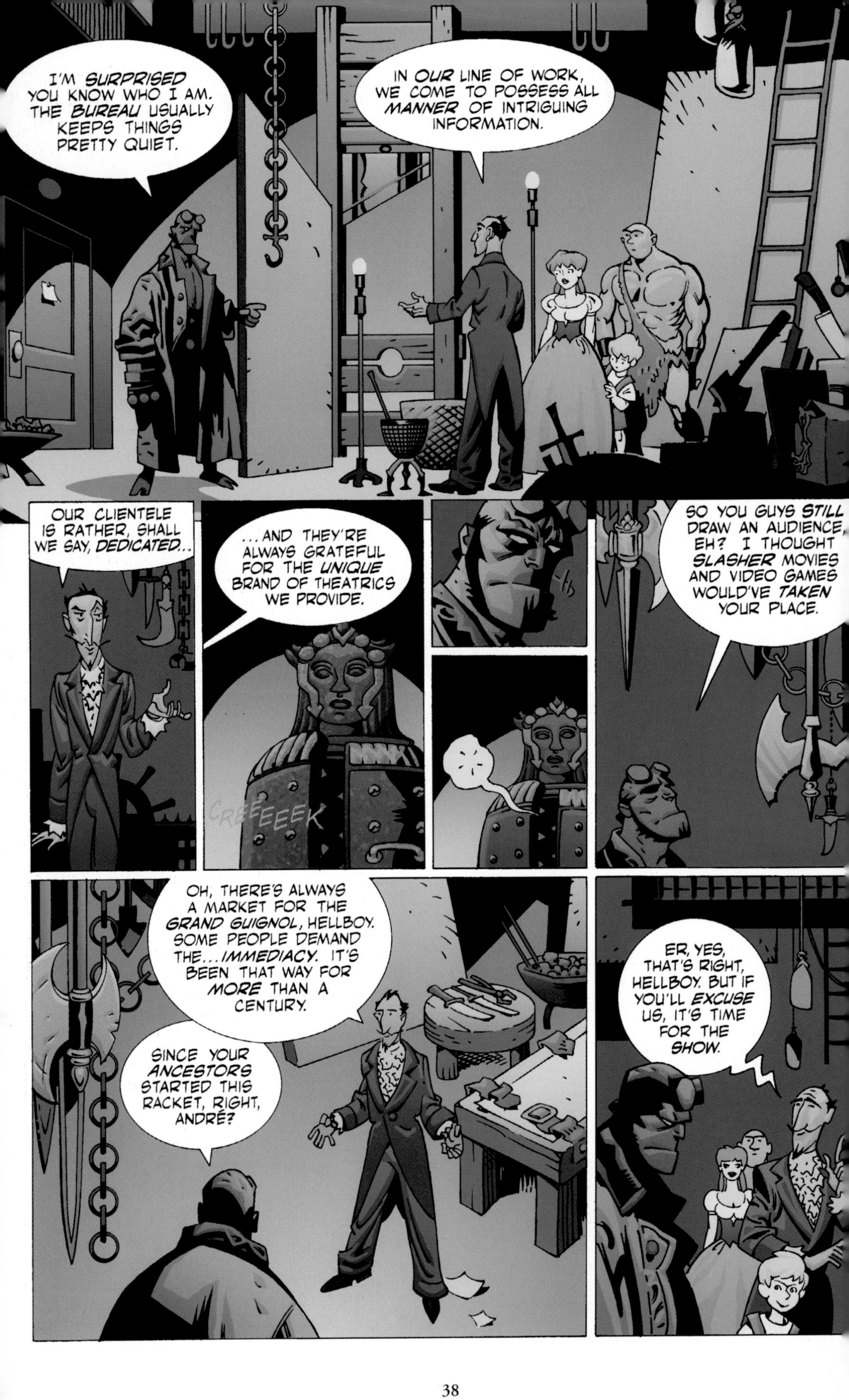
I'M SURPRISED YOU KNOW WHO I AM. THE BUREAU USUALLY KEEPS THINGS PRETTY QUIET.
IN OUR LINE OF WORK, WE COME TO POSSESS ALL MANNER OF INTRIGUING INFORMATION.
OUR CLIENTELE IS RATHER, SHALL WE SAY, DEDICATED...
...AND THEY'RE ALWAYS GRATEFUL FOR THE UNIQUE BRAND OF THEATRICS WE PROVIDE.
CREEEEEK
SO YOU GUYS STILL DRAW AN AUDIENCE, EH? I THOUGHT SLASHER MOVIES AND VIDEO GAMES WOULD'VE TAKEN YOUR PLACE.
OH, THERE'S ALWAYS A MARKET FOR THE GRAND GUIGNOL, HELLBOY. SOME PEOPLE DEMAND THE...IMMEDIACY. IT'S BEEN THAT WAY FOR MORE THAN A CENTURY.
SINCE YOUR ANCESTORS STARTED THIS RACKET, RIGHT, ANDRÉ?
ER, YES, THAT'S RIGHT, HELLBOY. BUT IF YOU'LL EXCUSE US, IT'S TIME FOR THE SHOW.

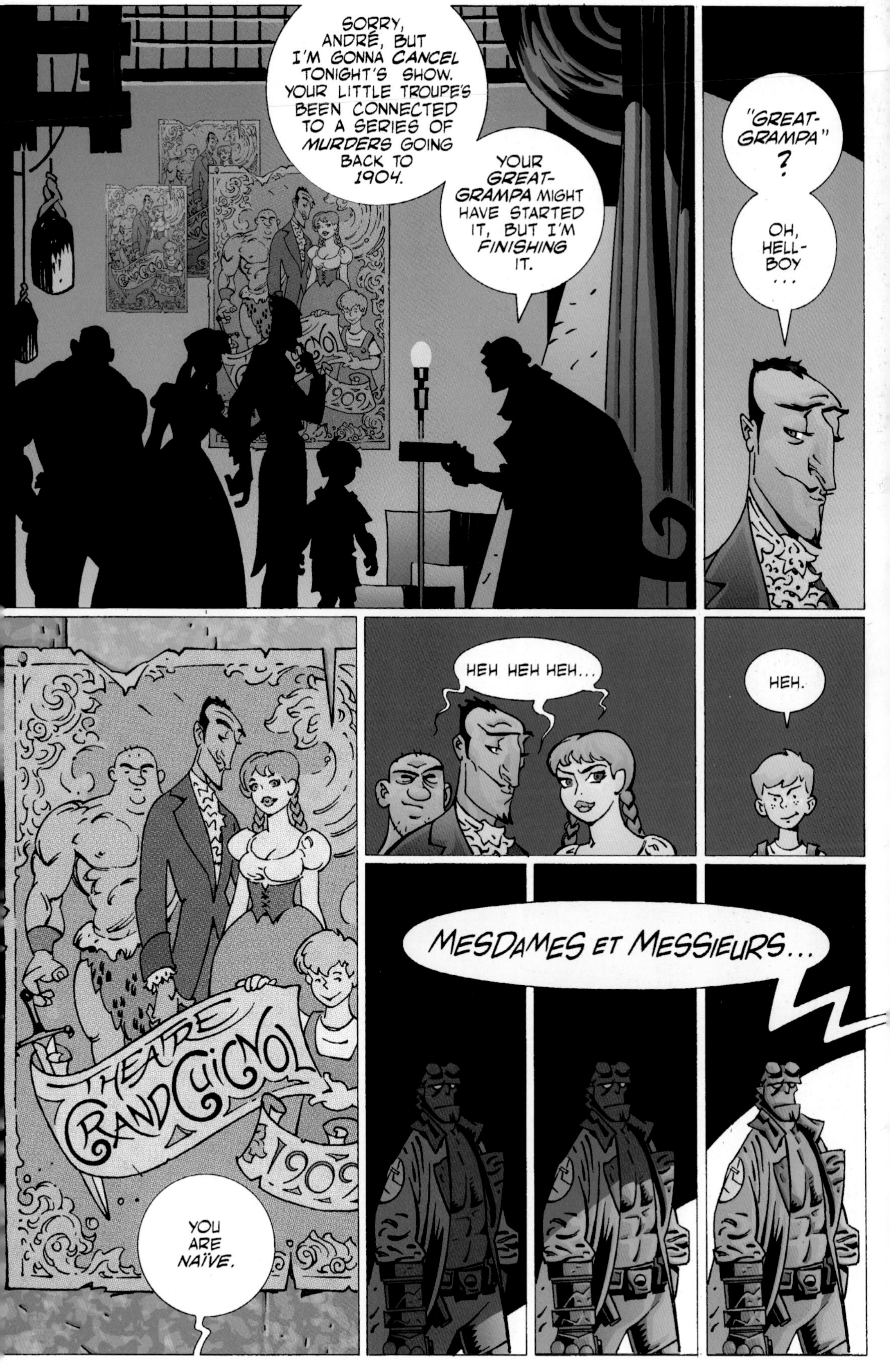
SORRY, ANDRÉ, BUT I'M GONNA CANCEL TONIGHT'S SHOW. YOUR LITTLE TROUPE'S BEEN CONNECTED TO A SERIES OF MURDERS GOING BACK TO 1904.
YOUR GREAT-GRAMPA MIGHT HAVE STARTED IT, BUT I'M FINISHING IT.
"GREAT-GRAMPA" ?
OH, HELL-BOY . . .
THEATRE GRAND GUIGNOL 1909
YOU ARE NAÏVE.
HEH HEH HEH...
HEH.
MESDAMES ET MESSIEURS...

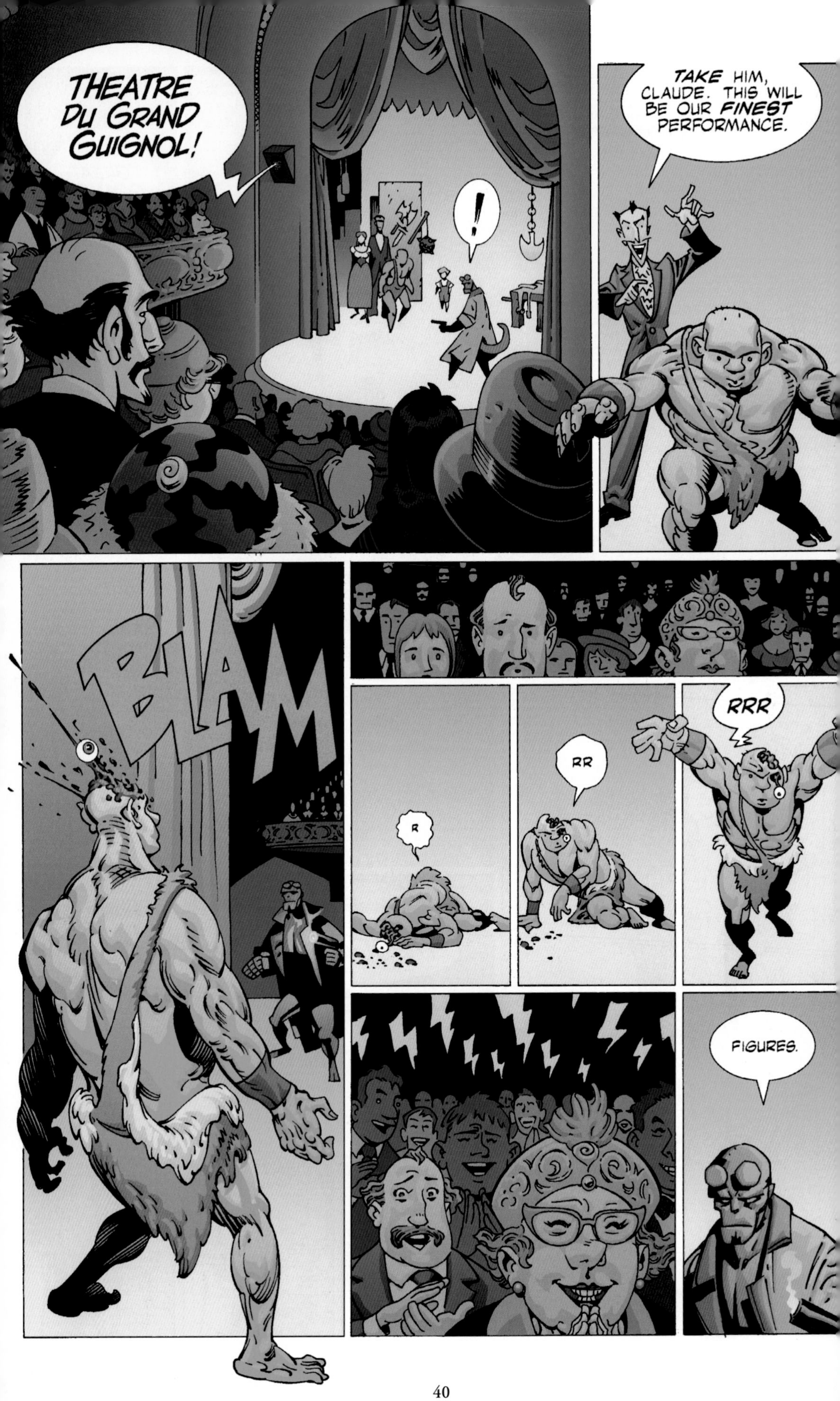
THEATRE DU GRAND GUIGNOL!
!
TAKE HIM, CLAUDE. THIS WILL BE OUR FINEST PERFORMANCE.
BLAM
R
RR
RRR
FIGURES.

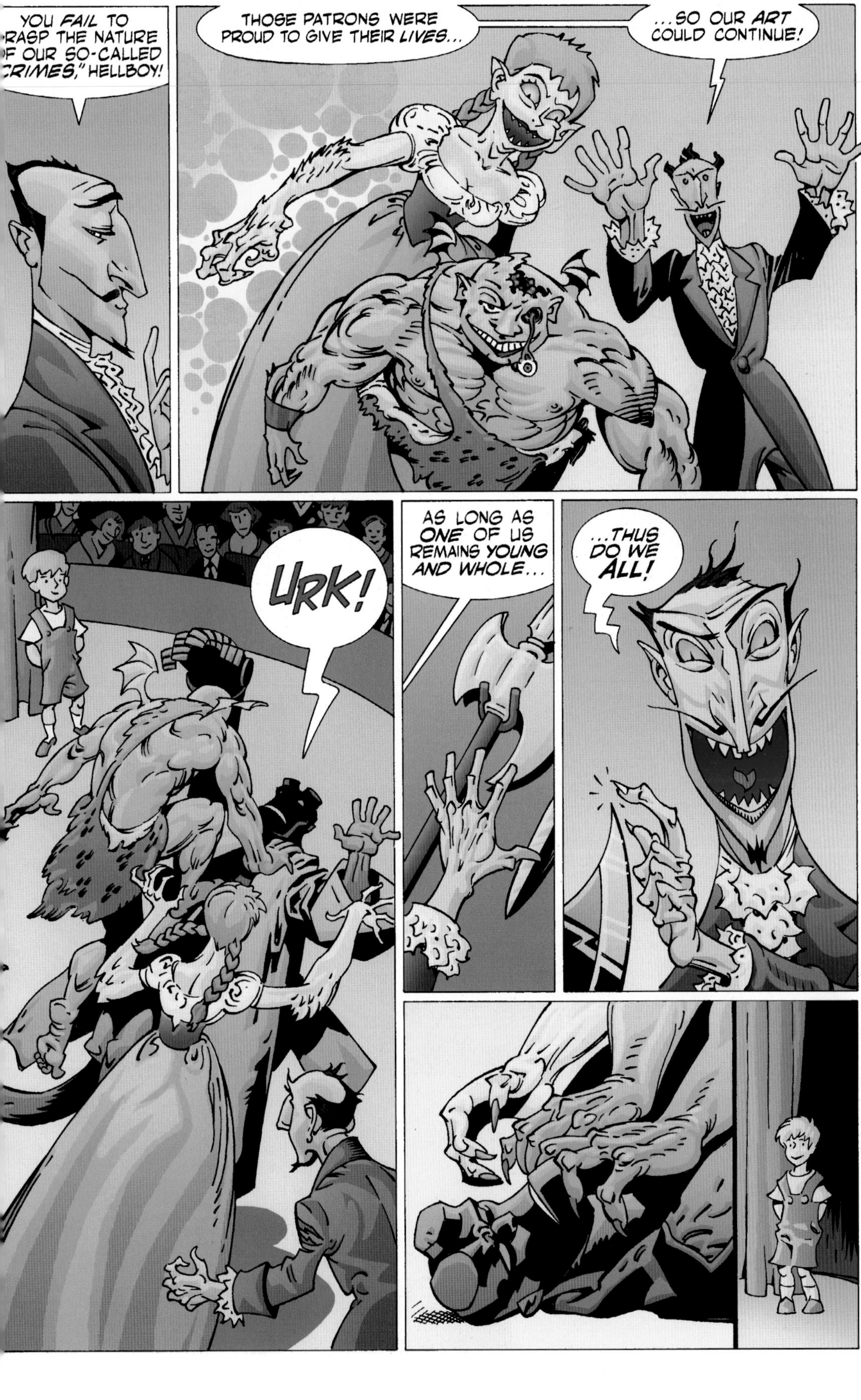
YOU FAIL TO RASP THE NATURE F OUR SO-CALLED CRIMES," HELLBOY!
THOSE PATRONS WERE PROUD TO GIVE THEIR LIVES...
...SO OUR ART COULD CONTINUE!
URK!
AS LONG AS ONE OF US REMAINS YOUNG AND WHOLE...
...THUS DO WE ALL!

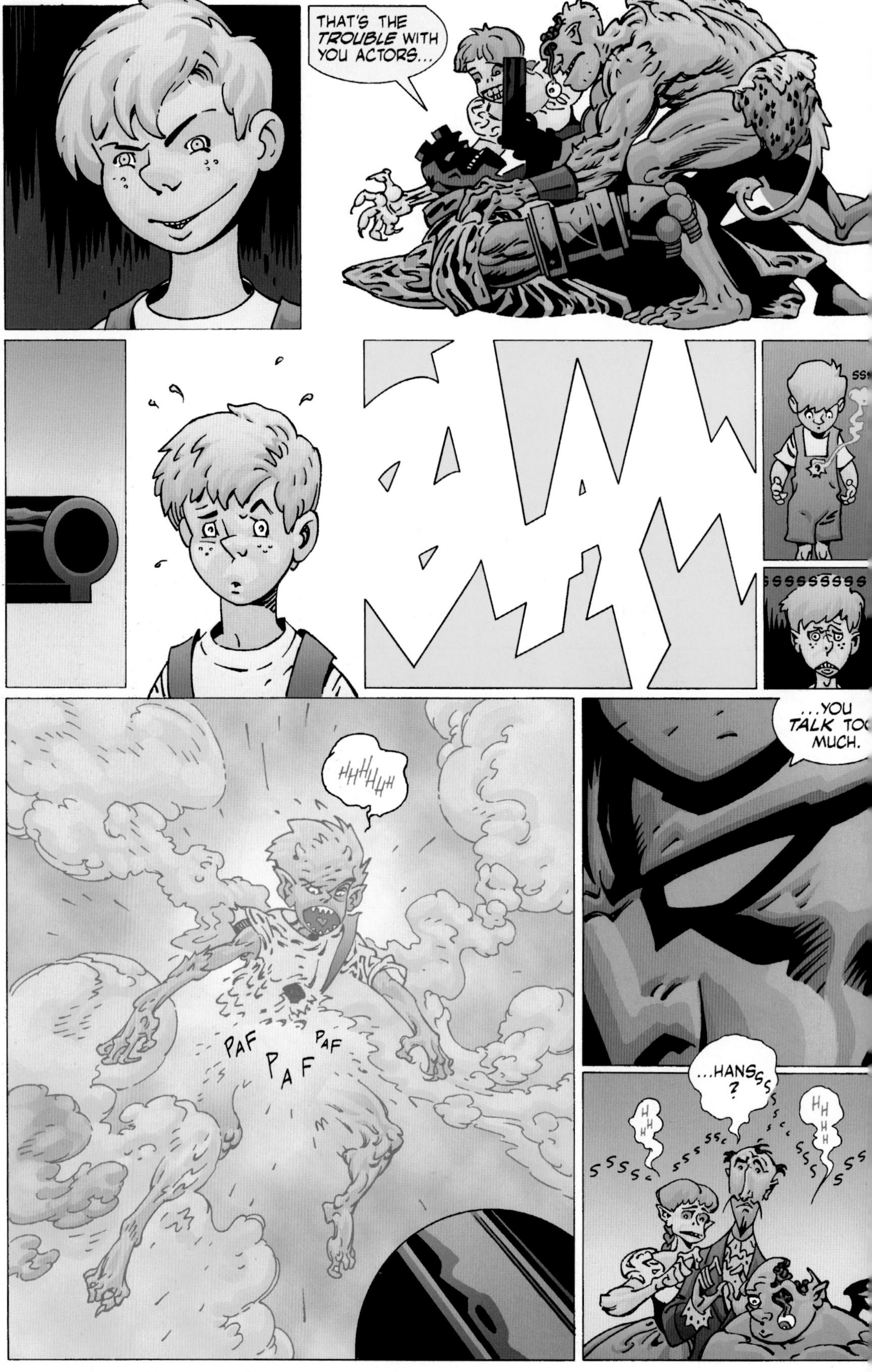
THAT'S THE TROUBLE WITH YOU ACTORS...
...YOU TALK TOO MUCH.
HHHHHH
PAF PAF PAF
...HANSSS ?
HHHH
HHHH
SSSS

AAAHHHHHHHHH **KAK**
SSSSSSSSSSSSSSS SKA-

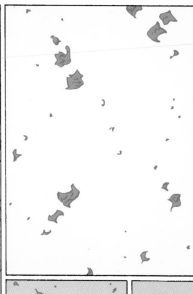

BRAVO BRAVO
BRAVO BRAVO BRAVO
BRAVO
BRAVO BRAVO

!?

HEH.

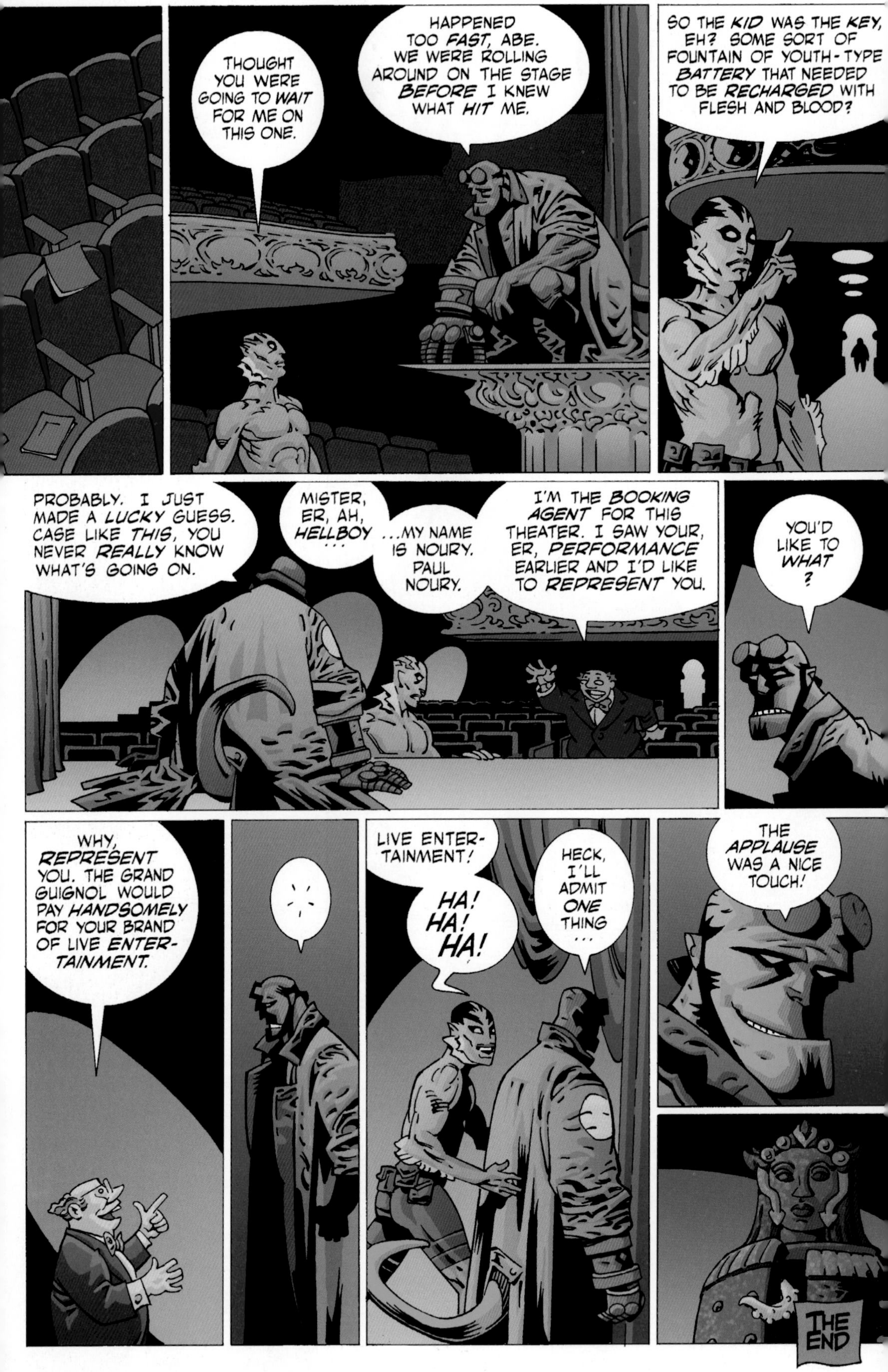
THOUGHT YOU WERE GOING TO WAIT FOR ME ON THIS ONE.
HAPPENED TOO FAST, ABE. WE WERE ROLLING AROUND ON THE STAGE BEFORE I KNEW WHAT HIT ME.
SO THE KID WAS THE KEY, EH? SOME SORT OF FOUNTAIN OF YOUTH-TYPE BATTERY THAT NEEDED TO BE RECHARGED WITH FLESH AND BLOOD?
PROBABLY. I JUST MADE A LUCKY GUESS. CASE LIKE THIS, YOU NEVER REALLY KNOW WHAT'S GOING ON.
MISTER, ER, AH, HELLBOY . . .
. . .MY NAME IS NOURY. PAUL NOURY.
I'M THE BOOKING AGENT FOR THIS THEATER. I SAW YOUR, ER, PERFORMANCE EARLIER AND I'D LIKE TO REPRESENT YOU.
YOU'D LIKE TO WHAT?
WHY, REPRESENT YOU. THE GRAND GUIGNOL WOULD PAY HANDSOMELY FOR YOUR BRAND OF LIVE ENTERTAINMENT.
LIVE ENTERTAINMENT!
HA! HA! HA!
HECK, I'LL ADMIT ONE THING . . .
THE APPLAUSE WAS A NICE TOUCH!
THE END

LOVE IS SCARIER THAN DEATH

PRINCE GEORGES COUNTY, MARYLAND. NIGHT ONE.

YOU COULDN'T GET A CAR WITH A BIGGER BACK SEAT?

IT WAS THIS OR A VW BUG. WE NEED TO LOOK AUTHENTIC IF WE'RE GOING TO DRAW GOATMAN OUT OF HIDING.

"GOATMAN?" SOUNDS LIKE AN URBAN LEGEND TO ME.

TELL THAT TO THE SIX DEAD KIDS.

YEAH, OKAY, I READ THE FILE, AGENT GRANGER.

BUT THE *FBI* CAN HANDLE A PSYCHO AXE MURDERER WITHOUT MY HELP.

MEET GOATMAN. HALF HUMAN, HALF GOAT. INSANE. CARRIES AROUND A BIG, BLOODY AXE. SOUND LIKE YOUR KIND OF ASSIGNMENT NOW?

YEAH, IF I BELIEVED IT. I *DON'T*.

BUT ASSUMING THAT THIS GUY *IS* REAL, YOU REALLY THINK WE'LL CATCH HIM JUST BY PARKING OUT HERE?

WE'RE BAIT. WE MIGHT NEED TO ACT LIKE IT.

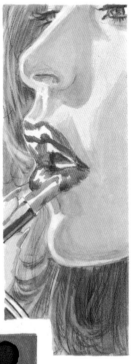

CHRIST. I'M TAKING A NAP. WAKE ME UP IF WE GET ATTACKED BY YOUR KILLER GOAT.

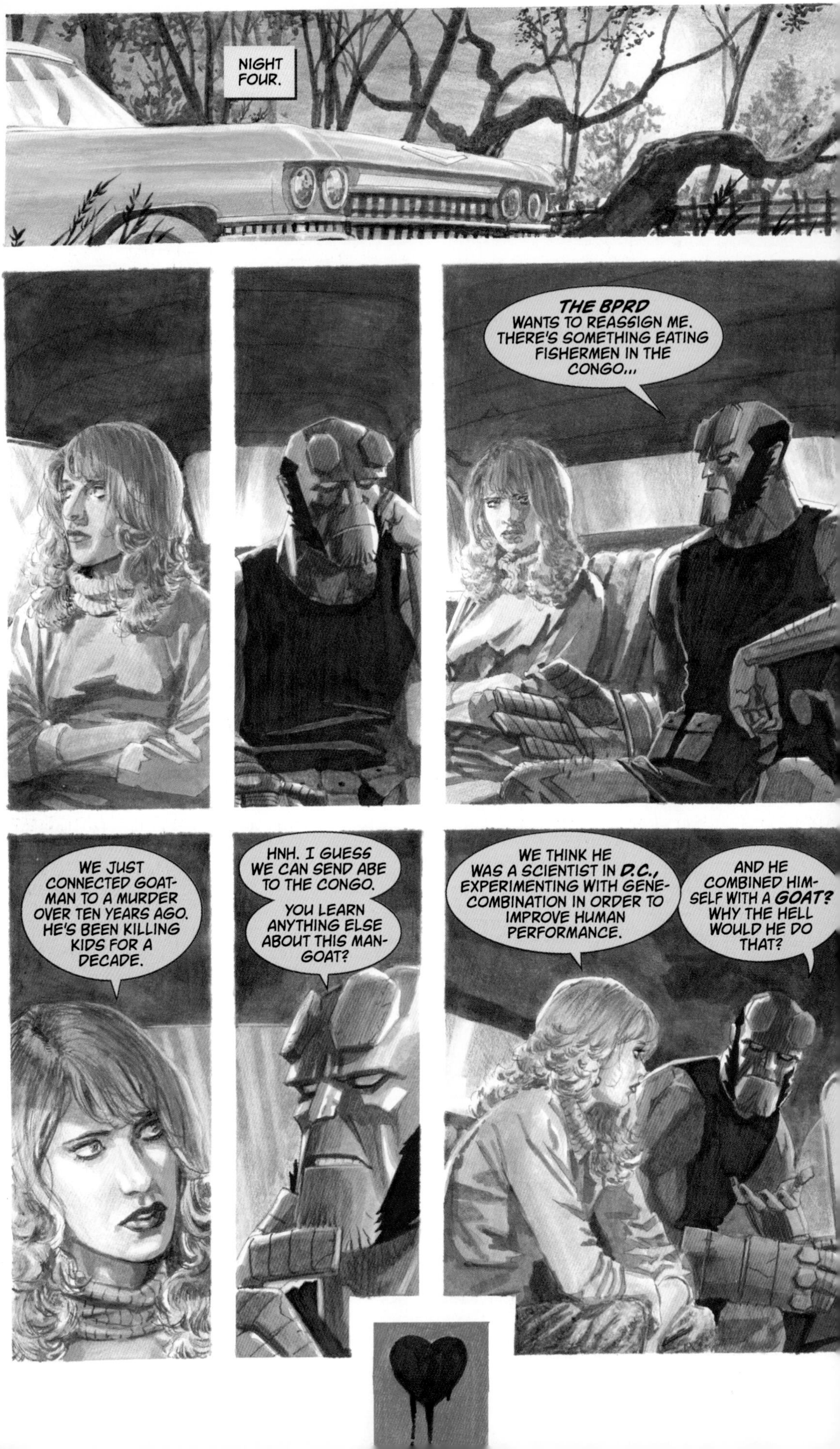
NIGHT FOUR.
THE BPRD WANTS TO REASSIGN ME. THERE'S SOMETHING EATING FISHERMEN IN THE CONGO...
WE JUST CONNECTED GOAT-MAN TO A MURDER OVER TEN YEARS AGO. HE'S BEEN KILLING KIDS FOR A DECADE.
HNH. I GUESS WE CAN SEND ABE TO THE CONGO.
YOU LEARN ANYTHING ELSE ABOUT THIS MAN-GOAT?
WE THINK HE WAS A SCIENTIST IN D.C., EXPERIMENTING WITH GENE-COMBINATION IN ORDER TO IMPROVE HUMAN PERFORMANCE.
AND HE COMBINED HIM-SELF WITH A GOAT? WHY THE HELL WOULD HE DO THAT?

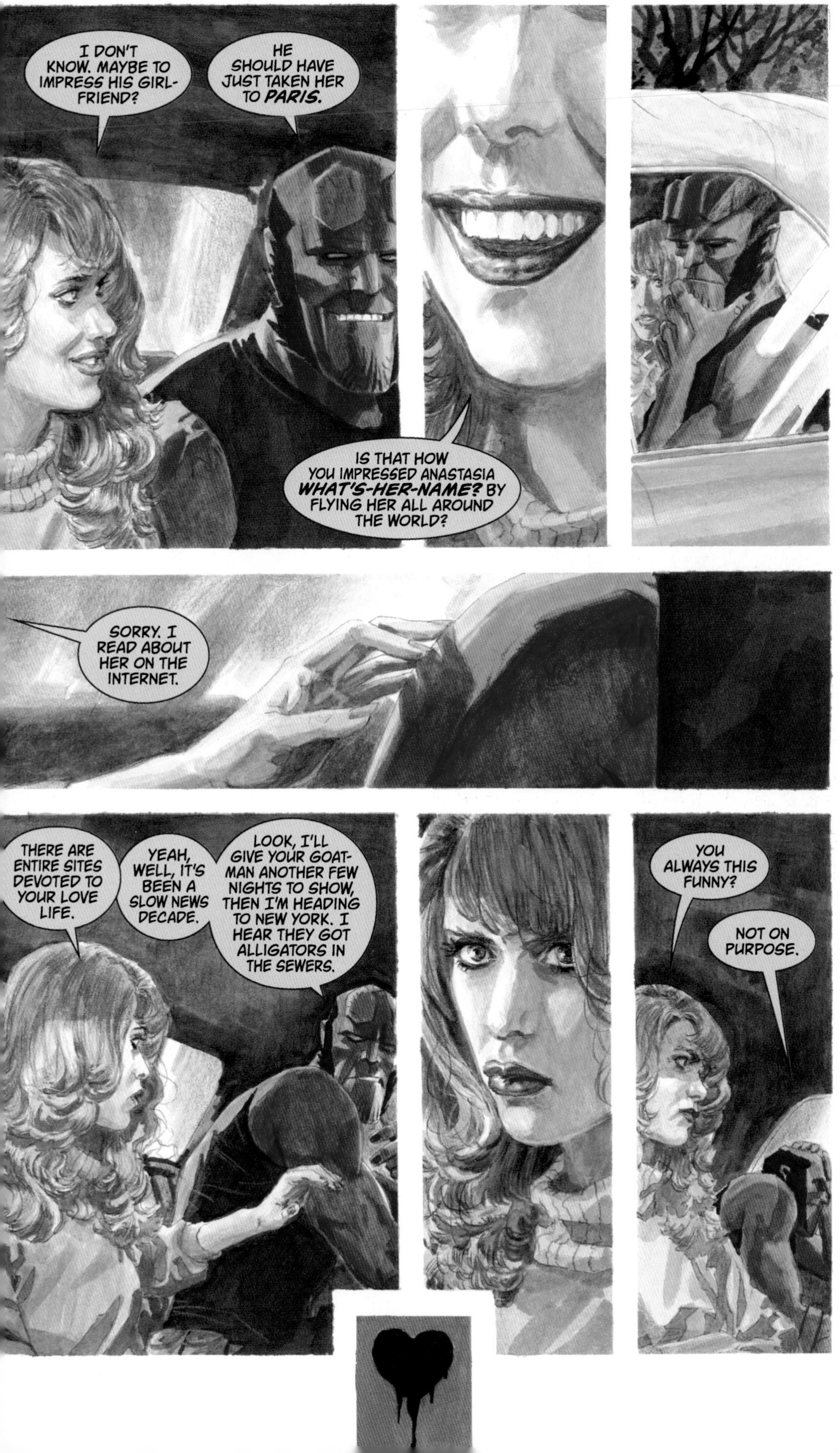
I DON'T KNOW. MAYBE TO IMPRESS HIS GIRL-FRIEND?
HE SHOULD HAVE JUST TAKEN HER TO *PARIS.*
IS THAT HOW YOU IMPRESSED ANASTASIA *WHAT'S-HER-NAME?* BY FLYING HER ALL AROUND THE WORLD?
SORRY. I READ ABOUT HER ON THE INTERNET.
THERE ARE ENTIRE SITES DEVOTED TO YOUR LOVE LIFE.
YEAH, WELL, IT'S BEEN A SLOW NEWS DECADE.
LOOK, I'LL GIVE YOUR GOAT-MAN ANOTHER FEW NIGHTS TO SHOW, THEN I'M HEADING TO NEW YORK. I HEAR THEY GOT ALLIGATORS IN THE SEWERS.
YOU ALWAYS THIS FUNNY?
NOT ON PURPOSE.

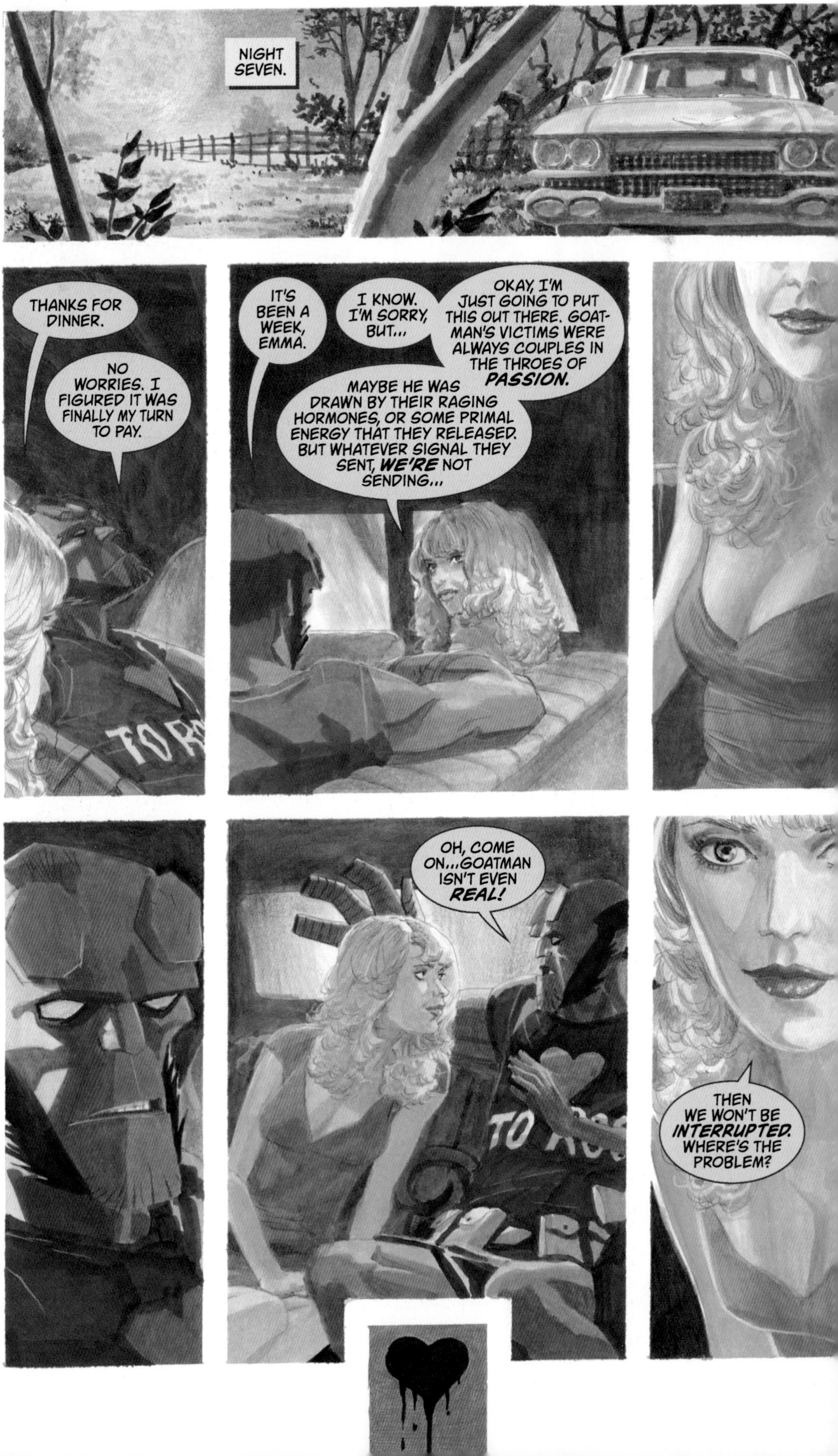
NIGHT SEVEN.
THANKS FOR DINNER.
NO WORRIES. I FIGURED IT WAS FINALLY MY TURN TO PAY.
IT'S BEEN A WEEK, EMMA.
I KNOW. I'M SORRY, BUT...
OKAY, I'M JUST GOING TO PUT THIS OUT THERE. GOATMAN'S VICTIMS WERE ALWAYS COUPLES IN THE THROES OF PASSION.
MAYBE HE WAS DRAWN BY THEIR RAGING HORMONES, OR SOME PRIMAL ENERGY THAT THEY RELEASED. BUT WHATEVER SIGNAL THEY SENT, WE'RE NOT SENDING...
OH, COME ON...GOATMAN ISN'T EVEN REAL!
THEN WE WON'T BE INTERRUPTED. WHERE'S THE PROBLEM?

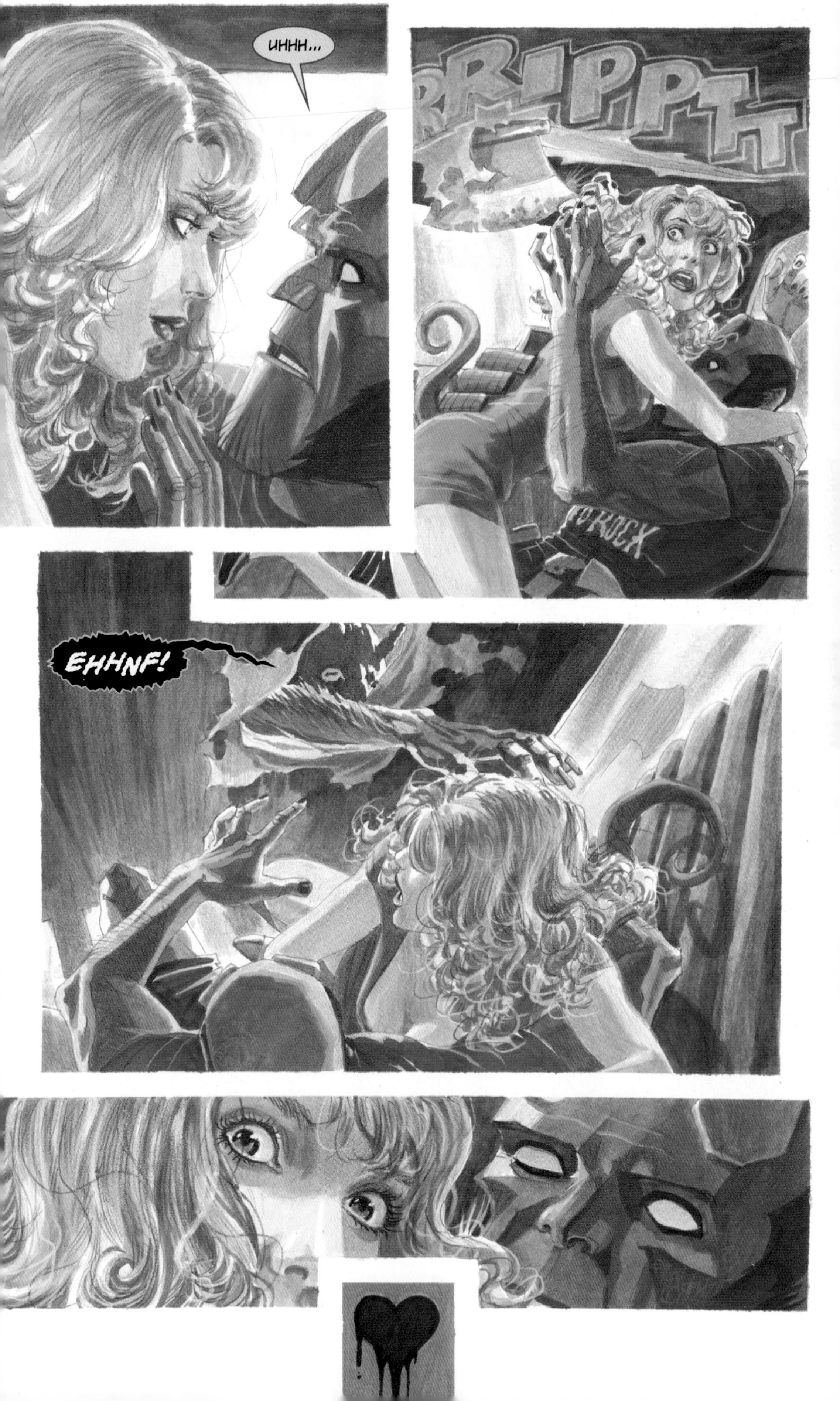
UHHH...
RRIPPTT
EHHNF!

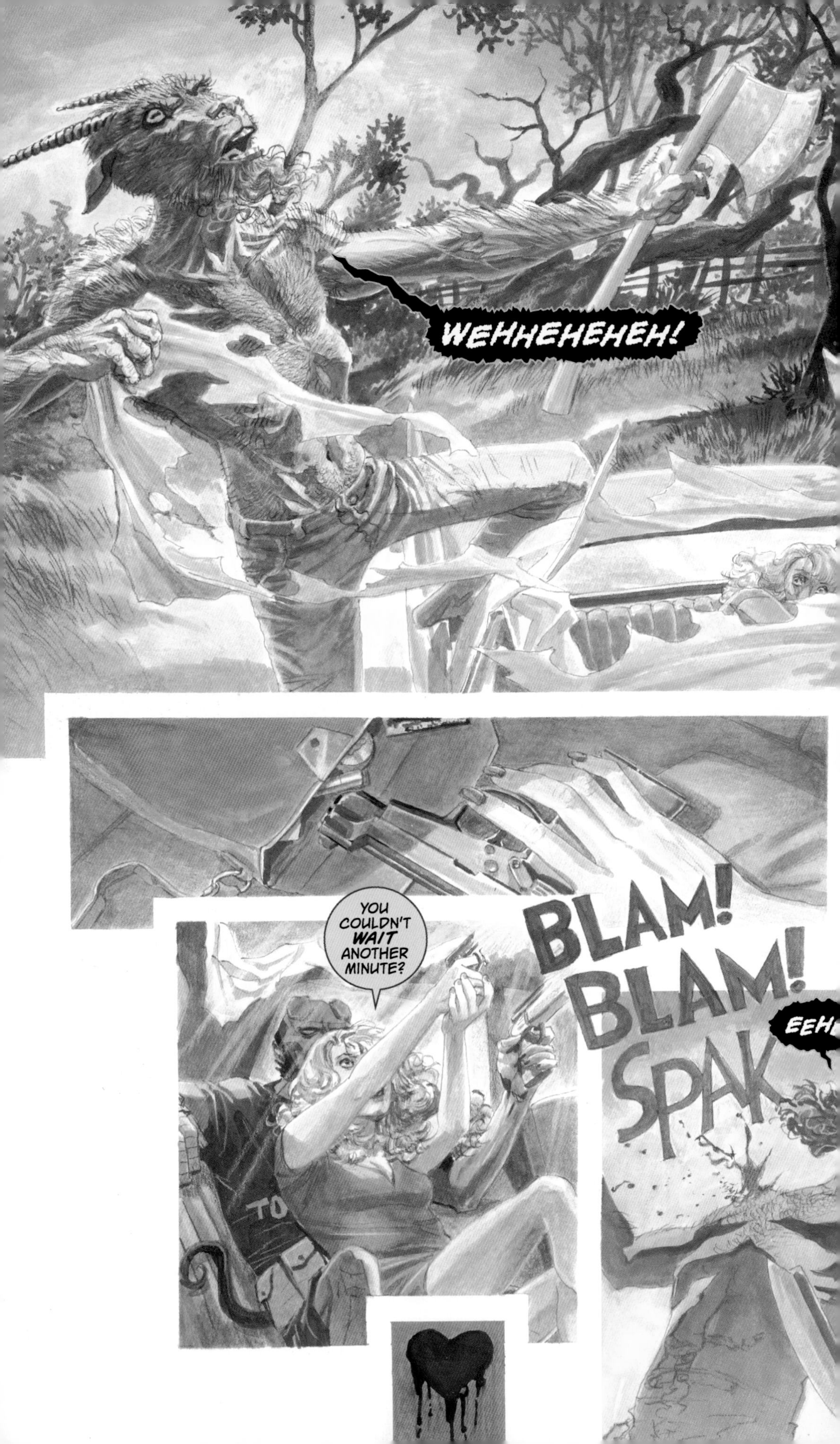
WEHHEHEHEH!
YOU COULDN'T WAIT ANOTHER MINUTE?
BLAM! BLAM!
SPAK
EEH

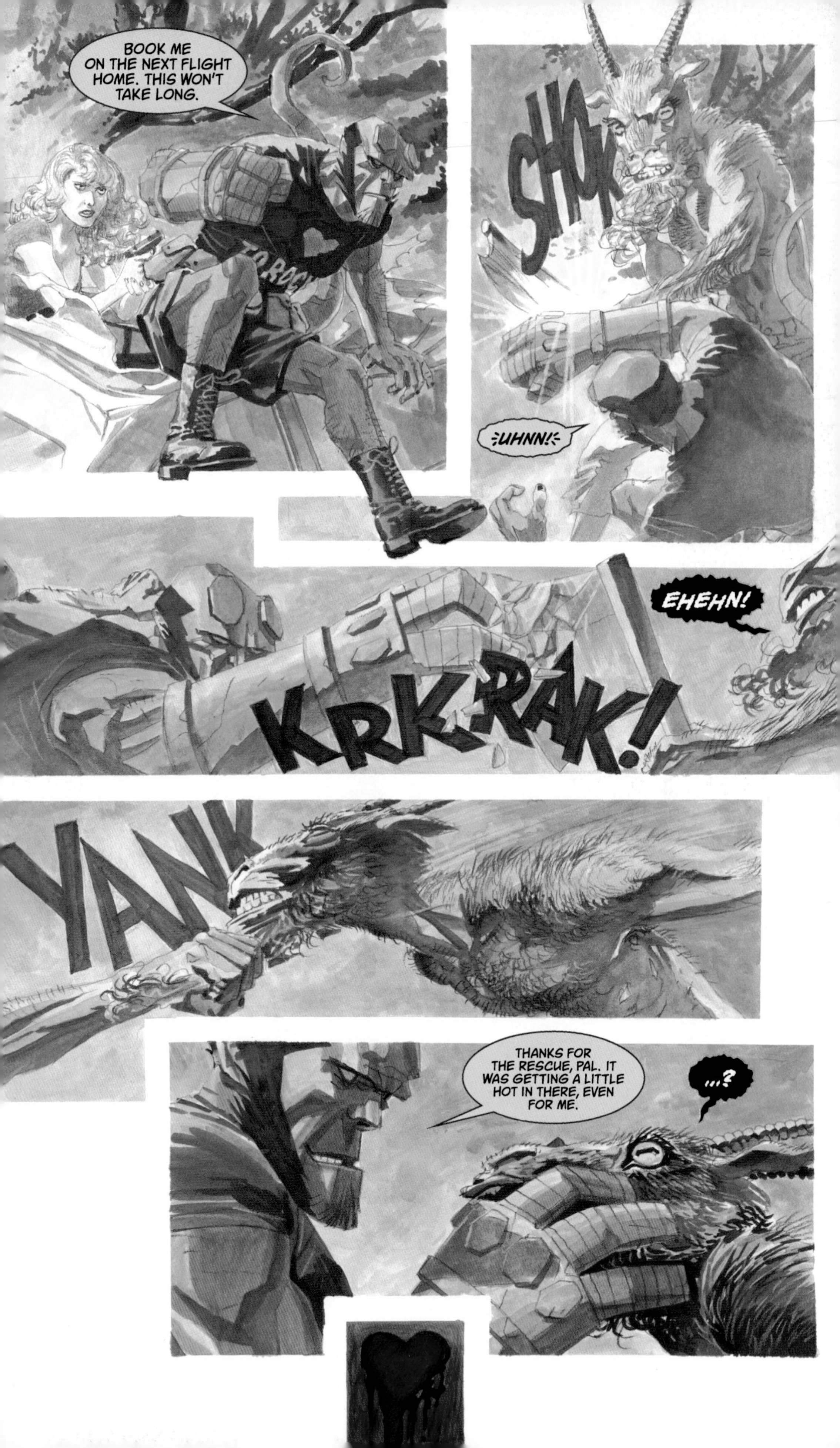
BOOK ME ON THE NEXT FLIGHT HOME. THIS WON'T TAKE LONG.
SHOK
UHNN!
EHEHN!
KRK-RAK!
YANK
THANKS FOR THE RESCUE, PAL. IT WAS GETTING A LITTLE HOT IN THERE, EVEN FOR ME.
...?

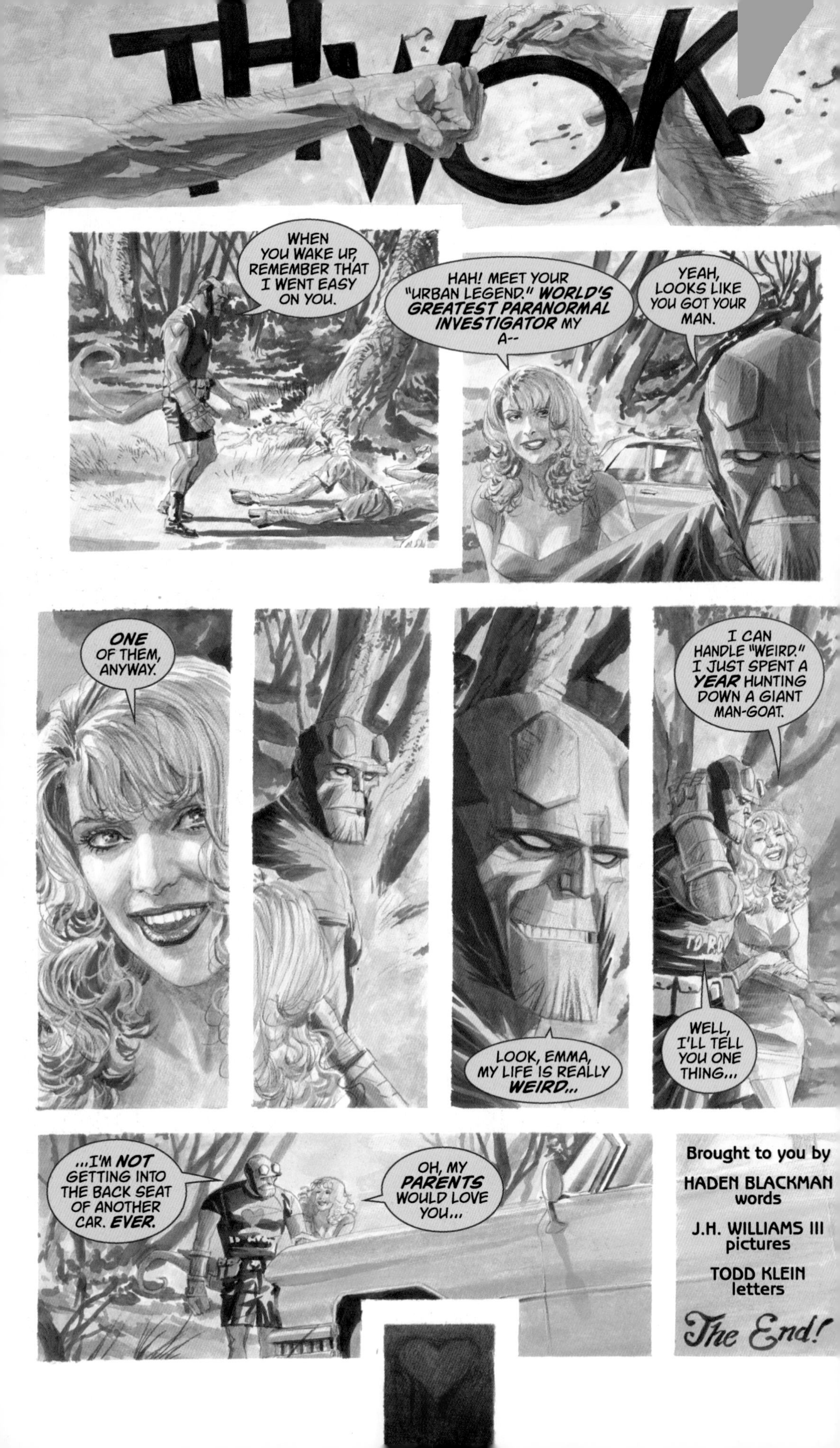
THWOK!
WHEN YOU WAKE UP, REMEMBER THAT I WENT EASY ON YOU.
HAH! MEET YOUR "URBAN LEGEND." WORLD'S GREATEST PARANORMAL INVESTIGATOR MY A--
YEAH, LOOKS LIKE YOU GOT YOUR MAN.
ONE OF THEM, ANYWAY.
LOOK, EMMA, MY LIFE IS REALLY WEIRD...
I CAN HANDLE "WEIRD." I JUST SPENT A YEAR HUNTING DOWN A GIANT MAN-GOAT.
WELL, I'LL TELL YOU ONE THING...
...I'M NOT GETTING INTO THE BACK SEAT OF ANOTHER CAR. EVER.
OH, MY PARENTS WOULD LOVE YOU...
Brought to you by
HADEN BLACKMAN words
J.H. WILLIAMS III pictures
TODD KLEIN letters
The End!

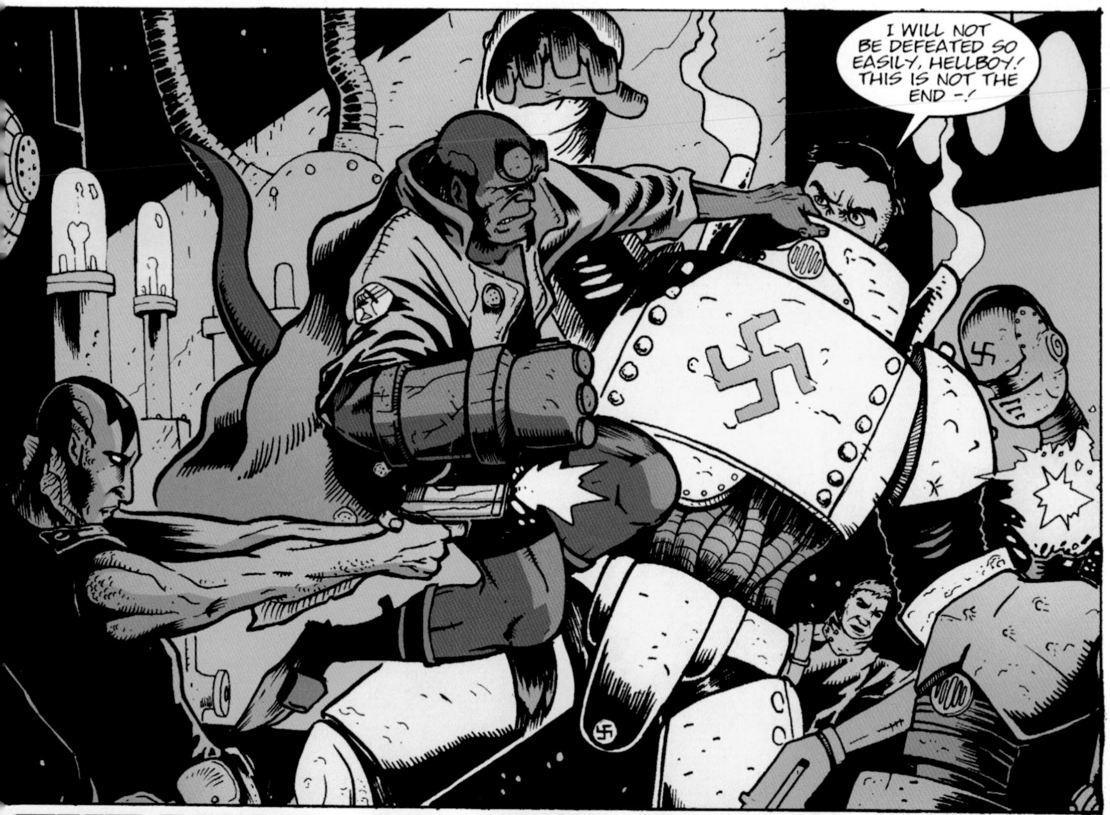
I WILL NOT BE DEFEATED SO EASILY, HELLBOY! THIS IS NOT THE END -!

THEATRE OF THE DEAD

WRITERS- FASSBENDER AND PASCOE
ARTIST- SIMEON WILKINS
COLORIST- DAVID SELF
LETTERER- ANNIE PARKHOUSE

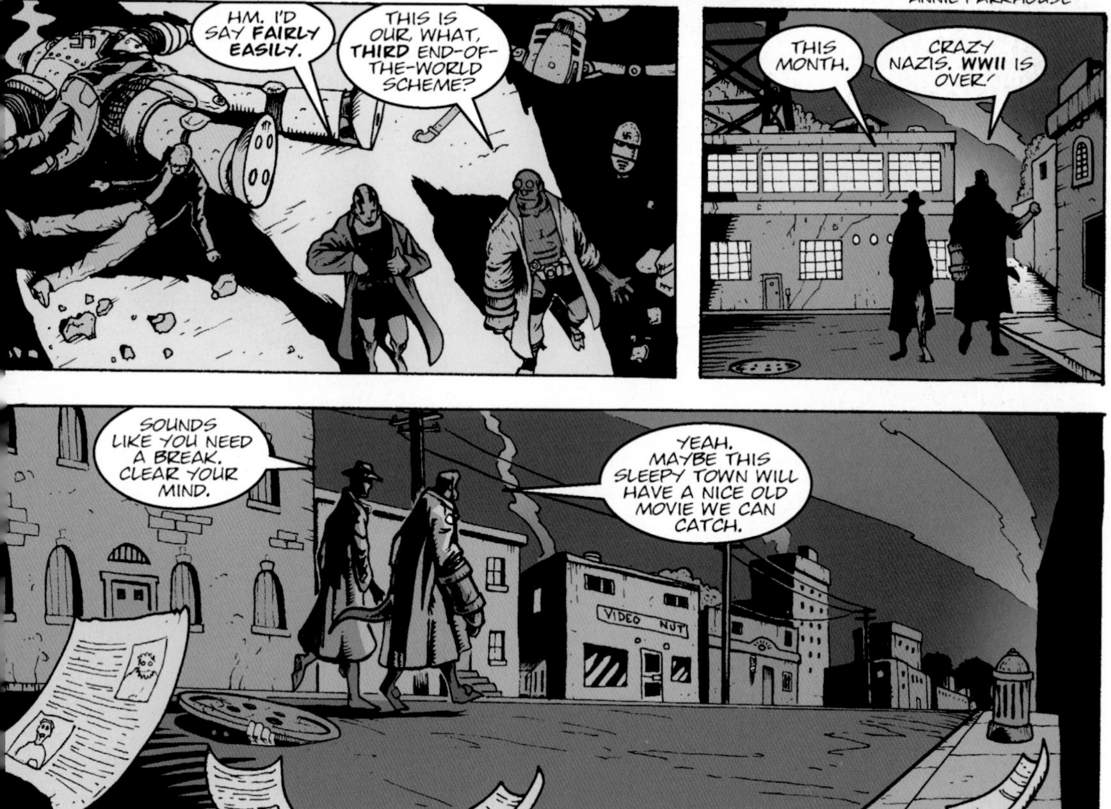
HM. I'D SAY FAIRLY EASILY.
THIS IS OUR, WHAT, THIRD END-OF-THE-WORLD SCHEME?
THIS MONTH.
CRAZY NAZIS. WWII IS OVER!
SOUNDS LIKE YOU NEED A BREAK. CLEAR YOUR MIND.
YEAH. MAYBE THIS SLEEPY TOWN WILL HAVE A NICE OLD MOVIE WE CAN CATCH.
VIDEO NUT

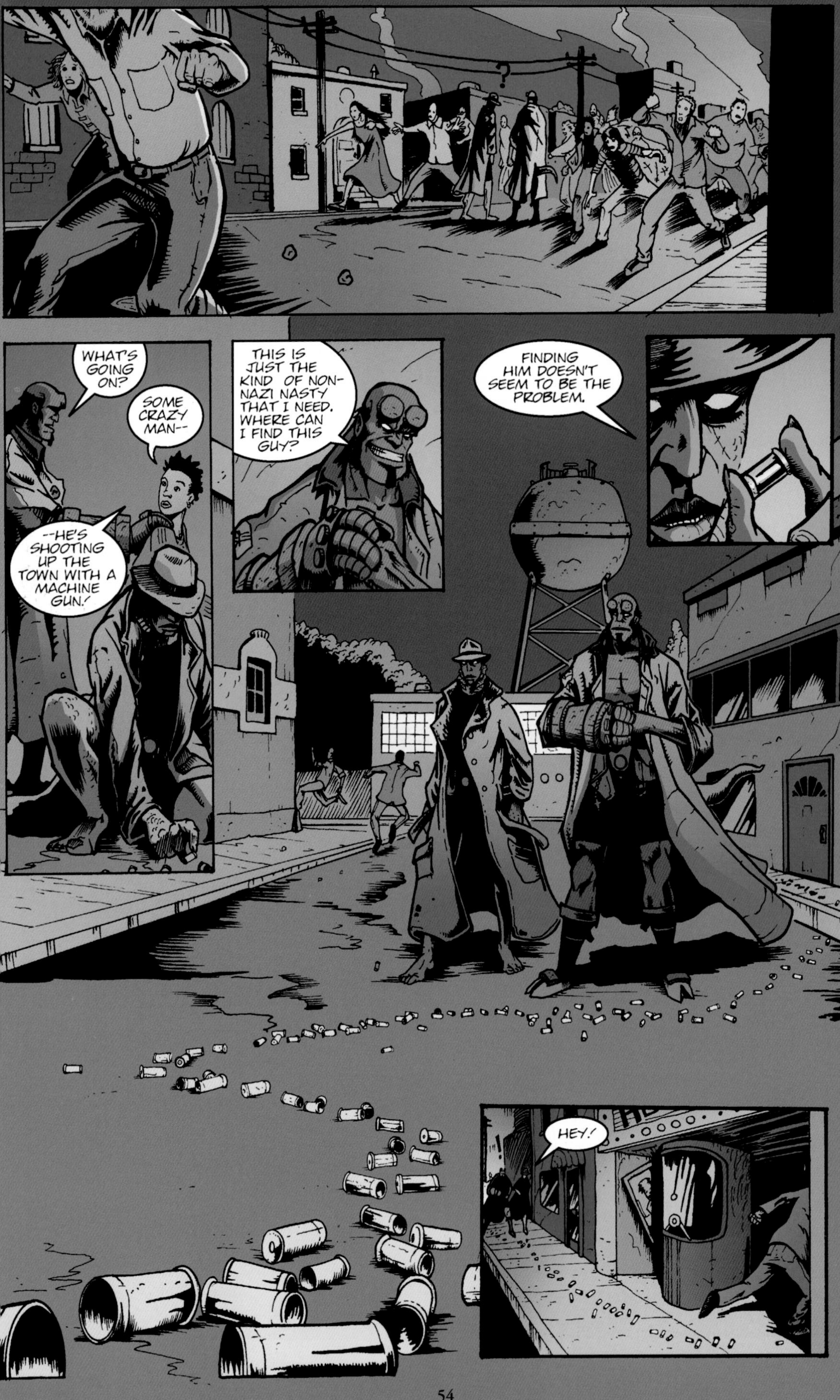

WHAT'S GOING ON?
SOME CRAZY MAN--
--HE'S SHOOTING UP THE TOWN WITH A MACHINE GUN!
THIS IS JUST THE KIND OF NON-NAZI NASTY THAT I NEED. WHERE CAN I FIND THIS GUY?
FINDING HIM DOESN'T SEEM TO BE THE PROBLEM.
HEY!

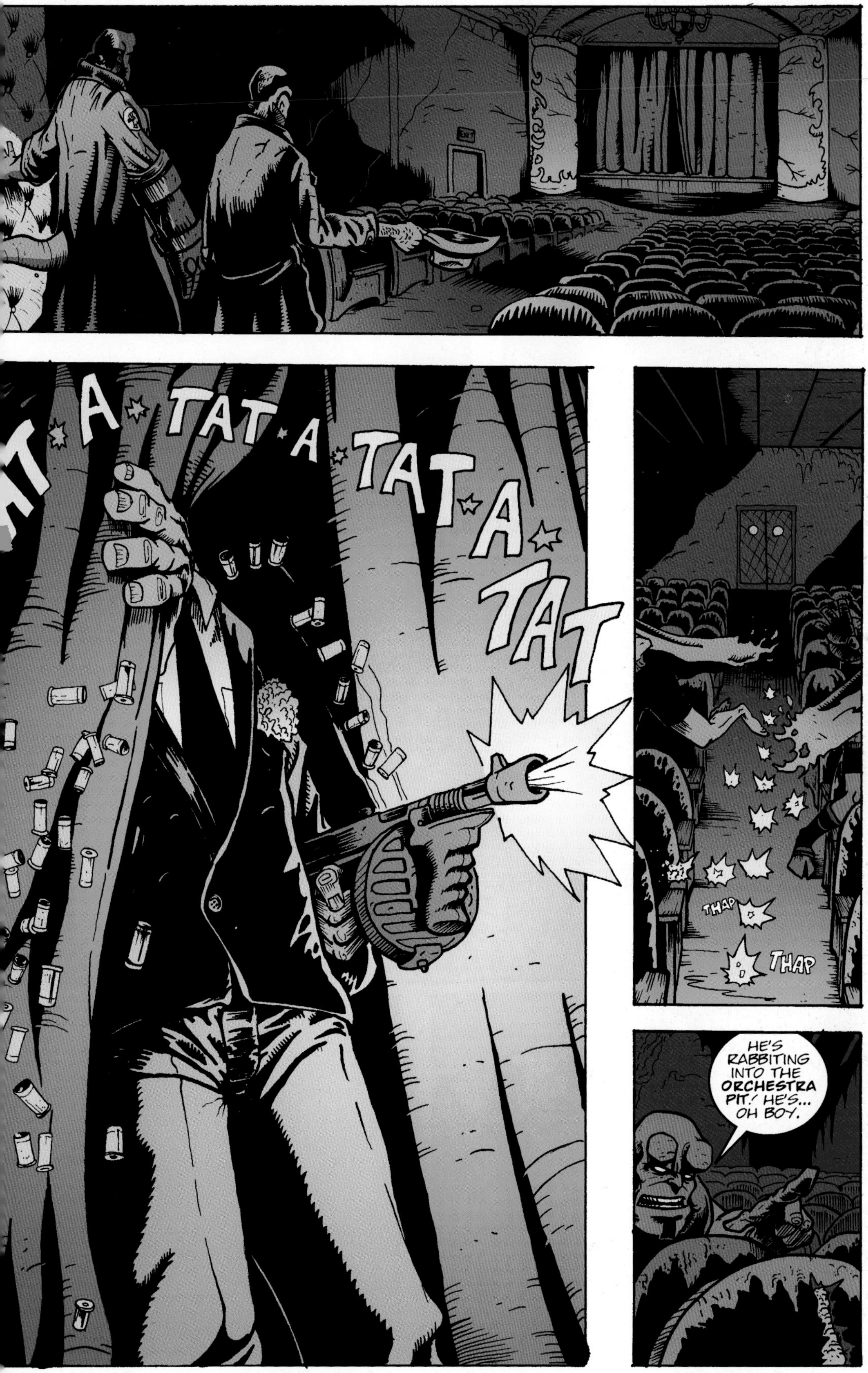
EXIT
AT A TAT A TAT A TAT
THAP
THAP
HE'S RABBITING INTO THE **ORCHESTRA PIT**! HE'S... OH BOY.

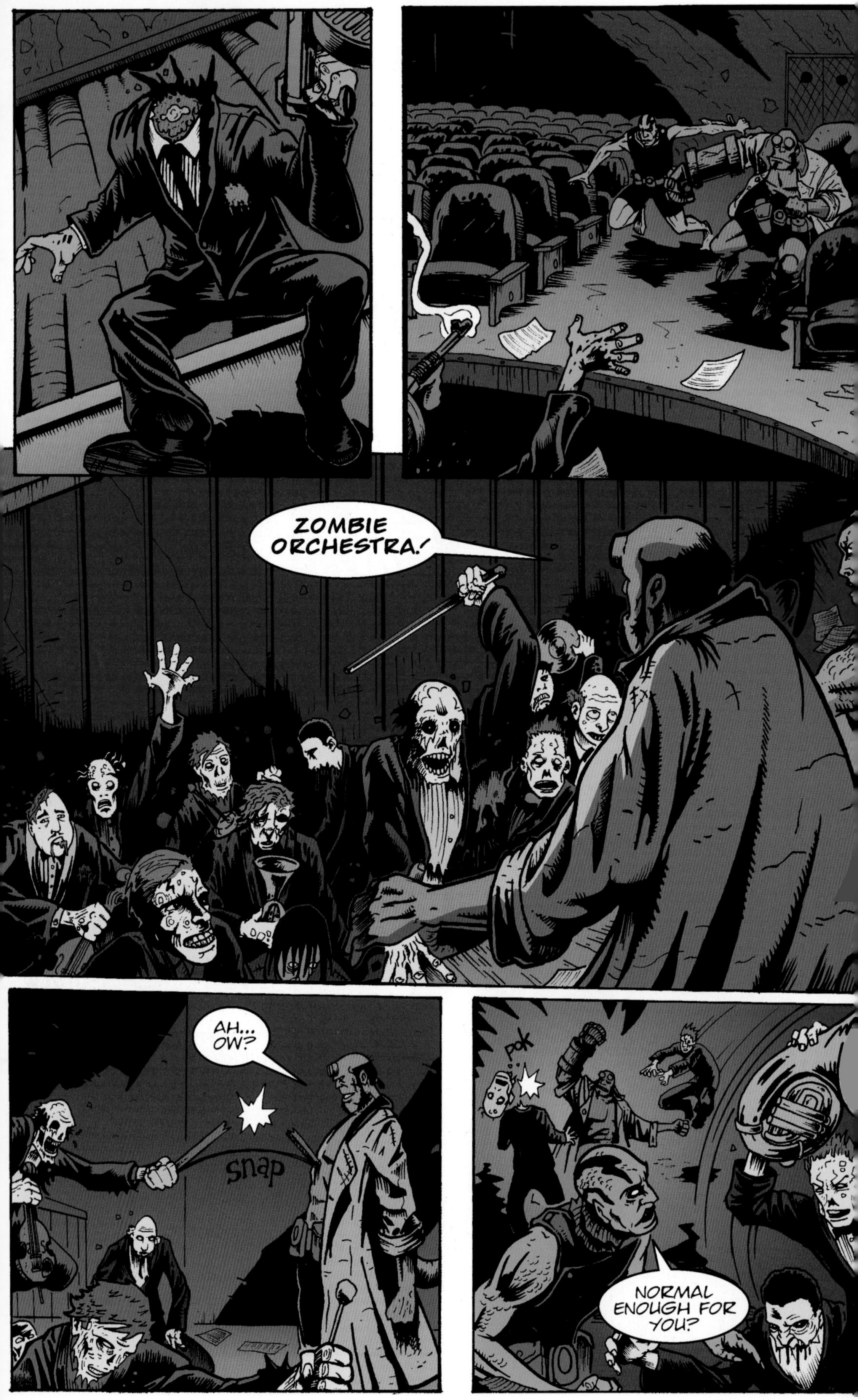
ZOMBIE ORCHESTRA!
AH... OW?
SNAP
POK
NORMAL ENOUGH FOR YOU?

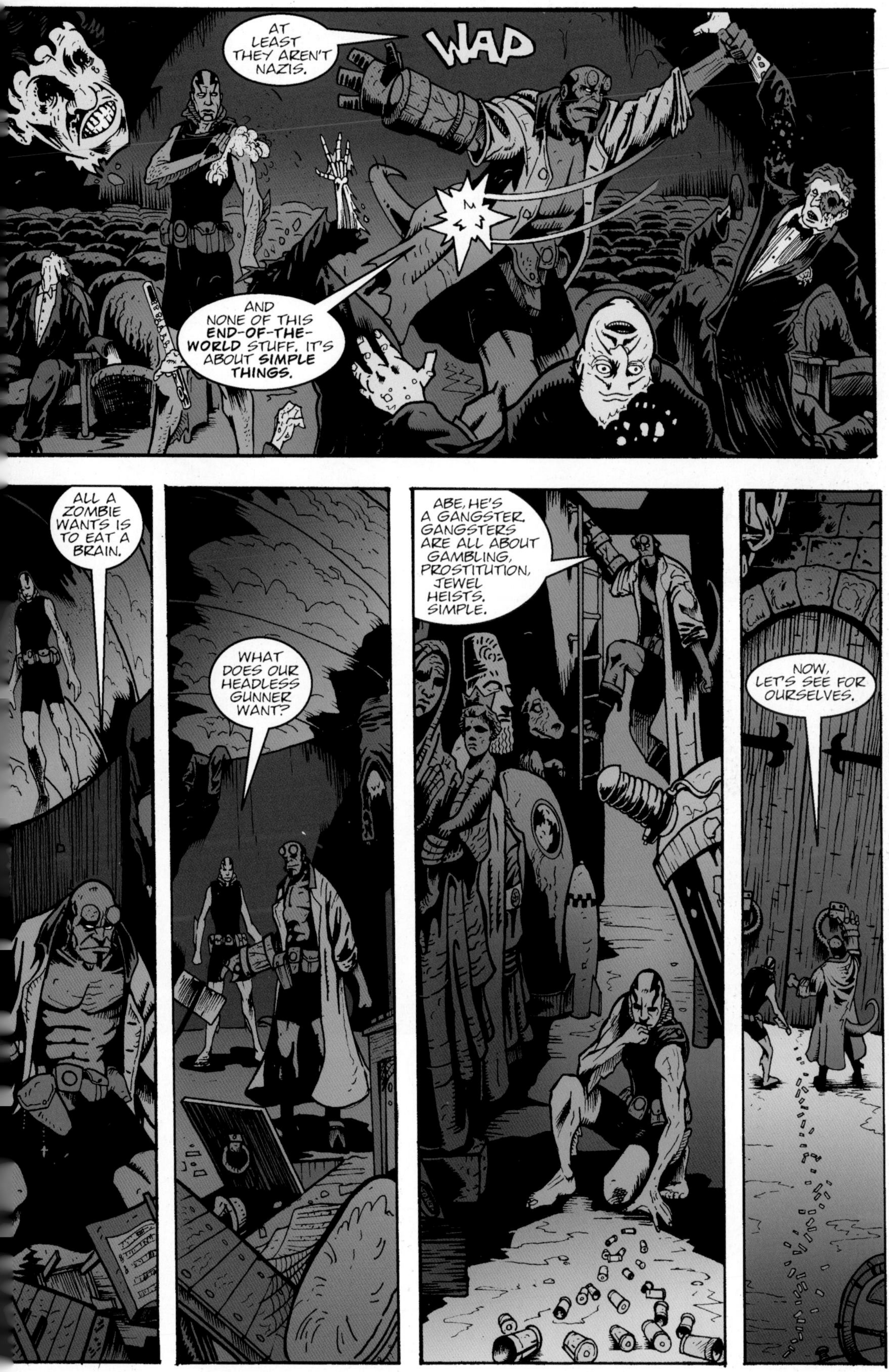
AT LEAST THEY AREN'T NAZIS.
WAP
AND NONE OF THIS **END-OF-THE-WORLD** STUFF. IT'S ABOUT **SIMPLE THINGS.**
ALL A ZOMBIE WANTS IS TO EAT A BRAIN.
WHAT DOES OUR HEADLESS GUNNER WANT?
ABE, HE'S A GANGSTER. GANGSTERS ARE ALL ABOUT GAMBLING, PROSTITUTION, JEWEL HEISTS. SIMPLE.
NOW, LET'S SEE FOR OURSELVES.

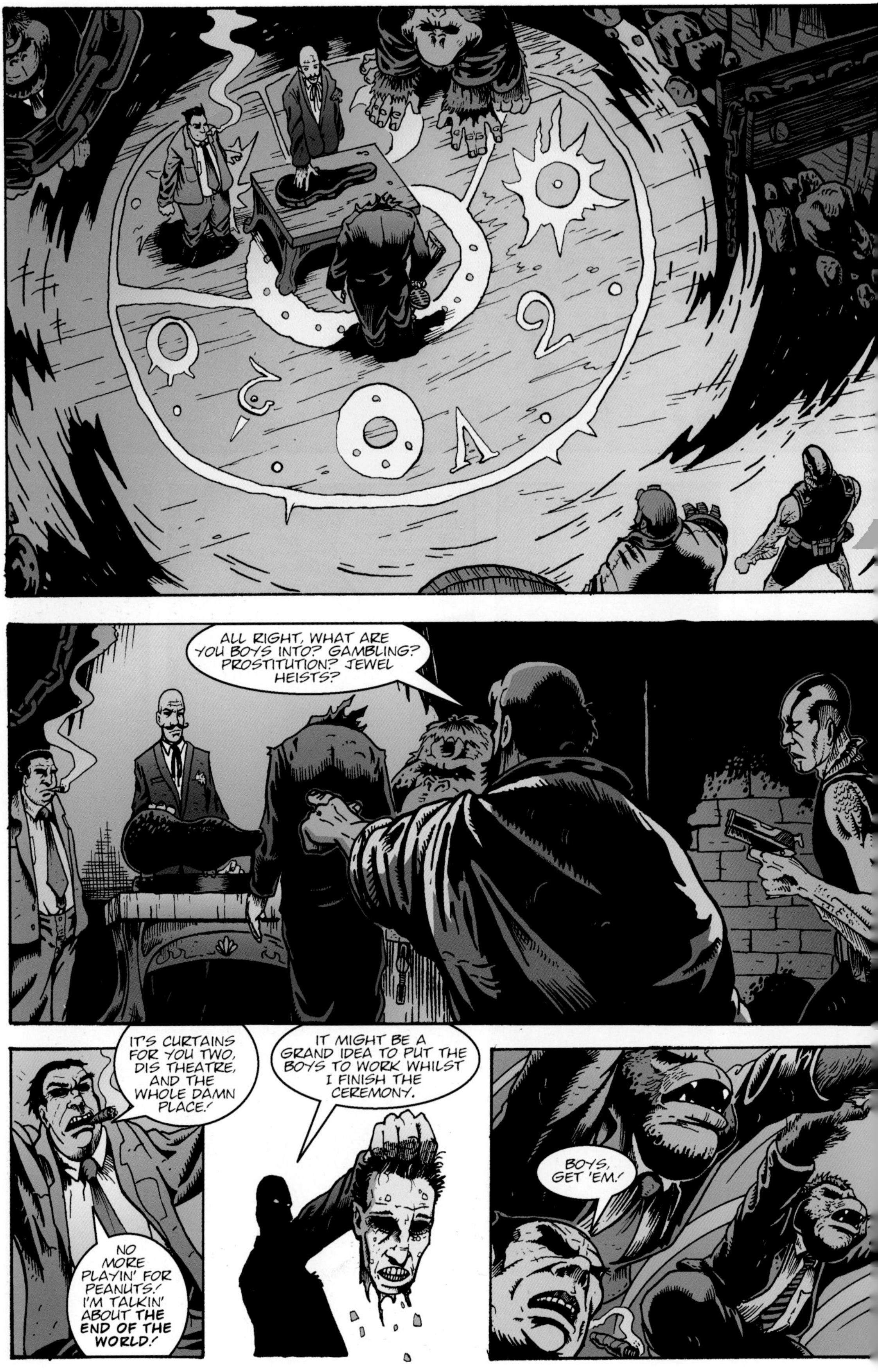
ALL RIGHT, WHAT ARE YOU BOYS INTO? GAMBLING? PROSTITUTION? JEWEL HEISTS?
IT'S CURTAINS FOR YOU TWO, DIS THEATRE, AND THE WHOLE DAMN PLACE!
NO MORE PLAYIN' FOR PEANUTS! I'M TALKIN' ABOUT THE END OF THE WORLD!
IT MIGHT BE A GRAND IDEA TO PUT THE BOYS TO WORK WHILST I FINISH THE CEREMONY.
BOYS, GET 'EM!

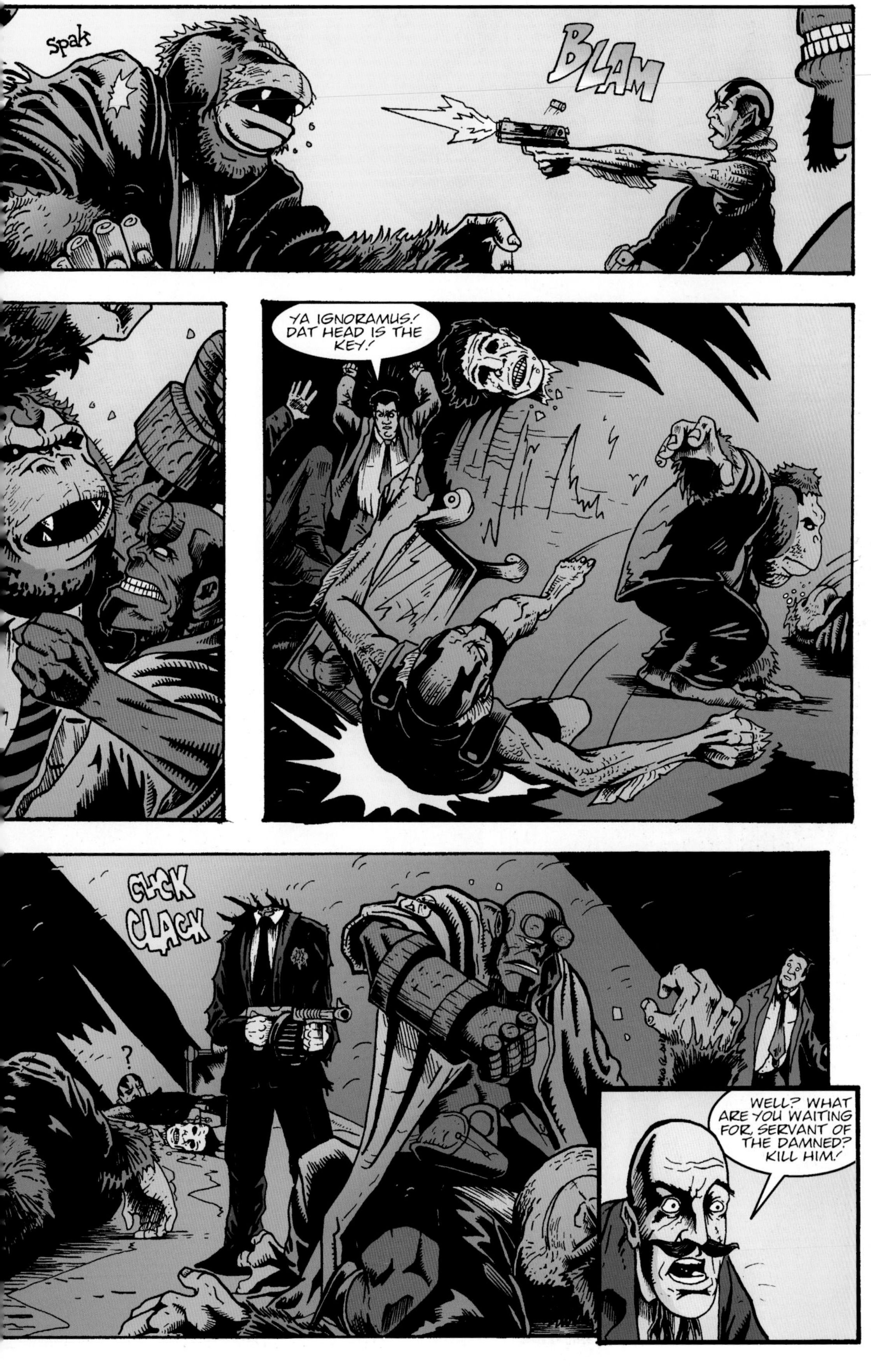
Spak
BLAM
YA IGNORAMUS! DAT HEAD IS THE KEY!
CLICK CLACK
?
WELL? WHAT ARE YOU WAITING FOR, SERVANT OF THE DAMNED? KILL HIM!

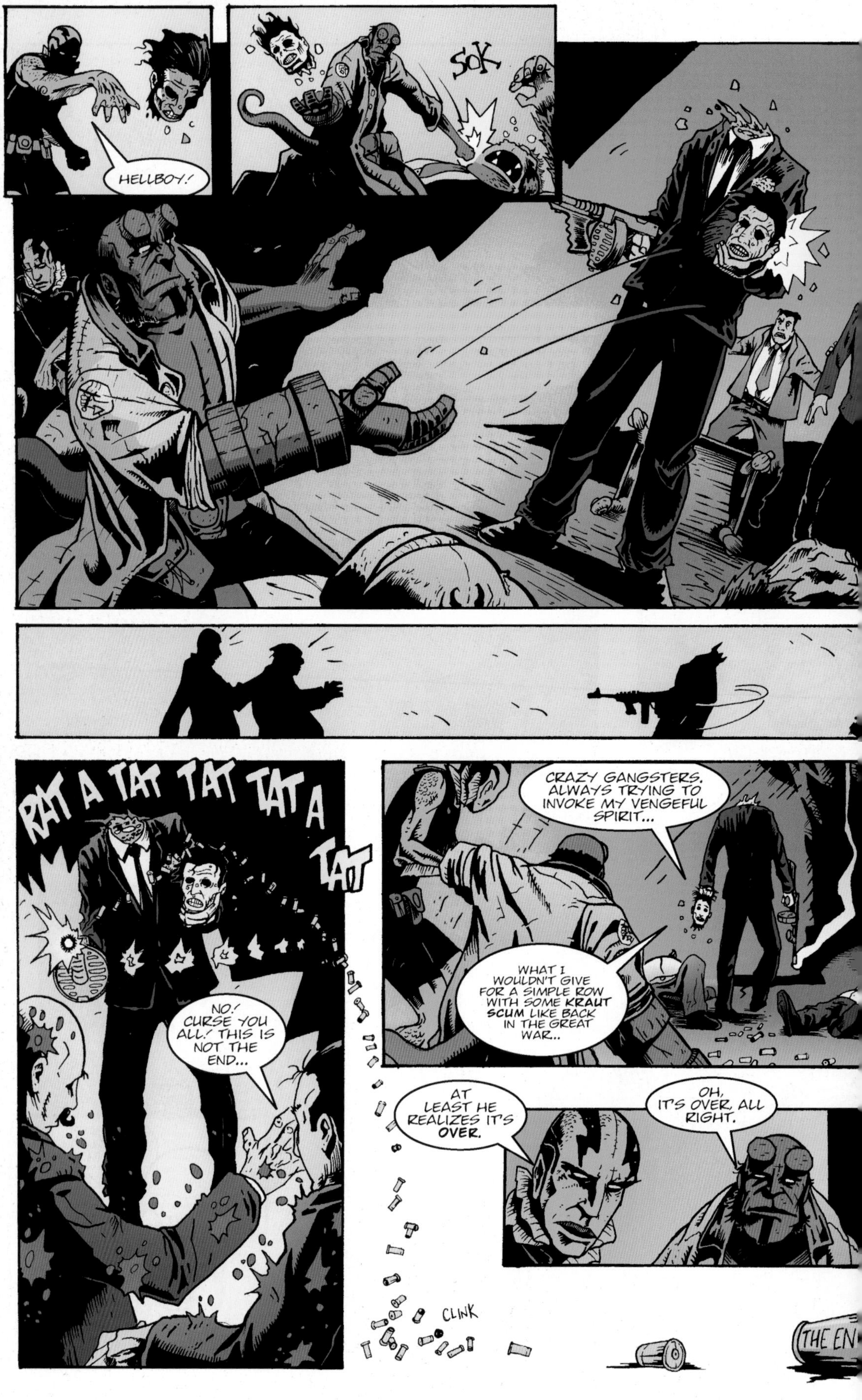
HELLBOY!
SOK
RAT A TAT TAT TAT A TAT
NO! CURSE YOU ALL! THIS IS NOT THE END...
CRAZY GANGSTERS. ALWAYS TRYING TO INVOKE MY VENGEFUL SPIRIT...
WHAT I WOULDN'T GIVE FOR A SIMPLE ROW WITH SOME KRAUT SCUM LIKE BACK IN THE GREAT WAR...
AT LEAST HE REALIZES IT'S OVER.
OH, IT'S OVER, ALL RIGHT.
CLINK
THE EN

ia asamiya &
kira yoshida
art and story

toy soldier

dave stewart
colors

clem robins
letters

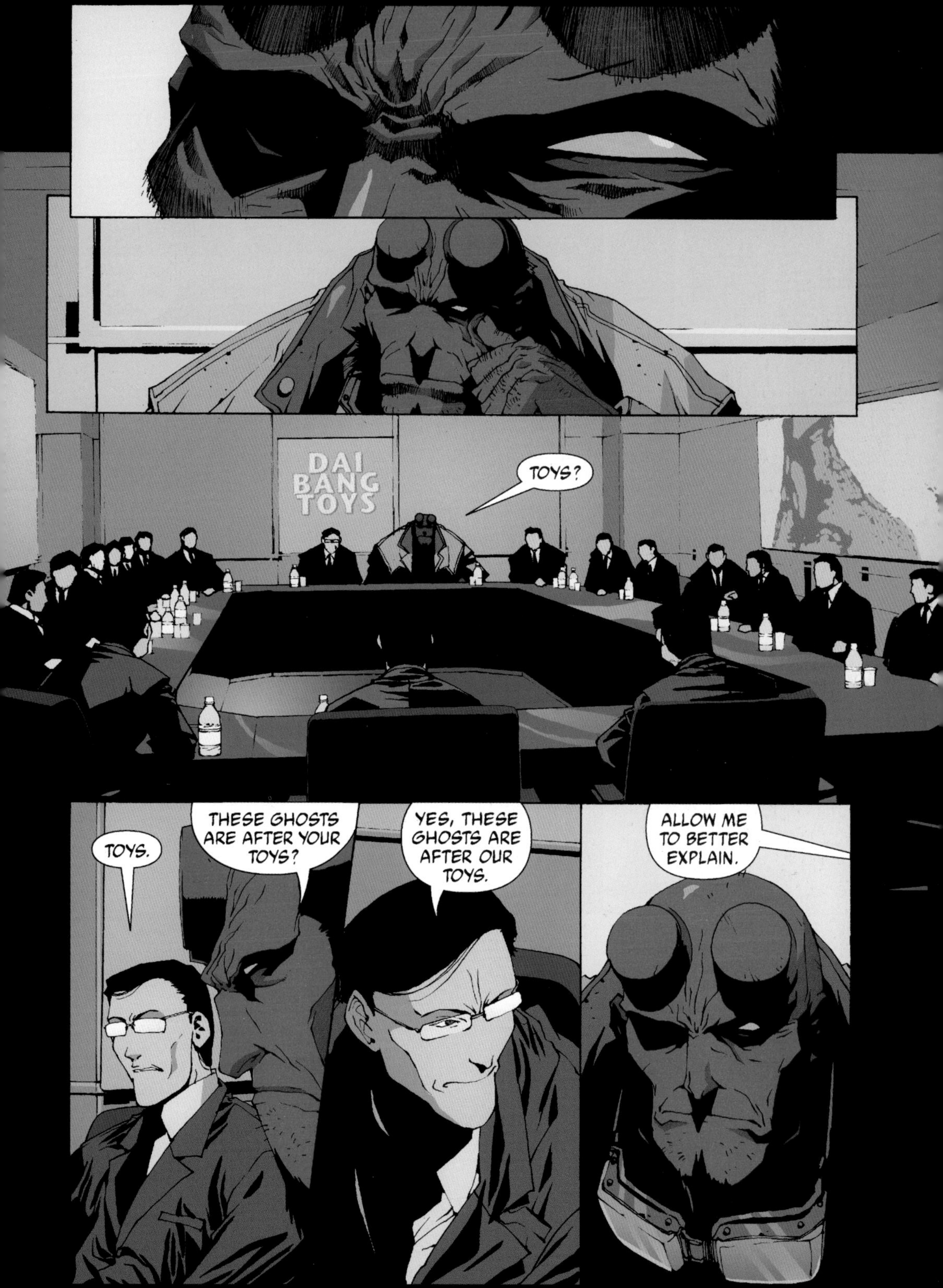
DAI BANG TOYS
TOYS?
TOYS.
THESE GHOSTS ARE AFTER YOUR TOYS?
YES, THESE GHOSTS ARE AFTER OUR TOYS.
ALLOW ME TO BETTER EXPLAIN.

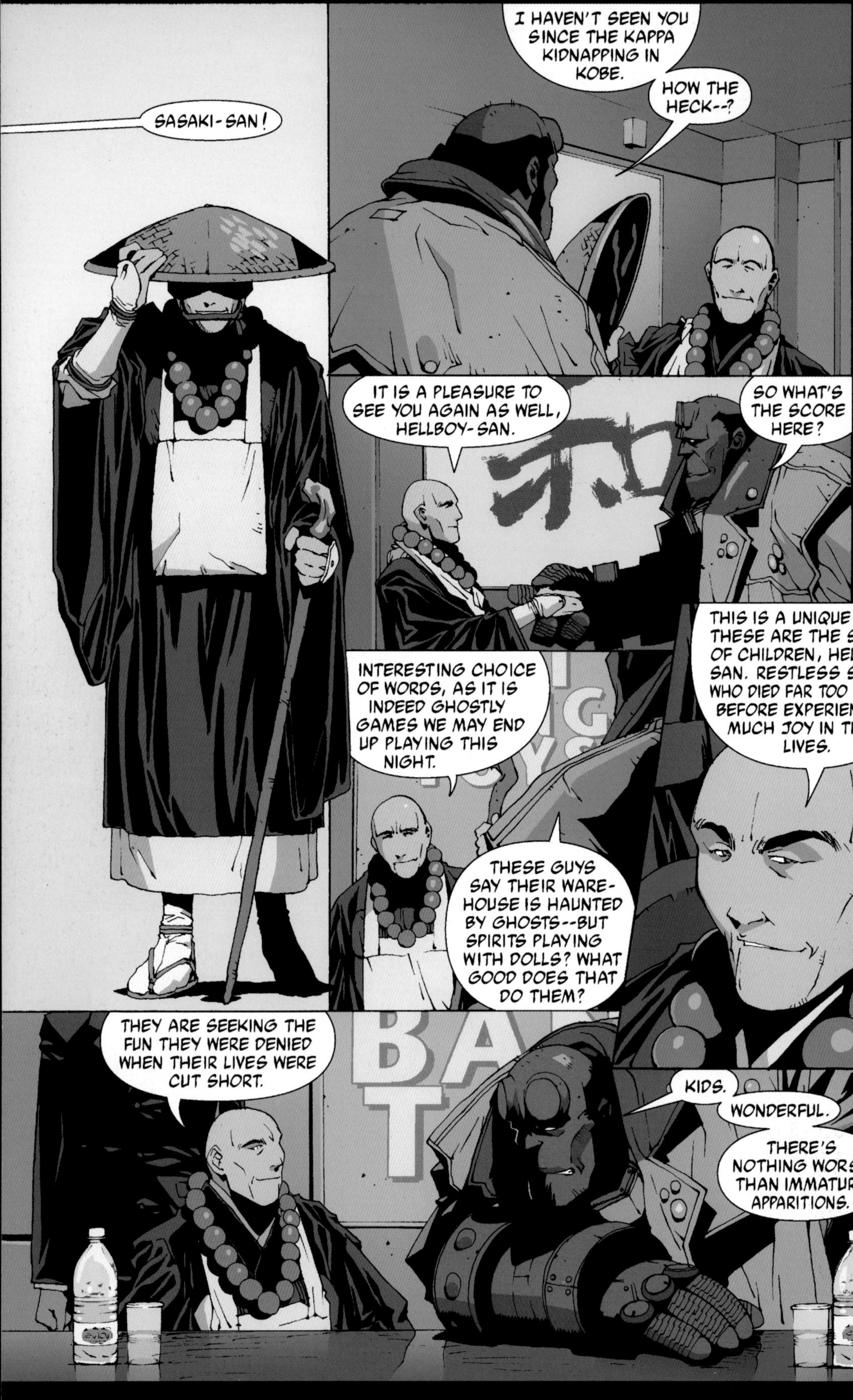
SASAKI-SAN!
I HAVEN'T SEEN YOU SINCE THE KAPPA KIDNAPPING IN KOBE.
HOW THE HECK--?
IT IS A PLEASURE TO SEE YOU AGAIN AS WELL, HELLBOY-SAN.
SO WHAT'S THE SCORE HERE?
INTERESTING CHOICE OF WORDS, AS IT IS INDEED GHOSTLY GAMES WE MAY END UP PLAYING THIS NIGHT.
THESE GUYS SAY THEIR WARE-HOUSE IS HAUNTED BY GHOSTS--BUT SPIRITS PLAYING WITH DOLLS? WHAT GOOD DOES THAT DO THEM?
THIS IS A UNIQUE CASE. THESE ARE THE SPIRITS OF CHILDREN, HELLBOY-SAN. RESTLESS SPIRITS WHO DIED FAR TOO YOUNG, BEFORE EXPERIENCING MUCH JOY IN THEIR LIVES.
THEY ARE SEEKING THE FUN THEY WERE DENIED WHEN THEIR LIVES WERE CUT SHORT.
KIDS.
WONDERFUL.
THERE'S NOTHING WORSE THAN IMMATURE APPARITIONS.

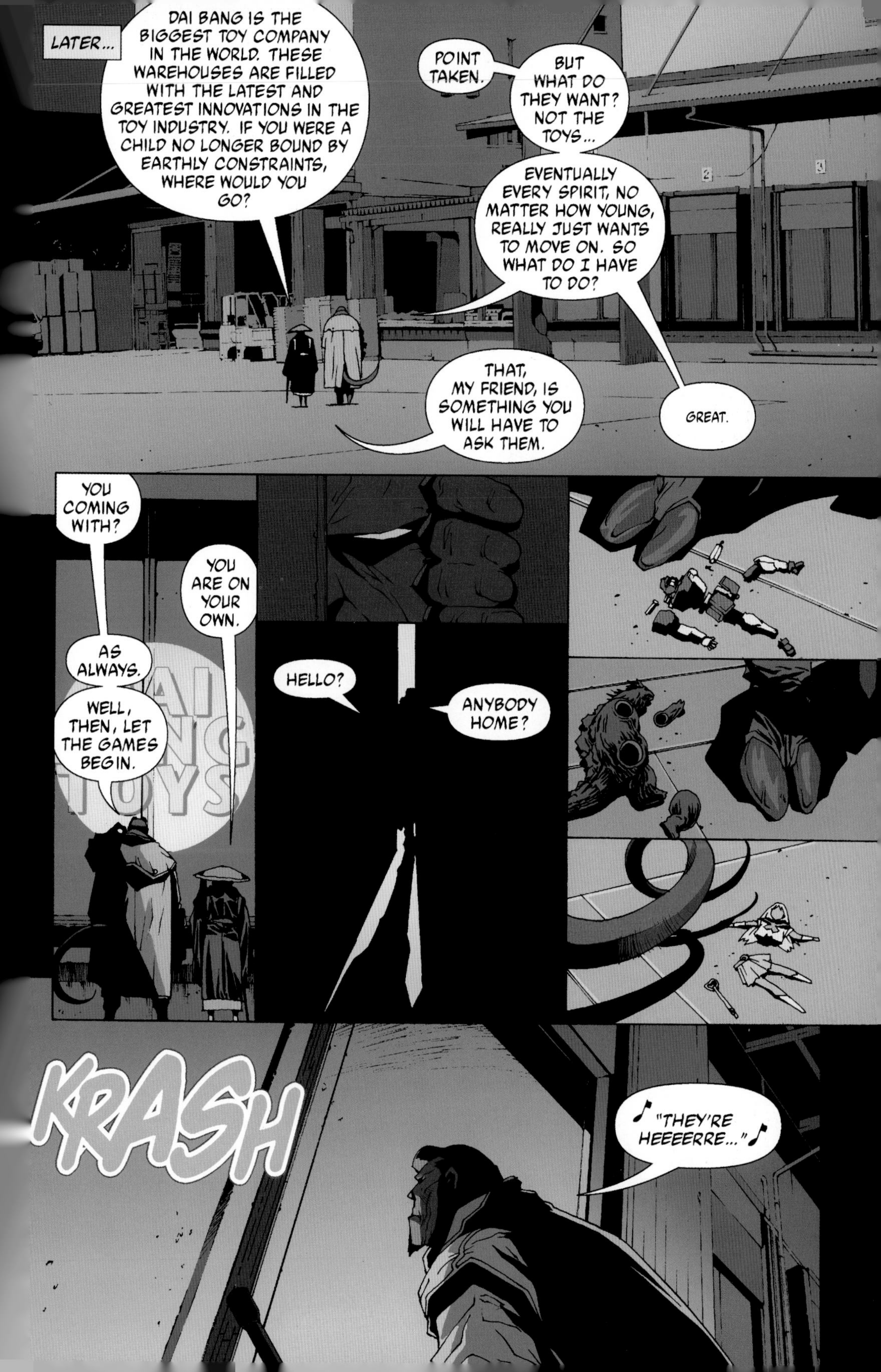

LATER...
DAI BANG IS THE BIGGEST TOY COMPANY IN THE WORLD. THESE WAREHOUSES ARE FILLED WITH THE LATEST AND GREATEST INNOVATIONS IN THE TOY INDUSTRY. IF YOU WERE A CHILD NO LONGER BOUND BY EARTHLY CONSTRAINTS, WHERE WOULD YOU GO?
POINT TAKEN.
BUT WHAT DO THEY WANT? NOT THE TOYS...
EVENTUALLY EVERY SPIRIT, NO MATTER HOW YOUNG, REALLY JUST WANTS TO MOVE ON. SO WHAT DO I HAVE TO DO?
THAT, MY FRIEND, IS SOMETHING YOU WILL HAVE TO ASK THEM.
GREAT.
YOU COMING WITH?
YOU ARE ON YOUR OWN.
AS ALWAYS.
WELL, THEN, LET THE GAMES BEGIN.
TOYS
HELLO?
ANYBODY HOME?
KRASH
♪ "THEY'RE HEEEERRE..." ♪

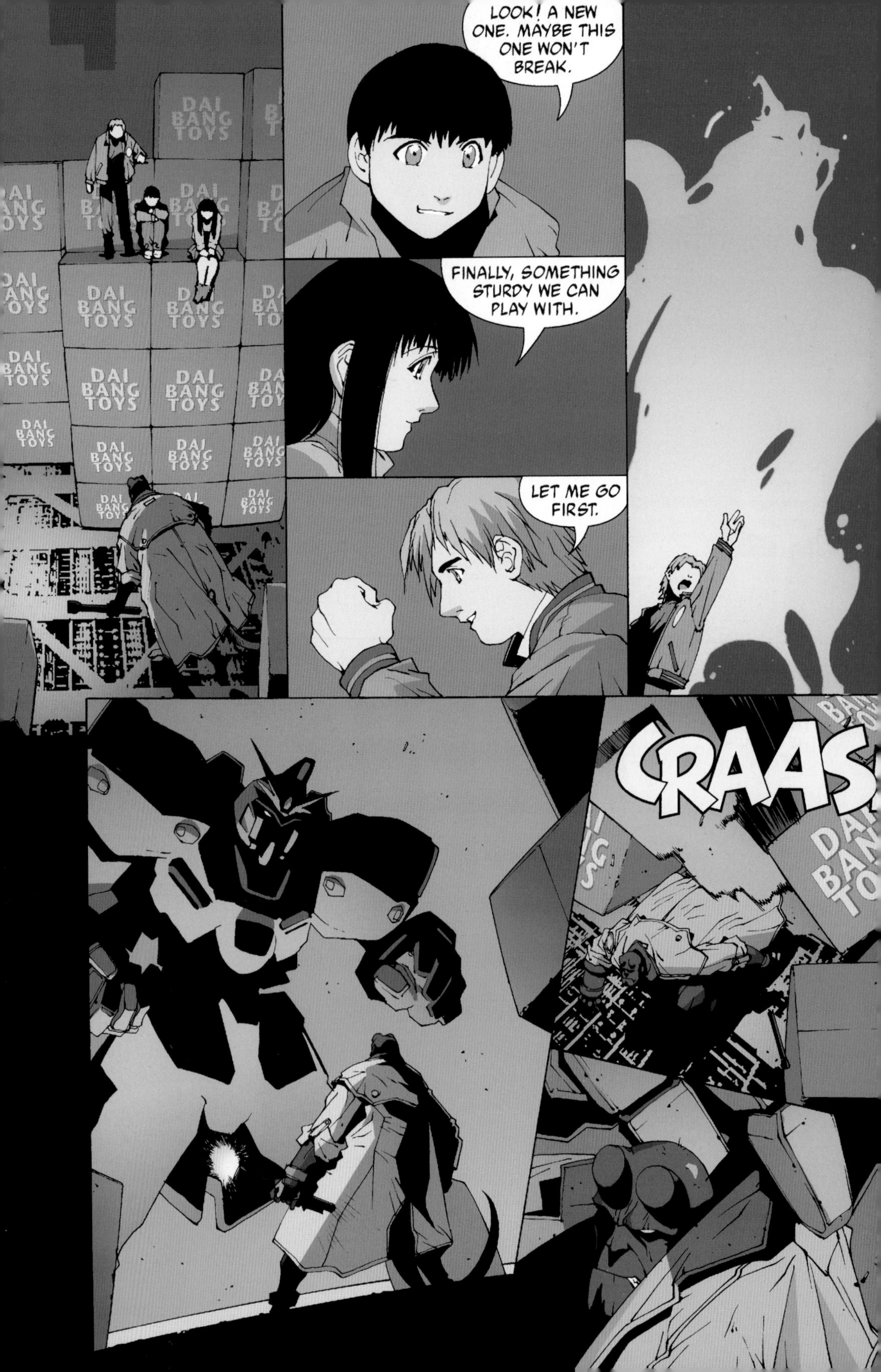
DAI BANG TOYS
LOOK! A NEW ONE. MAYBE THIS ONE WON'T BREAK.
FINALLY, SOMETHING STURDY WE CAN PLAY WITH.
LET ME GO FIRST.
CRAAS

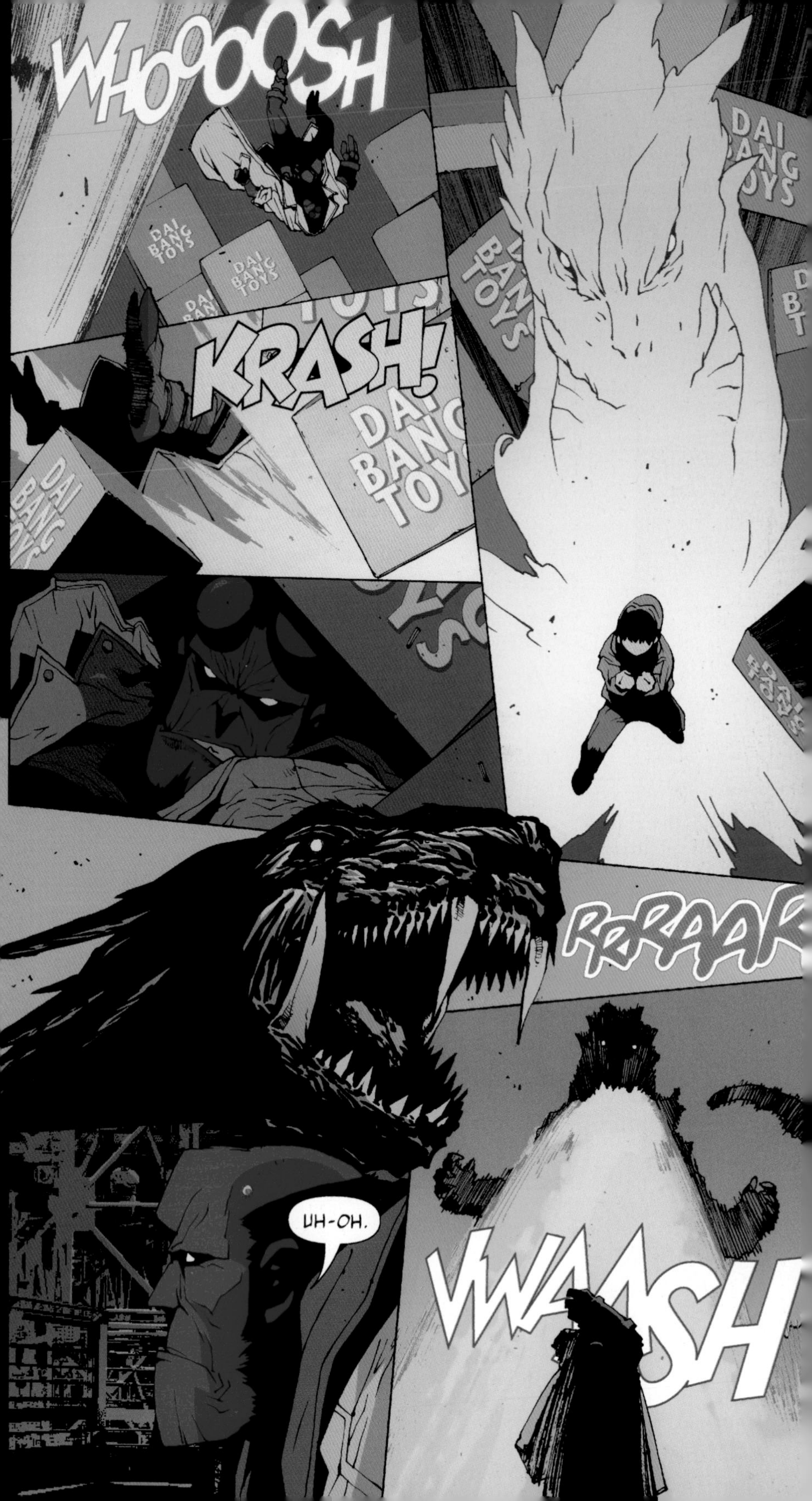
WHOOOOSH
DAI BANG TOYS
DAI BANG TOYS
KRASH!
DAI BANG TOYS
DAI BANG TOYS
DAI BANG TOYS
DAI BANG TOYS
RRRAAAR
UH-OH.
VWAASH

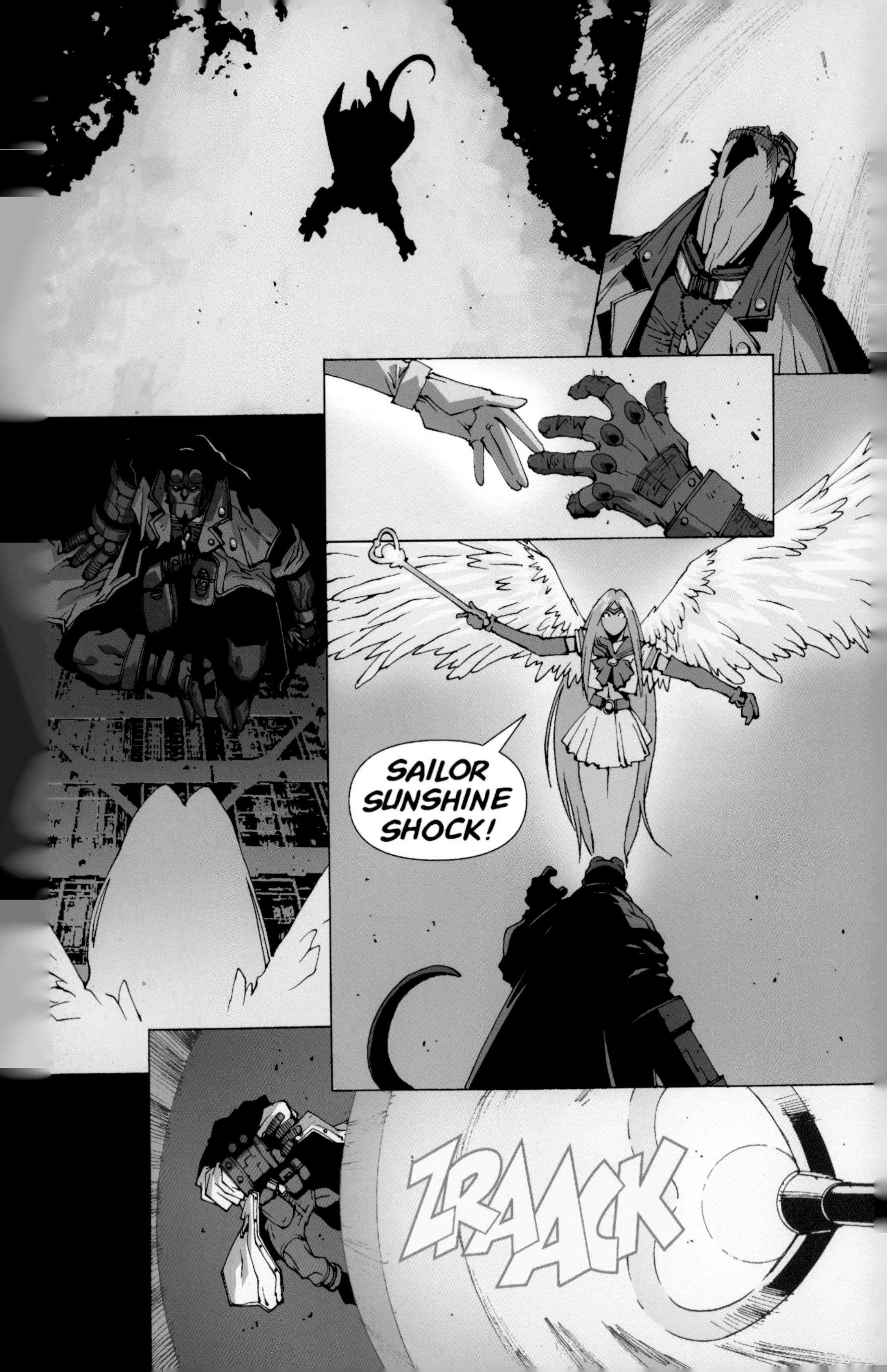
SAILOR SUNSHINE SHOCK!
ZRAACK

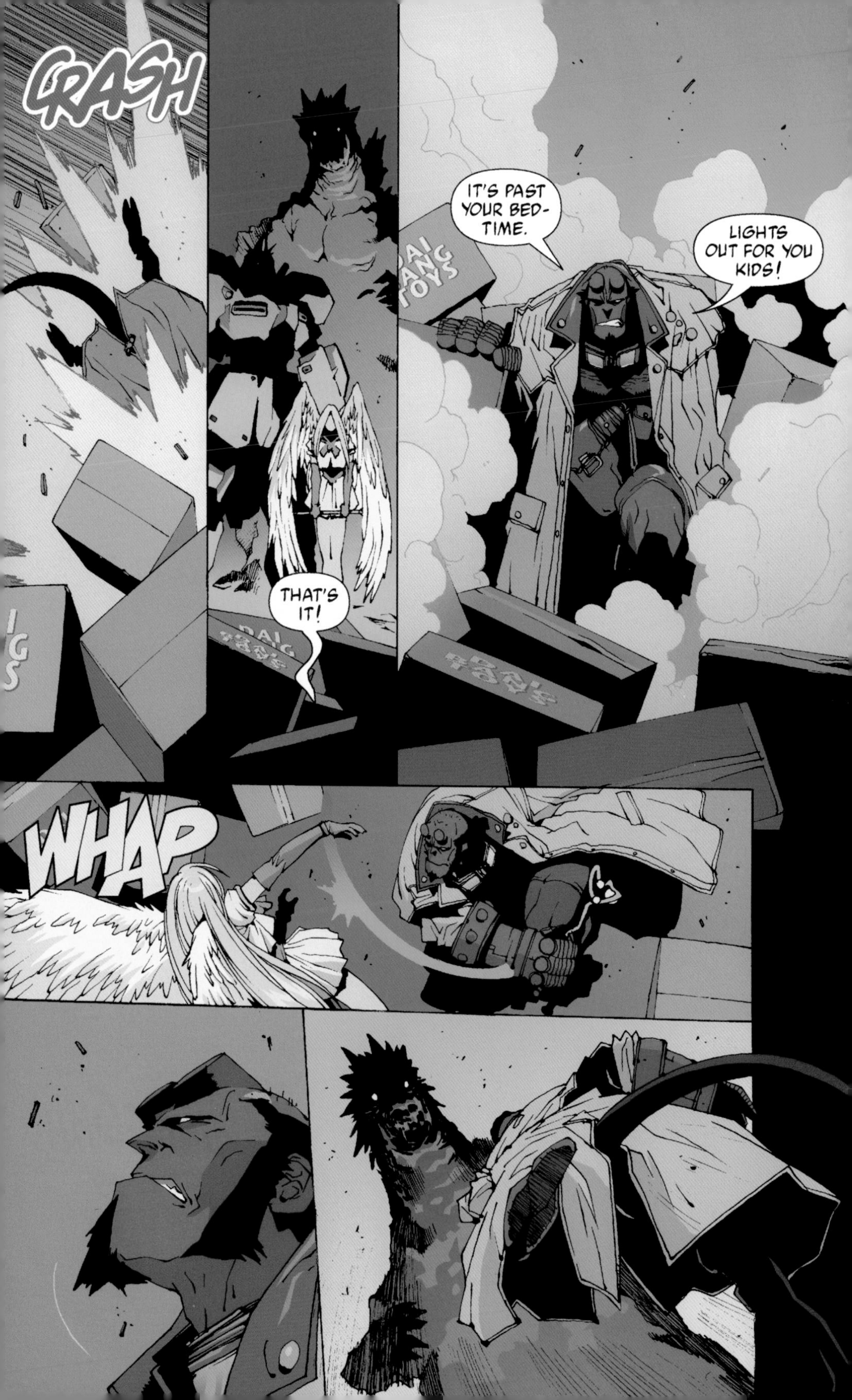
CRASH
IT'S PAST YOUR BED-TIME.
LIGHTS OUT FOR YOU KIDS!
THAT'S IT!
WHAP

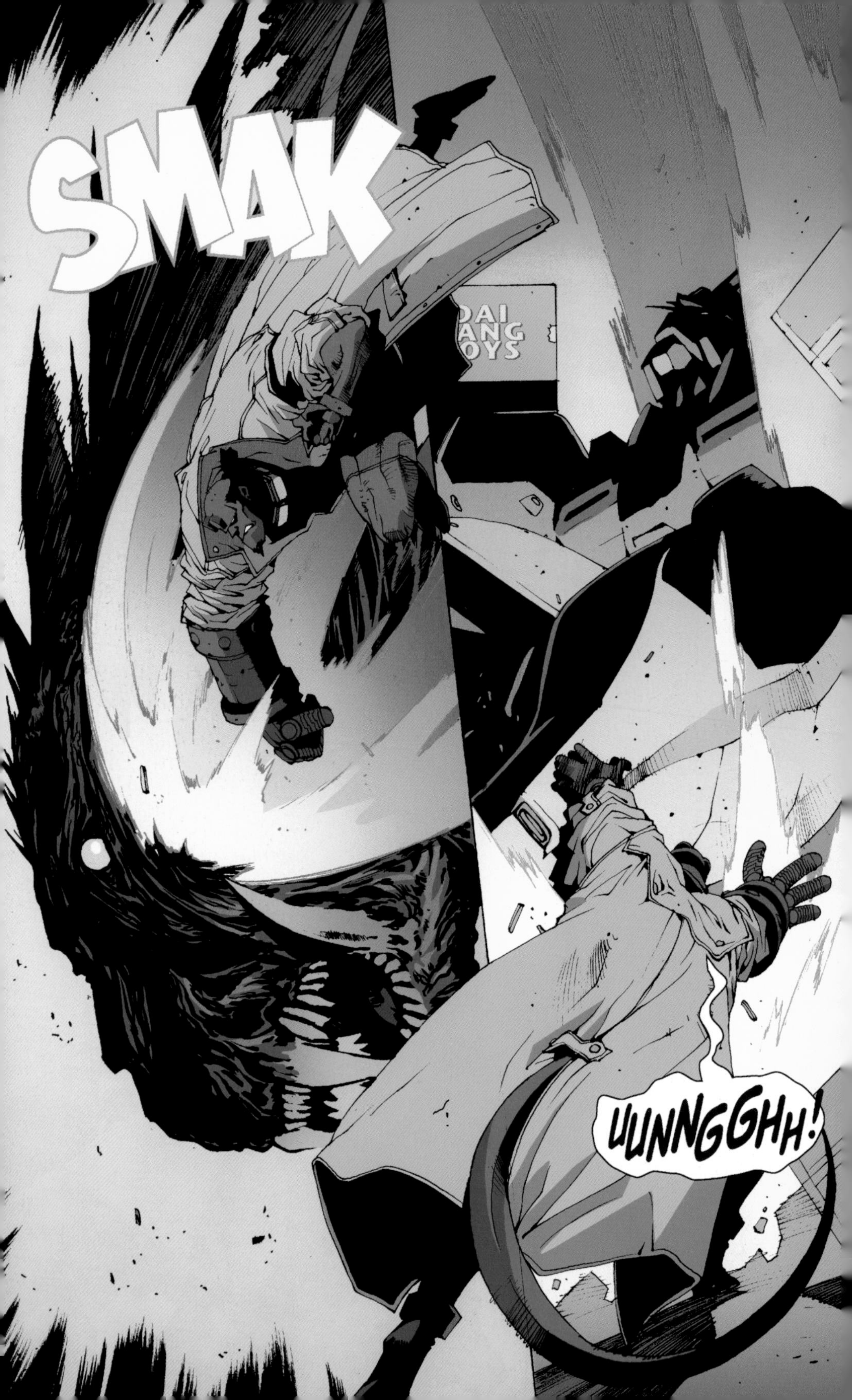
SMAK
UUNNGGHH!

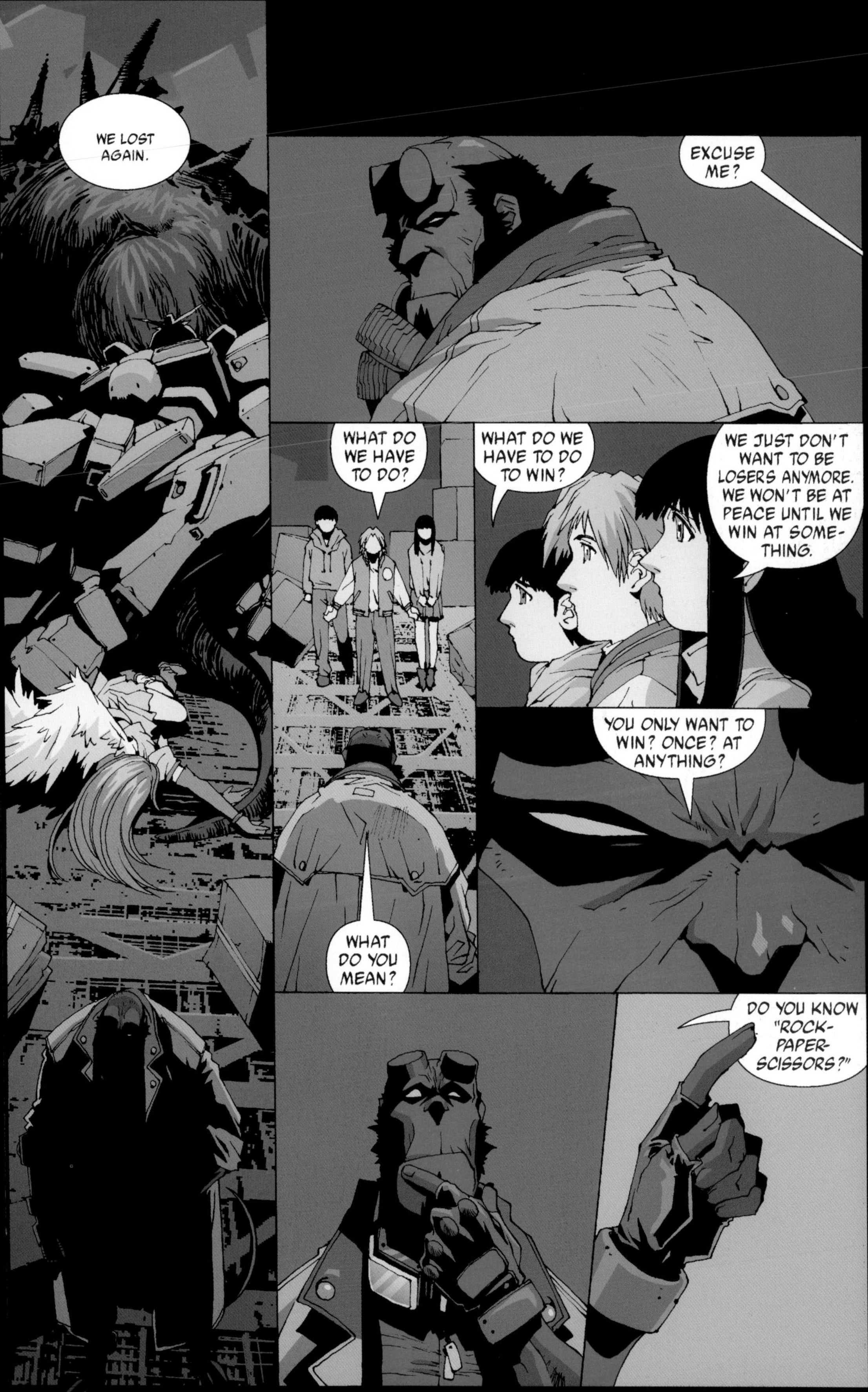
WE LOST AGAIN.
EXCUSE ME?
WHAT DO WE HAVE TO DO?
WHAT DO WE HAVE TO DO TO WIN?
WE JUST DON'T WANT TO BE LOSERS ANYMORE. WE WON'T BE AT PEACE UNTIL WE WIN AT SOME-THING.
WHAT DO YOU MEAN?
YOU ONLY WANT TO WIN? ONCE? AT ANYTHING?
DO YOU KNOW "ROCK-PAPER-SCISSORS?"

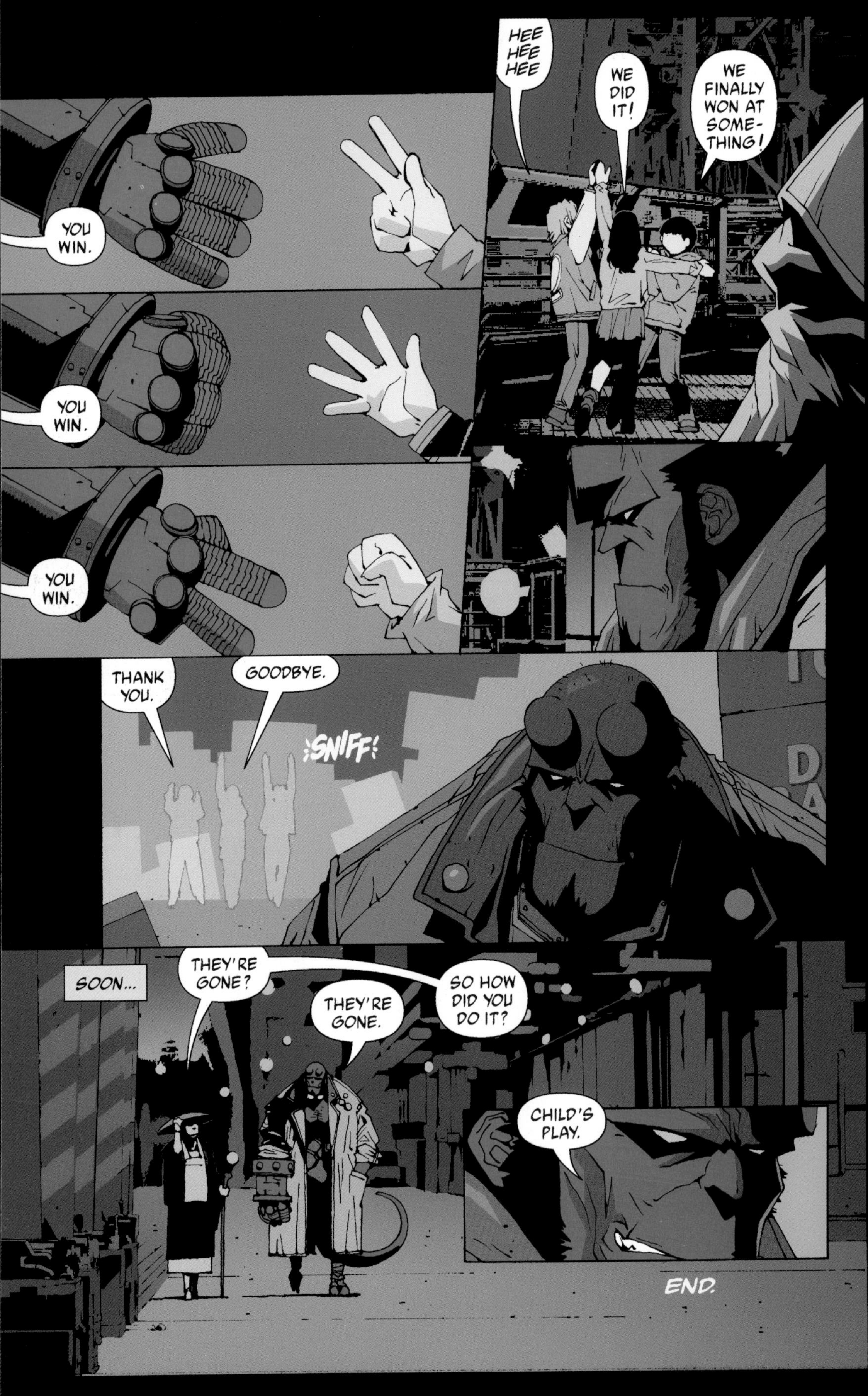
YOU WIN.
HEE HEE HEE
WE DID IT!
WE FINALLY WON AT SOME-THING!
YOU WIN.
YOU WIN.
THANK YOU.
GOODBYE.
SNIFF!
SOON...
THEY'RE GONE?
THEY'RE GONE.
SO HOW DID YOU DO IT?
CHILD'S PLAY.
END.

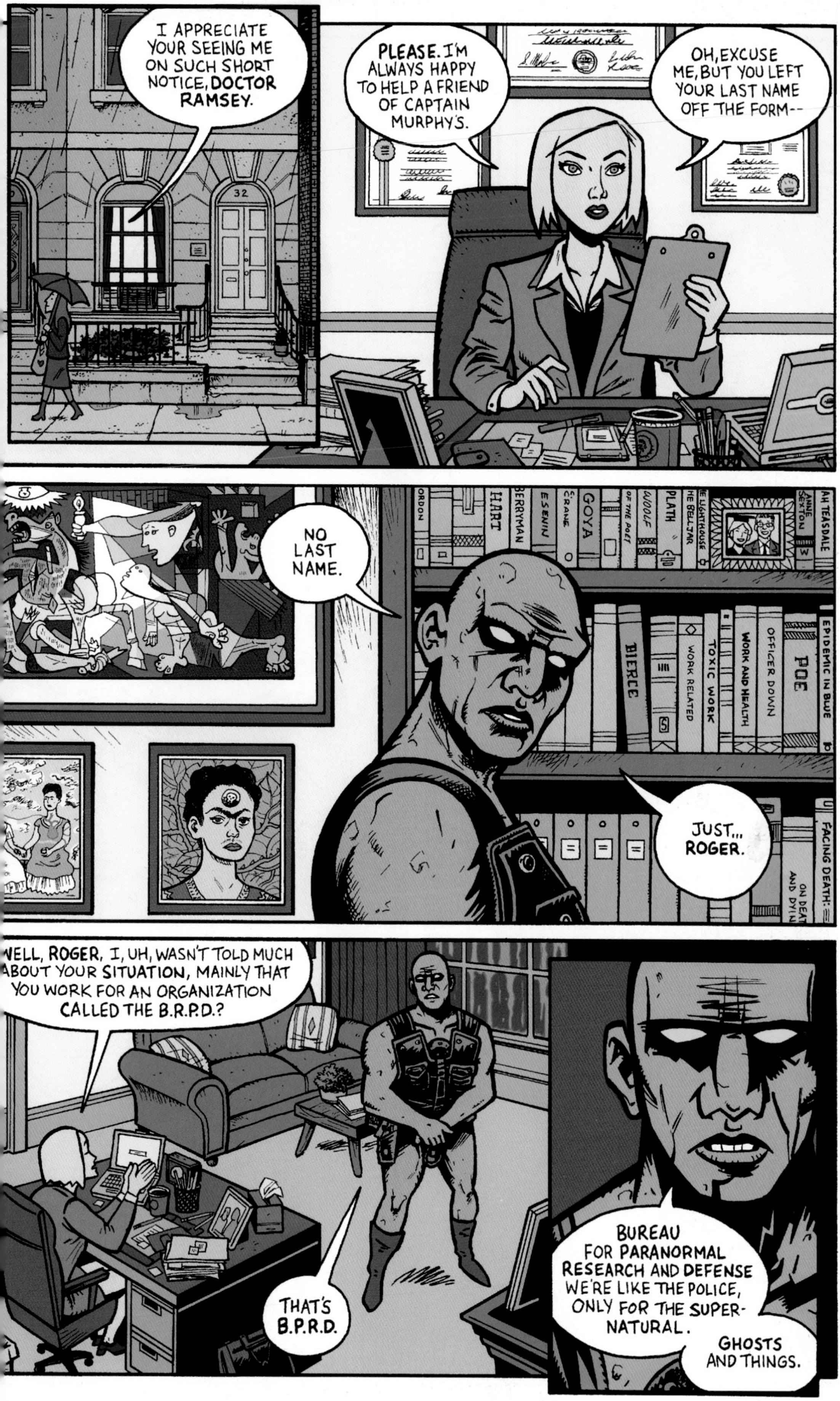

I APPRECIATE YOUR SEEING ME ON SUCH SHORT NOTICE, DOCTOR RAMSEY.
PLEASE. I'M ALWAYS HAPPY TO HELP A FRIEND OF CAPTAIN MURPHY'S.
OH, EXCUSE ME, BUT YOU LEFT YOUR LAST NAME OFF THE FORM--
NO LAST NAME.
JUST... ROGER.
WELL, ROGER, I, UH, WASN'T TOLD MUCH ABOUT YOUR SITUATION, MAINLY THAT YOU WORK FOR AN ORGANIZATION CALLED THE B.R.P.D.?
THAT'S B.P.R.D.
BUREAU FOR PARANORMAL RESEARCH AND DEFENSE WE'RE LIKE THE POLICE, ONLY FOR THE SUPER-NATURAL.
GHOSTS AND THINGS.

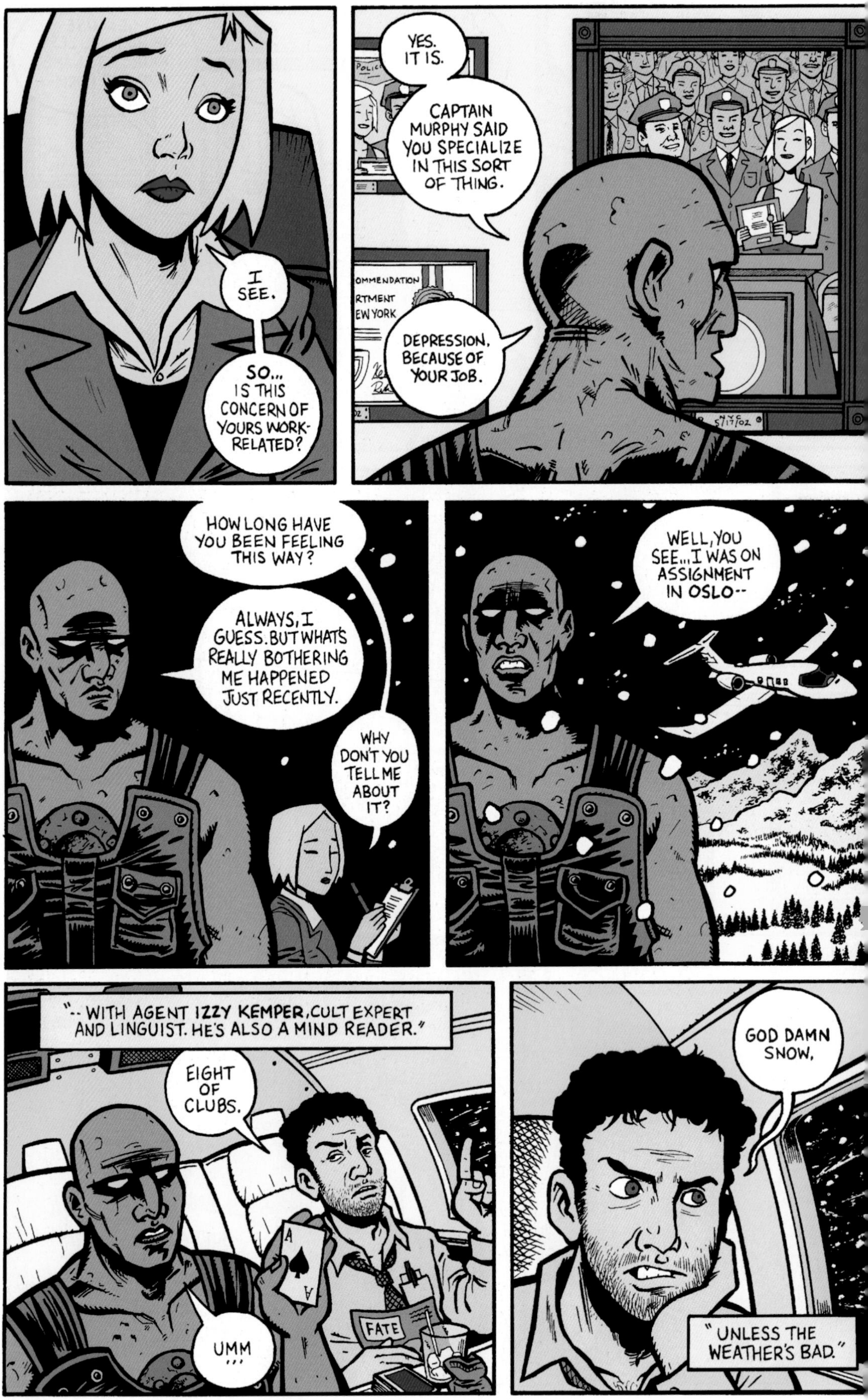

I SEE.
SO... IS THIS CONCERN OF YOURS WORK-RELATED?
YES. IT IS.
CAPTAIN MURPHY SAID YOU SPECIALIZE IN THIS SORT OF THING.
DEPRESSION, BECAUSE OF YOUR JOB.
HOW LONG HAVE YOU BEEN FEELING THIS WAY?
ALWAYS, I GUESS. BUT WHAT'S REALLY BOTHERING ME HAPPENED JUST RECENTLY.
WHY DON'T YOU TELL ME ABOUT IT?
WELL, YOU SEE... I WAS ON ASSIGNMENT IN OSLO--
"-- WITH AGENT IZZY KEMPER, CULT EXPERT AND LINGUIST. HE'S ALSO A MIND READER."
EIGHT OF CLUBS.
UMM ...
FATE
GOD DAMN SNOW,
"UNLESS THE WEATHER'S BAD."

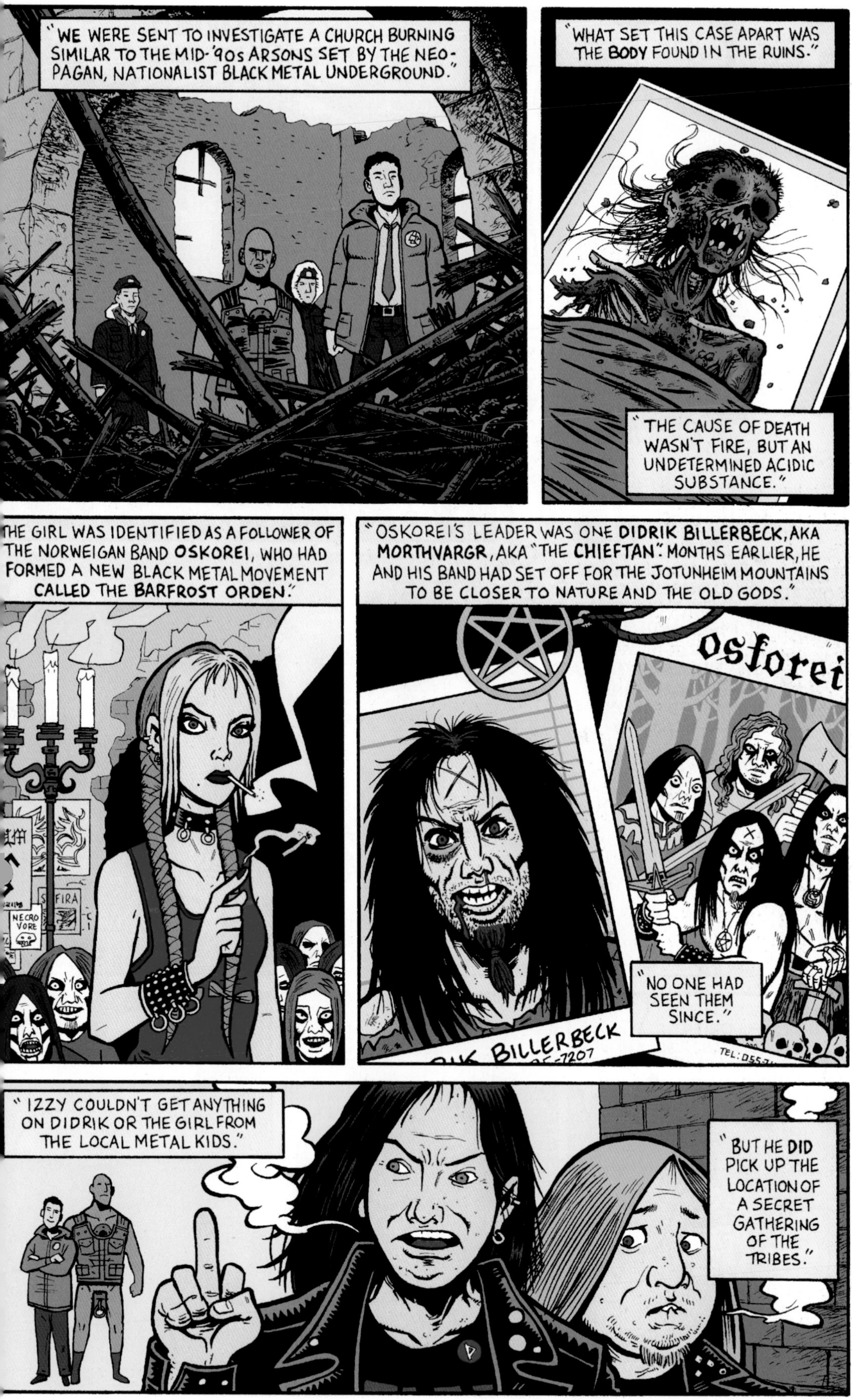
"WE WERE SENT TO INVESTIGATE A CHURCH BURNING SIMILAR TO THE MID-'90s ARSONS SET BY THE NEO-PAGAN, NATIONALIST BLACK METAL UNDERGROUND."
"WHAT SET THIS CASE APART WAS THE BODY FOUND IN THE RUINS."
"THE CAUSE OF DEATH WASN'T FIRE, BUT AN UNDETERMINED ACIDIC SUBSTANCE."
THE GIRL WAS IDENTIFIED AS A FOLLOWER OF THE NORWEIGAN BAND OSKOREI, WHO HAD FORMED A NEW BLACK METAL MOVEMENT CALLED THE BARFROST ORDEN."
NECRO VORE
"OSKOREI'S LEADER WAS ONE DIDRIK BILLERBECK, AKA MORTHVARGR, AKA "THE CHIEFTAN". MONTHS EARLIER, HE AND HIS BAND HAD SET OFF FOR THE JOTUNHEIM MOUNTAINS TO BE CLOSER TO NATURE AND THE OLD GODS."
osforei
"NO ONE HAD SEEN THEM SINCE."
BILLERBECK
"IZZY COULDN'T GET ANYTHING ON DIDRIK OR THE GIRL FROM THE LOCAL METAL KIDS."
"BUT HE DID PICK UP THE LOCATION OF A SECRET GATHERING OF THE TRIBES."

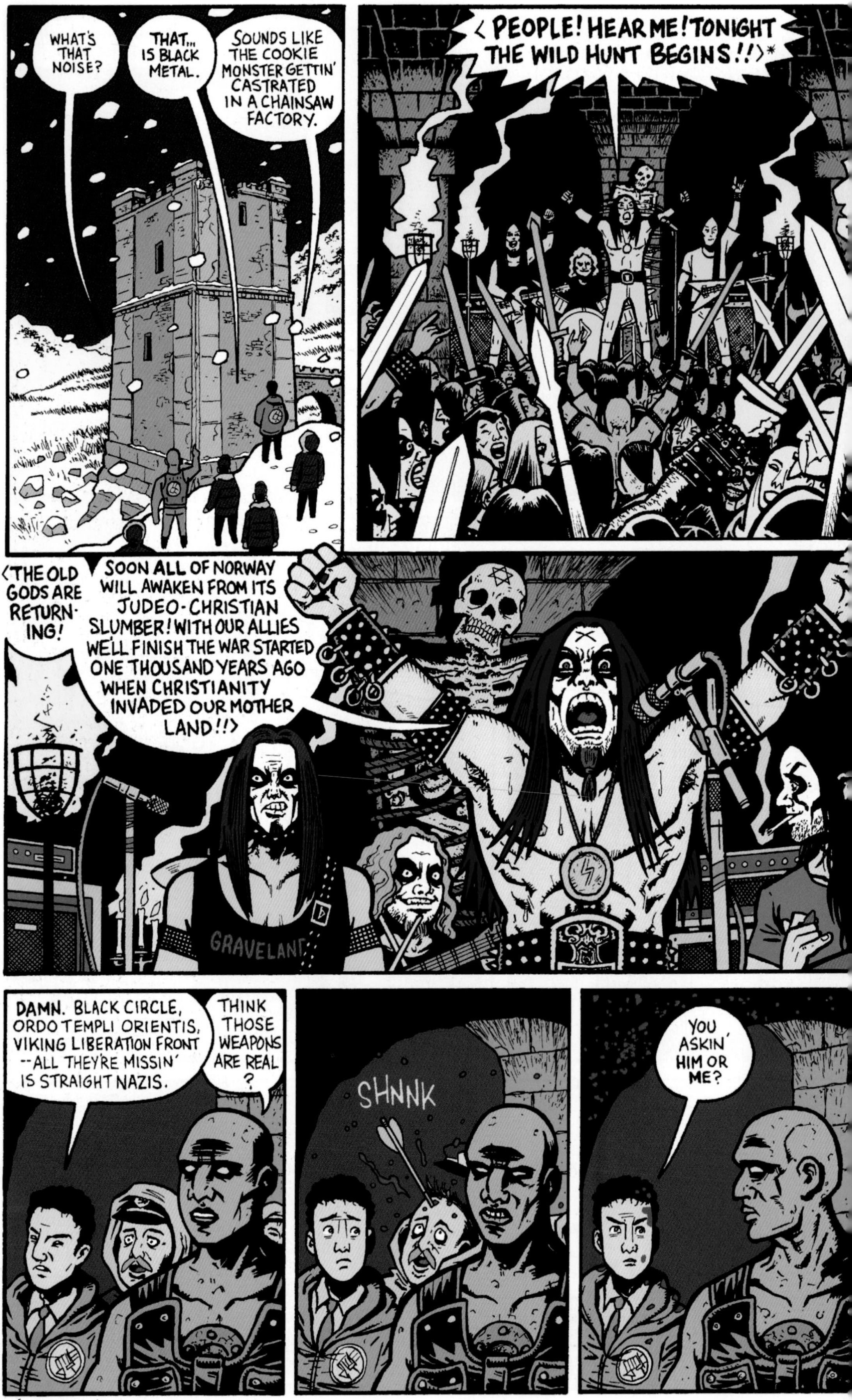
WHAT'S THAT NOISE?
THAT... IS BLACK METAL.
SOUNDS LIKE THE COOKIE MONSTER GETTIN' CASTRATED IN A CHAINSAW FACTORY.
< PEOPLE! HEAR ME! TONIGHT THE WILD HUNT BEGINS!!>*
<THE OLD GODS ARE RETURNING!
SOON ALL OF NORWAY WILL AWAKEN FROM ITS JUDEO-CHRISTIAN SLUMBER! WITH OUR ALLIES WE'LL FINISH THE WAR STARTED ONE THOUSAND YEARS AGO WHEN CHRISTIANITY INVADED OUR MOTHER LAND!!>
GRAVELAND
DAMN. BLACK CIRCLE, ORDO TEMPLI ORIENTIS, VIKING LIBERATION FRONT --ALL THEY'RE MISSIN' IS STRAIGHT NAZIS.
THINK THOSE WEAPONS ARE REAL?
SHNNK
YOU ASKIN' HIM OR ME?

<*NORWEGIAN>

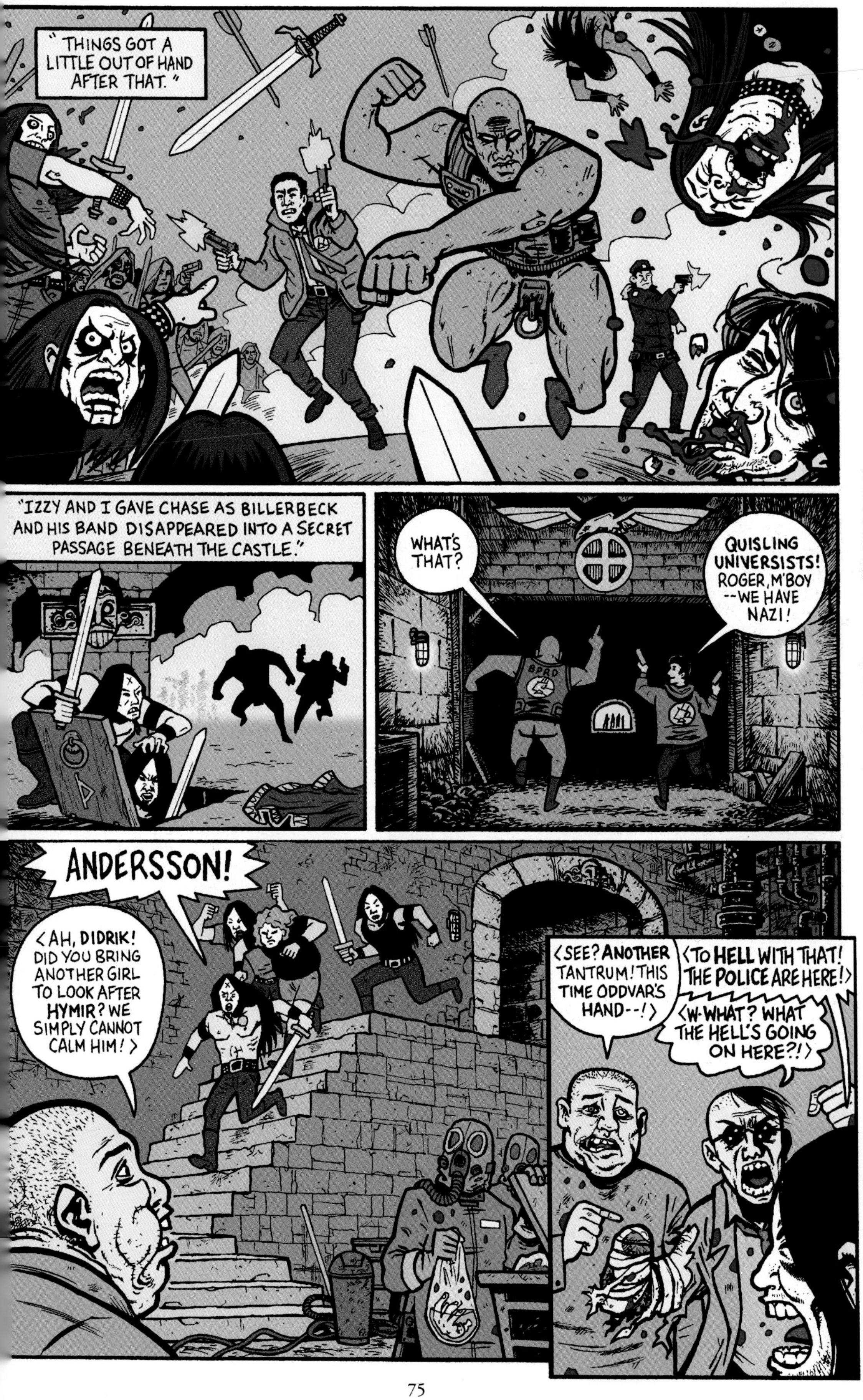
"THINGS GOT A LITTLE OUT OF HAND AFTER THAT."
"IZZY AND I GAVE CHASE AS BILLERBECK AND HIS BAND DISAPPEARED INTO A SECRET PASSAGE BENEATH THE CASTLE."
WHAT'S THAT?
QUISLING UNIVERSISTS! ROGER, M'BOY --WE HAVE NAZI!
BPRD
ANDERSSON!
<AH, DIDRIK! DID YOU BRING ANOTHER GIRL TO LOOK AFTER HYMIR? WE SIMPLY CANNOT CALM HIM!>
<SEE? ANOTHER TANTRUM! THIS TIME ODDVAR'S HAND--!>
<TO HELL WITH THAT! THE POLICE ARE HERE!>
<W-WHAT? WHAT THE HELL'S GOING ON HERE?!>

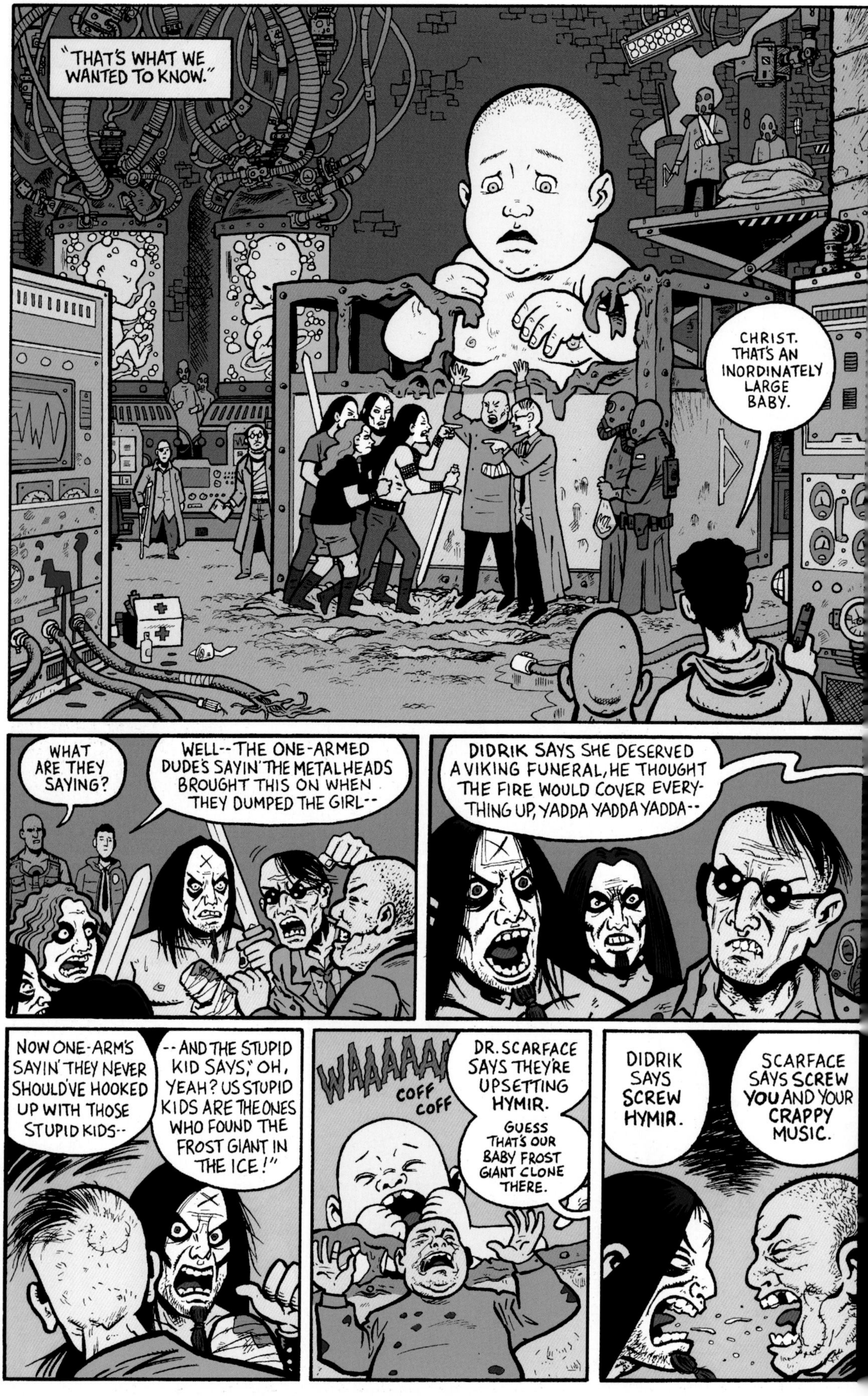
"THAT'S WHAT WE WANTED TO KNOW."
CHRIST. THAT'S AN INORDINATELY LARGE BABY.
WHAT ARE THEY SAYING?
WELL--THE ONE-ARMED DUDE'S SAYIN' THE METALHEADS BROUGHT THIS ON WHEN THEY DUMPED THE GIRL--
DIDRIK SAYS SHE DESERVED A VIKING FUNERAL, HE THOUGHT THE FIRE WOULD COVER EVERYTHING UP, YADDA YADDA YADDA--
NOW ONE-ARM'S SAYIN' THEY NEVER SHOULD'VE HOOKED UP WITH THOSE STUPID KIDS--
--AND THE STUPID KID SAYS, "OH, YEAH? US STUPID KIDS ARE THE ONES WHO FOUND THE FROST GIANT IN THE ICE!"
WAAAAA
COFF COFF
DR. SCARFACE SAYS THEY'RE UPSETTING HYMIR.
GUESS THAT'S OUR BABY FROST GIANT CLONE THERE.
DIDRIK SAYS SCREW HYMIR.
SCARFACE SAYS SCREW YOU AND YOUR CRAPPY MUSIC.

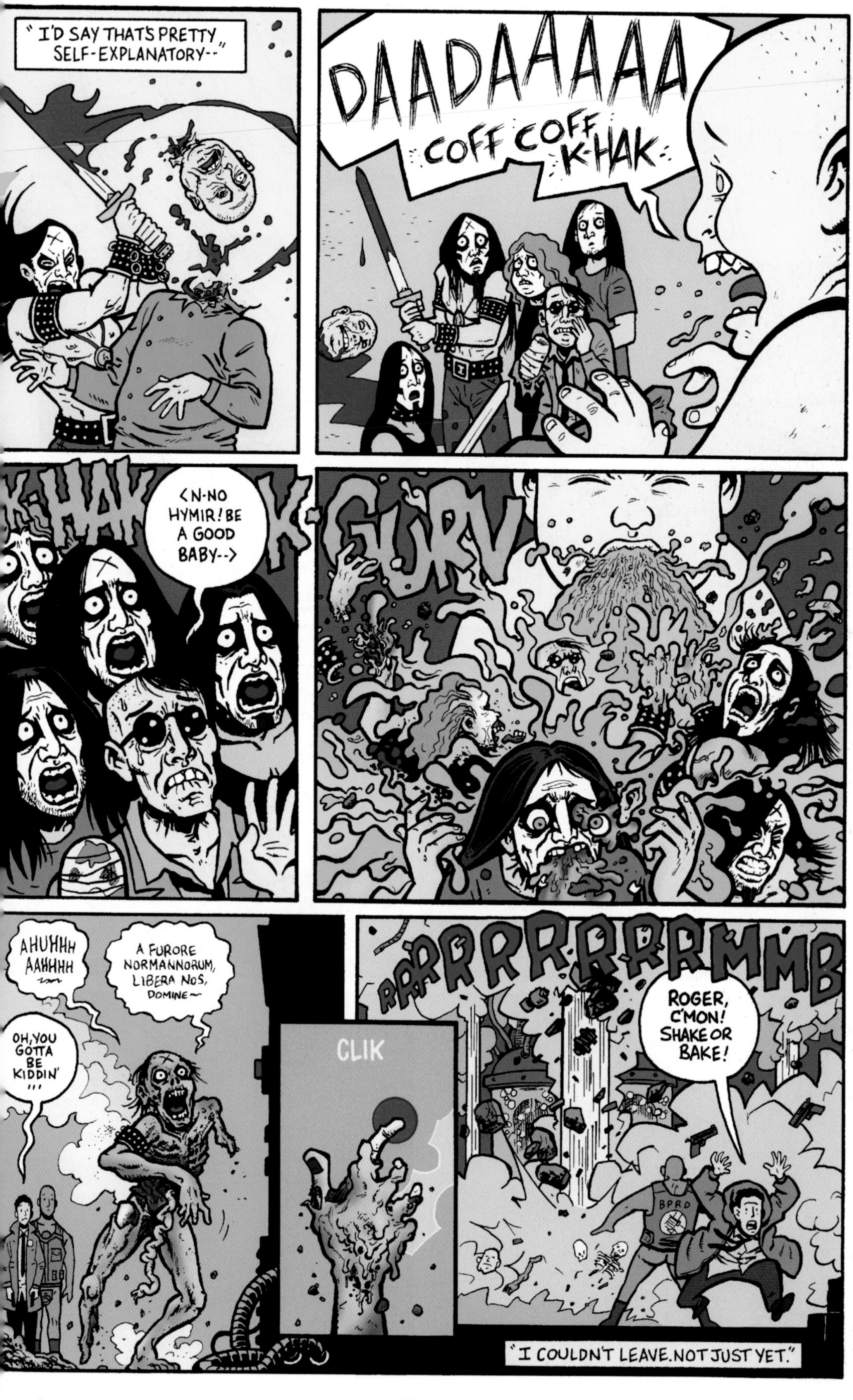
"I'D SAY THAT'S PRETTY SELF-EXPLANATORY--"
DAADAAAAA
COFF COFF K-HAK
K-HAK
<N-NO HYMIR! BE A GOOD BABY-->
K-GURV
AHUHHH AAHHHH
A FURORE NORMANNORUM, LIBERA NOS, DOMINE~
OH, YOU GOTTA BE KIDDIN'...
CLIK
RRRRRRRRRRMMB
ROGER, C'MON! SHAKE OR BAKE!
"I COULDN'T LEAVE. NOT JUST YET."

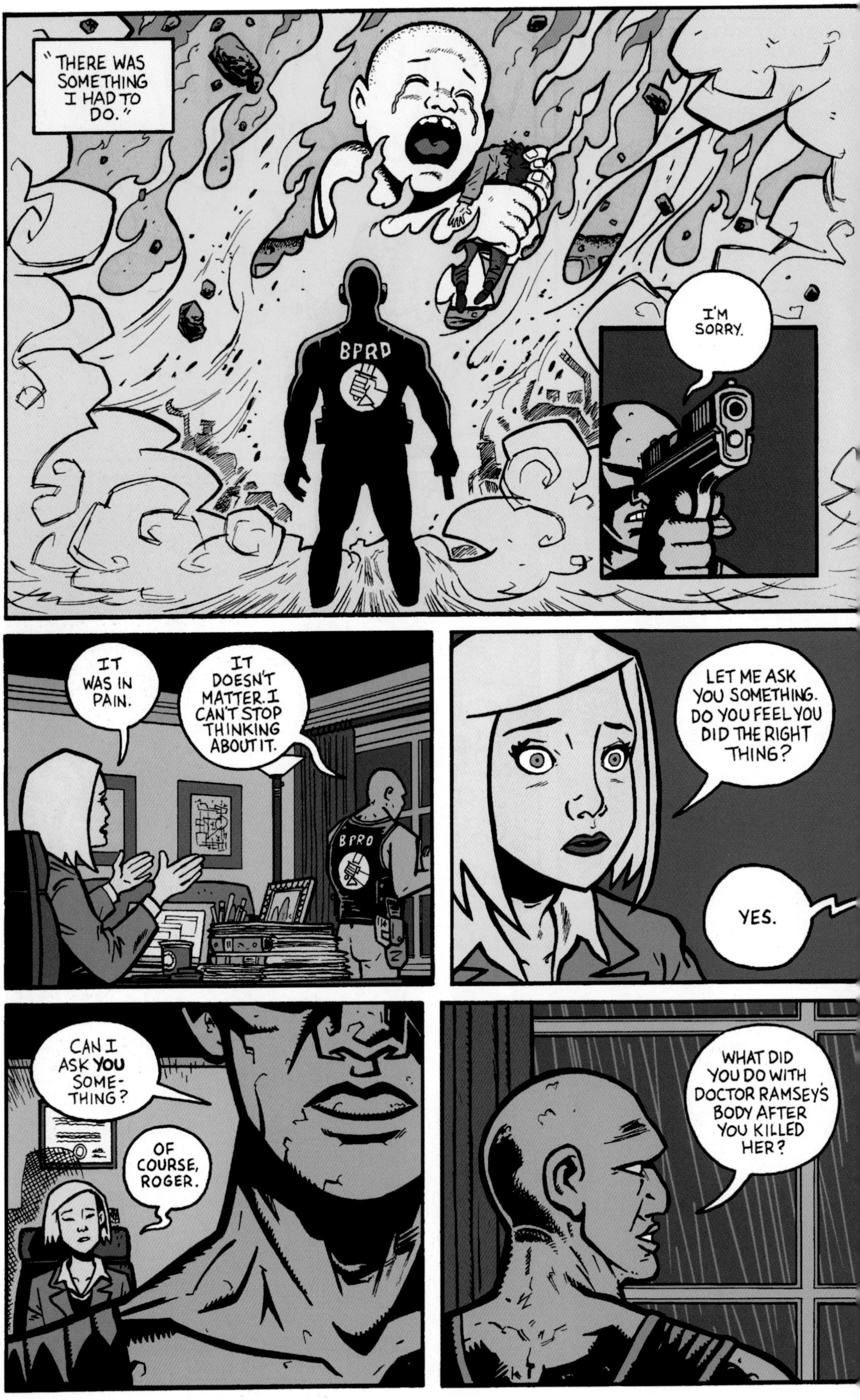
"THERE WAS SOMETHING I HAD TO DO."
I'M SORRY.
BPRD
IT WAS IN PAIN.
IT DOESN'T MATTER. I CAN'T STOP THINKING ABOUT IT.
LET ME ASK YOU SOMETHING. DO YOU FEEL YOU DID THE RIGHT THING?
YES.
CAN I ASK **YOU** SOME-THING?
OF COURSE, ROGER.
WHAT DID YOU DO WITH DOCTOR RAMSEY'S BODY AFTER YOU KILLED HER?

She's buried out back, with her dog.

How long have you known?

Since Officer D'Amico's suicide. Your former patient --or victim-- had friends in high places.

We found lesions in his brain caused by psychic vampirism. We suspected a temhot. A grief eater.

And here you are.

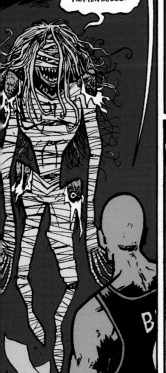

What would you have done if I hadn't revealed myself?

Thrown salt in your eyes, to see if you cried blood.

Hmm. Your masters taught you well, homunculus.

RAKK

But not well enough.

Stupider still. Your gun is useless here.

That's why I brought this.

Black and Decker cordless, rigged with nails from your victim's coffin--

K·CHUNT

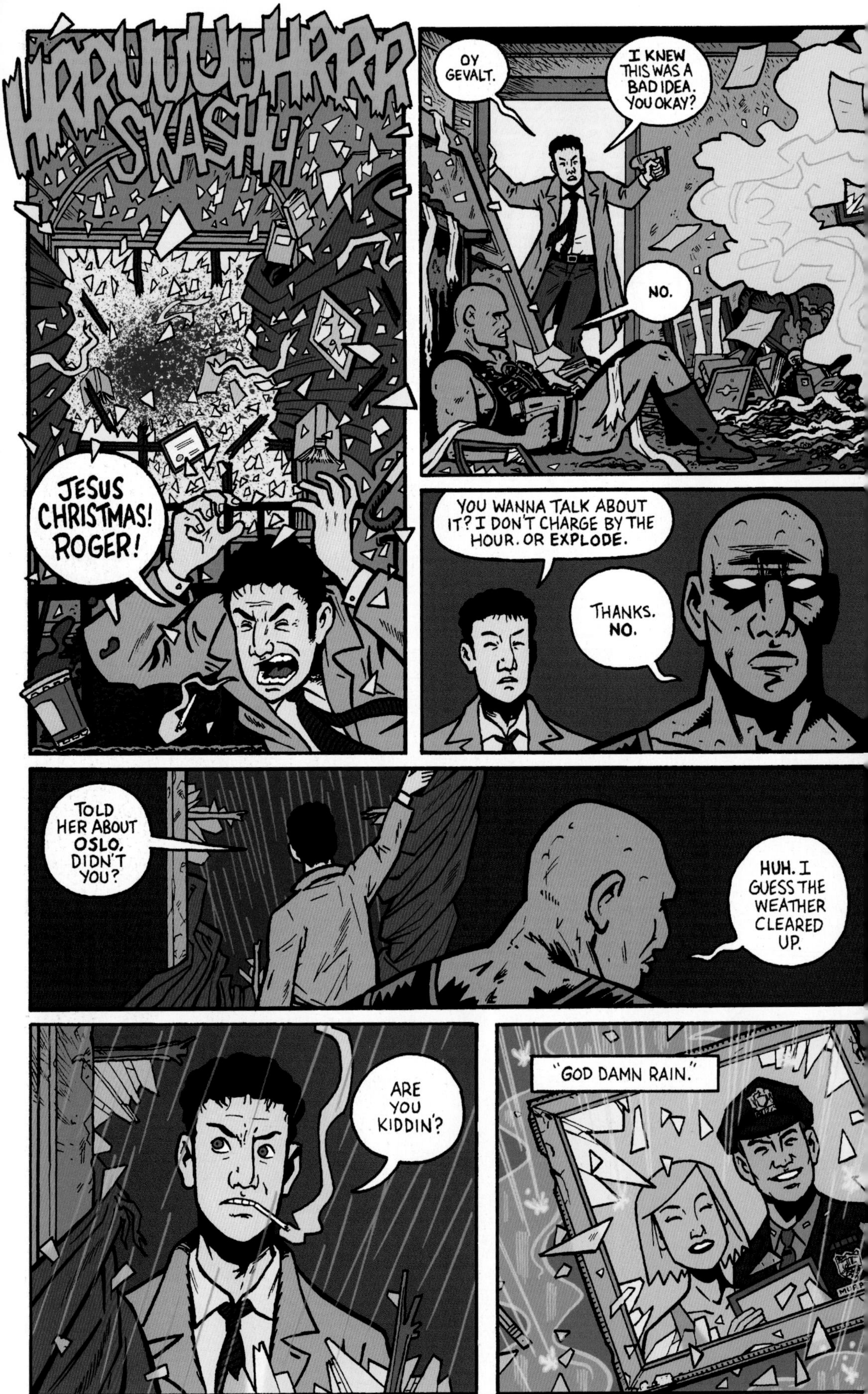
HRRUUUUHRRR SKASHH
JESUS CHRISTMAS! ROGER!
OY GEVALT.
I KNEW THIS WAS A BAD IDEA. YOU OKAY?
NO.
YOU WANNA TALK ABOUT IT? I DON'T CHARGE BY THE HOUR. OR EXPLODE.
THANKS. NO.
TOLD HER ABOUT OSLO, DIDN'T YOU?
HUH. I GUESS THE WEATHER CLEARED UP.
ARE YOU KIDDIN'?
"GOD DAMN RAIN."

PROFESSIONAL HELP • EVAN DORKIN (SCRIPT/ART) • SARAH DYER (COLORS/DIALOGUE ASSIST) THE END

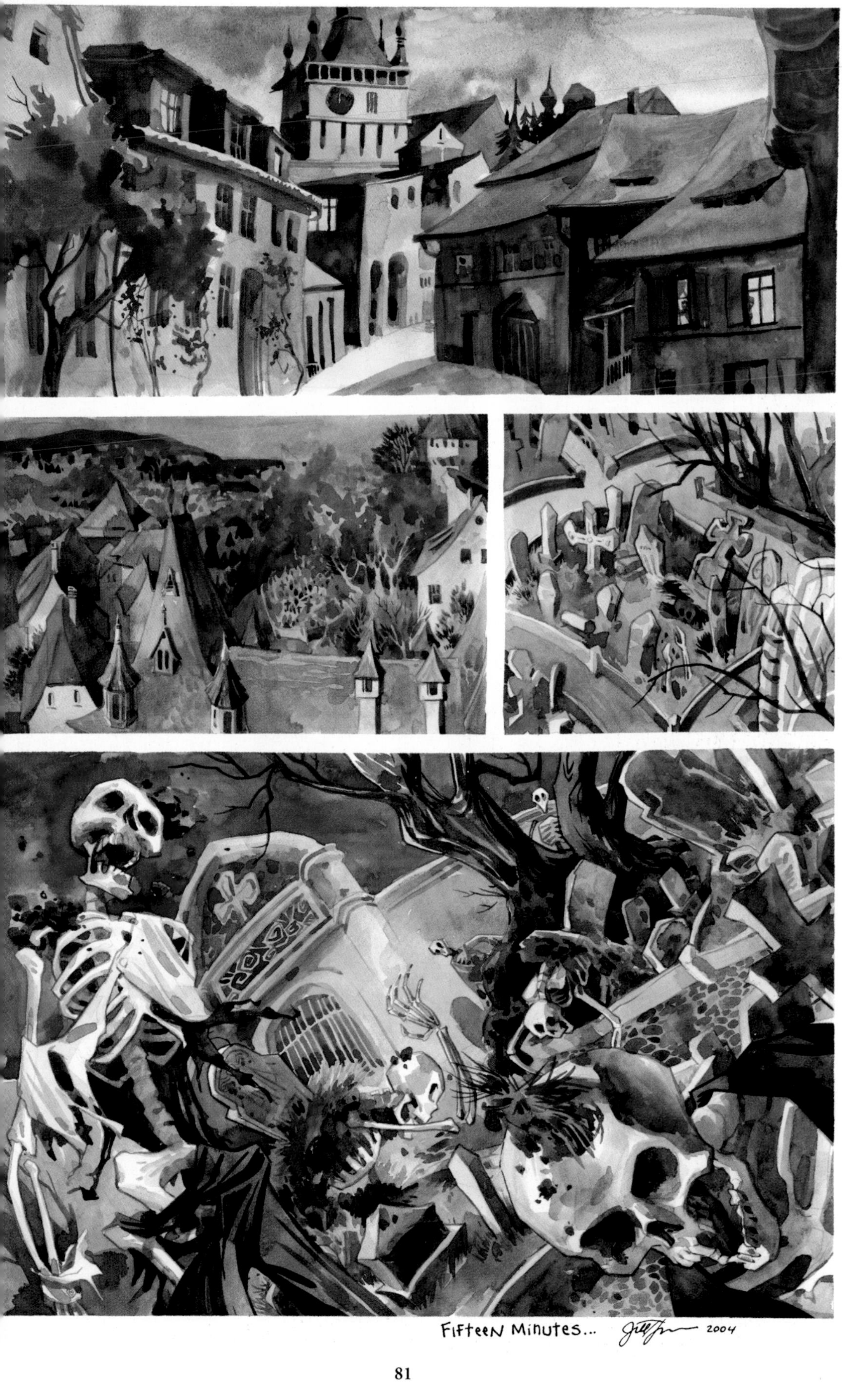

Fifteen Minutes... 2004

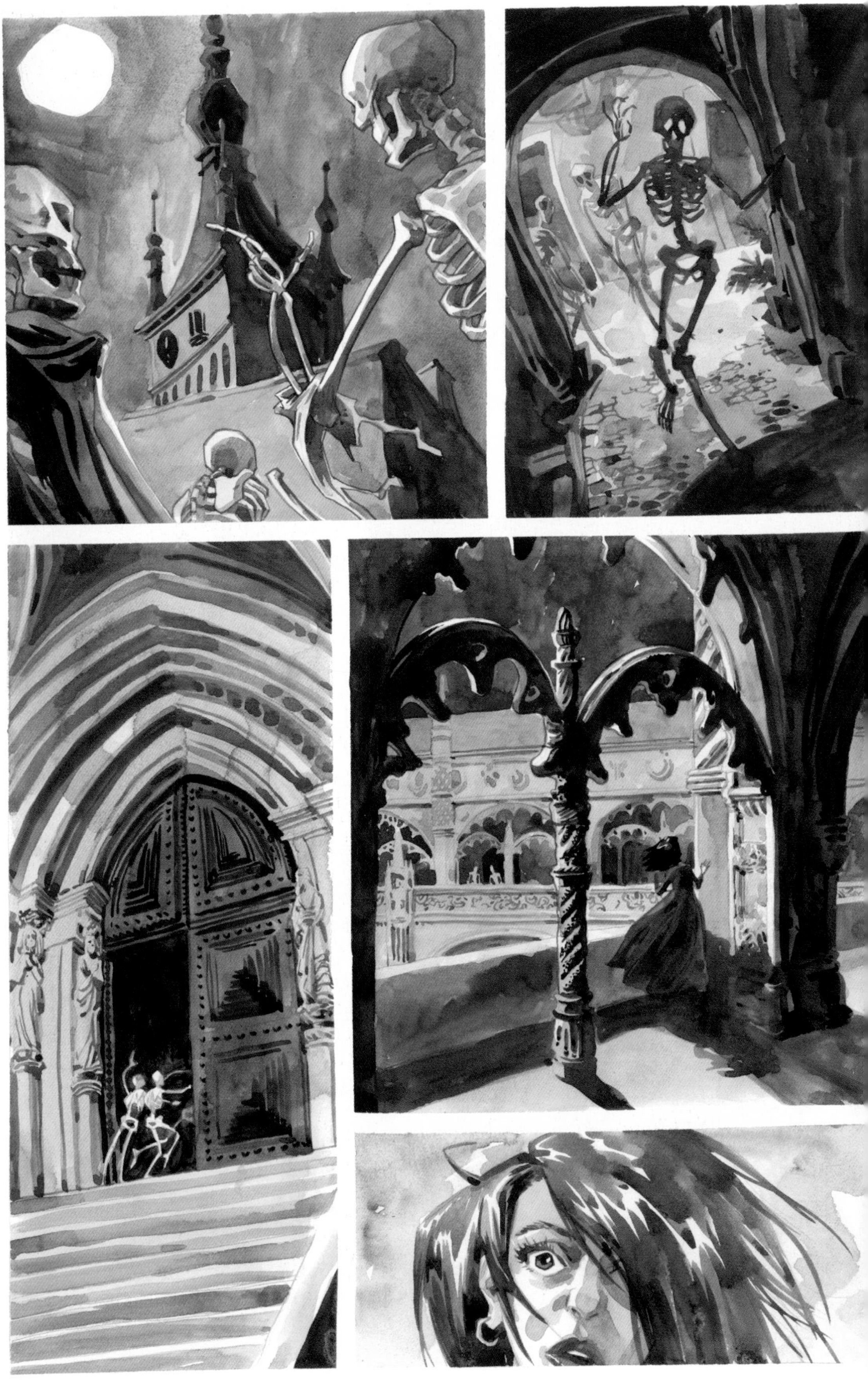

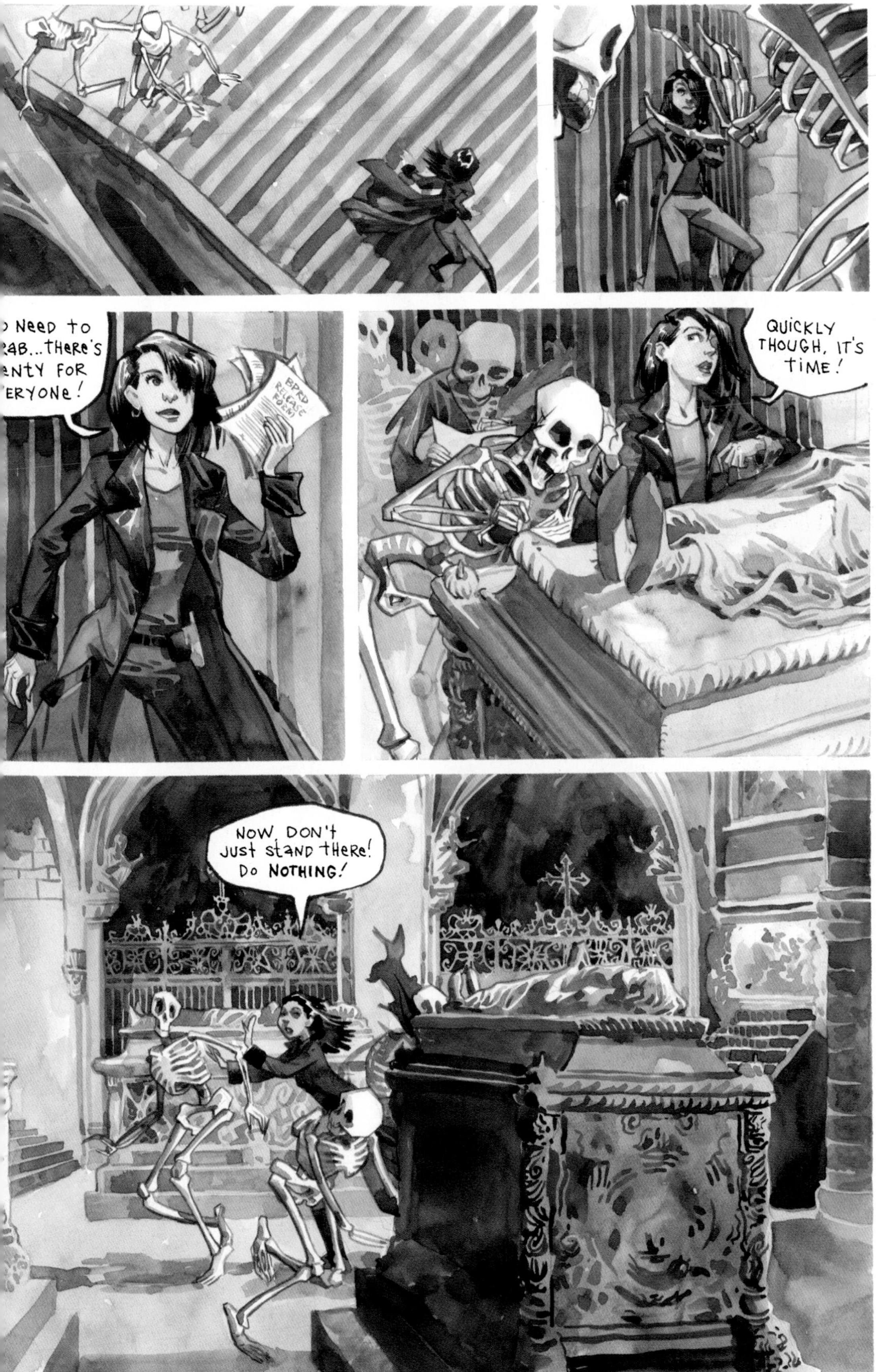

D NEED TO
RAB...THERE'S
ENTY FOR
ERYONE!
BPRD RELEASE FORM
QUICKLY THOUGH, IT'S TIME!
NOW, DON'T JUST STAND THERE! DO NOTHING!

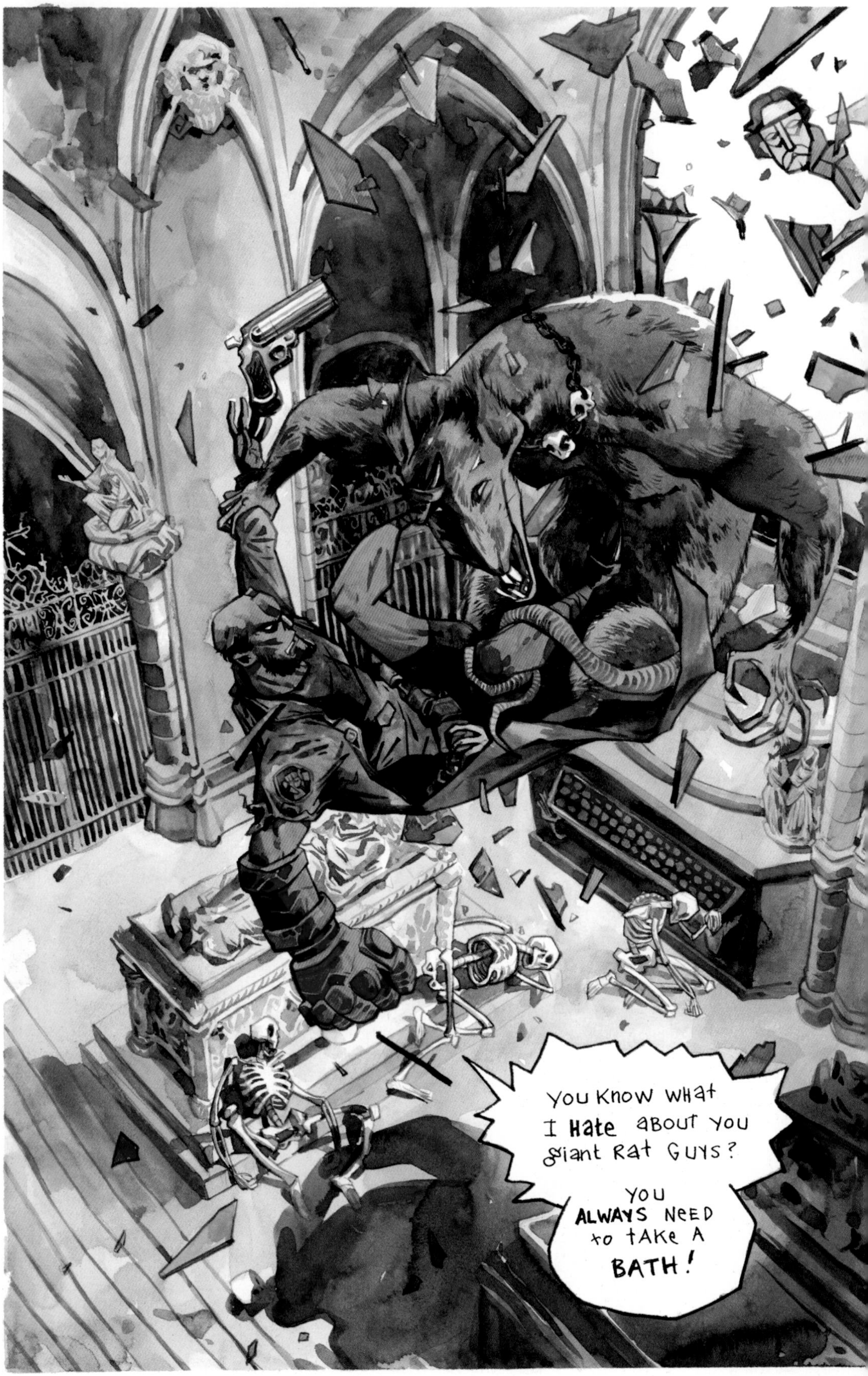
You know what I hate about you giant rat guys?
You always need to take a bath!

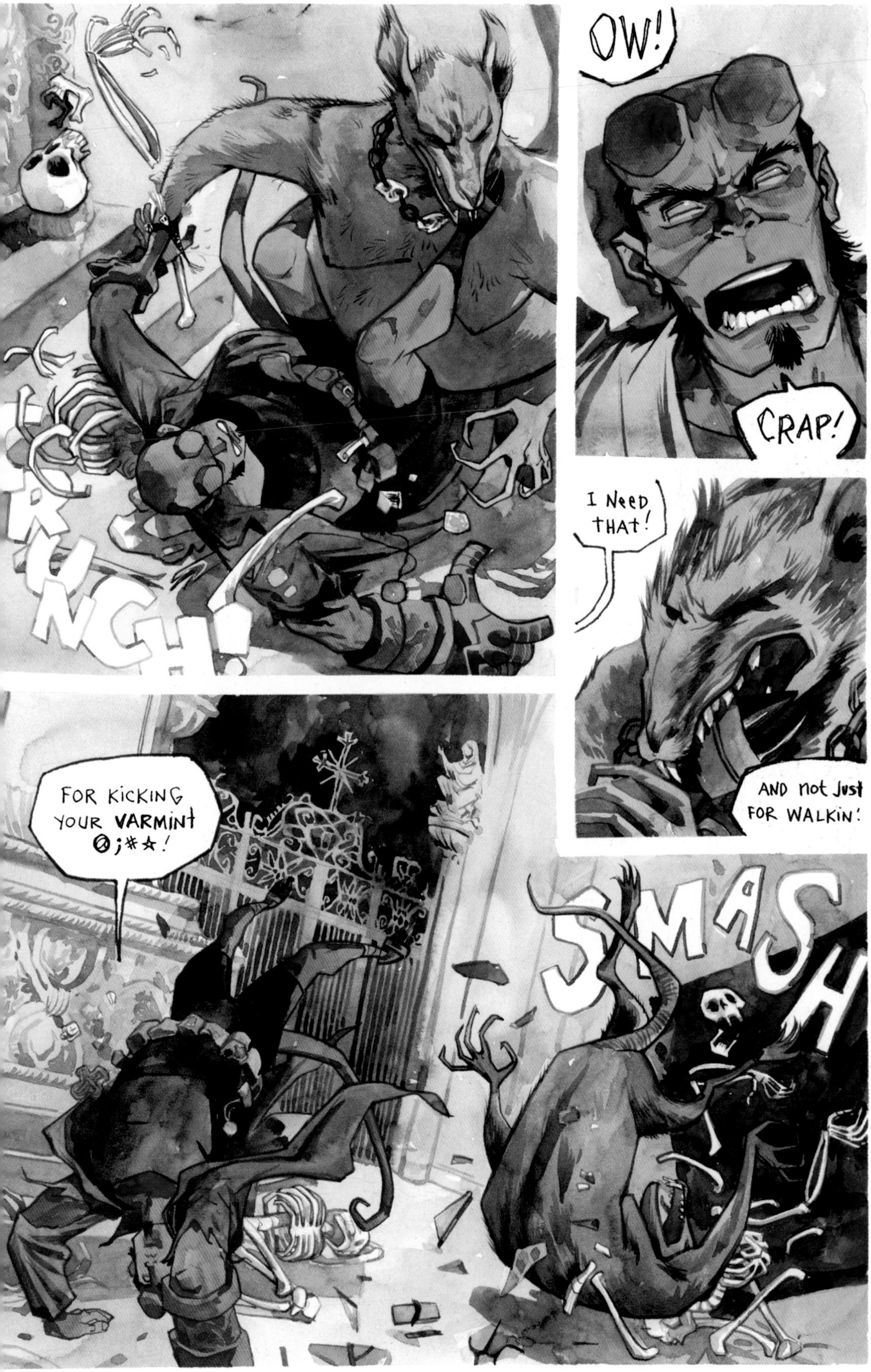

RUNCH!
OW!
CRAP!
I NEED THAT!
AND NOT JUST FOR WALKIN'!
FOR KICKING YOUR VARMINT @;#*!
SMASH

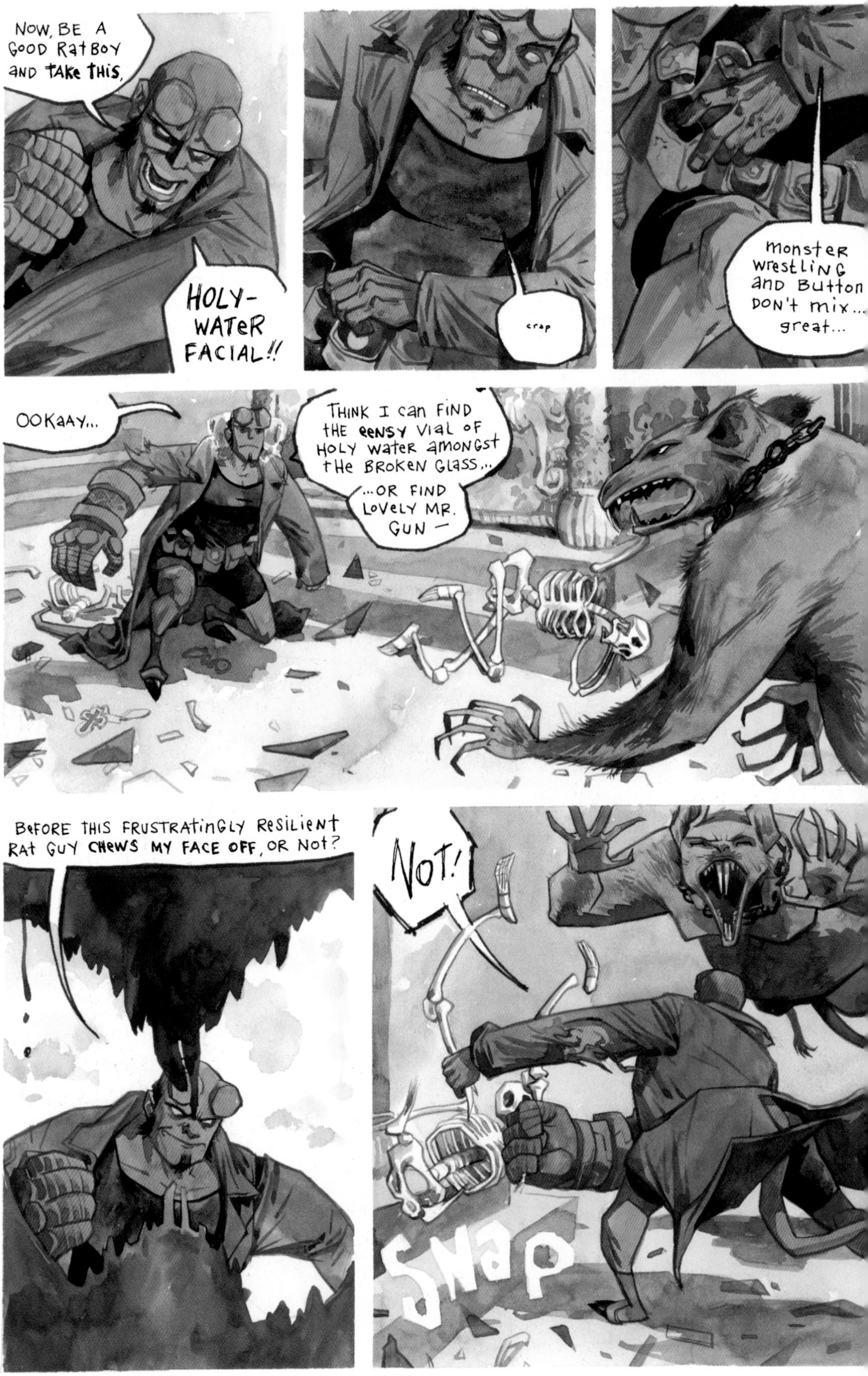
NOW, BE A GOOD RatBOY AND TAKE THIS,
HOLY-WATER FACIAL!!
crap
monster wrestling and Button DON't mix... great...
OOKaay...
THINK I can FIND THE eensy vial OF HOLY water amongst tHe BROKEN GLASS...
...OR FIND Lovely MR. GUN —
BEFORE THIS FRUSTRATINGLY RESILIENT Rat GUY CHEWS MY FACE OFF, OR Not?
Not!
SNAP

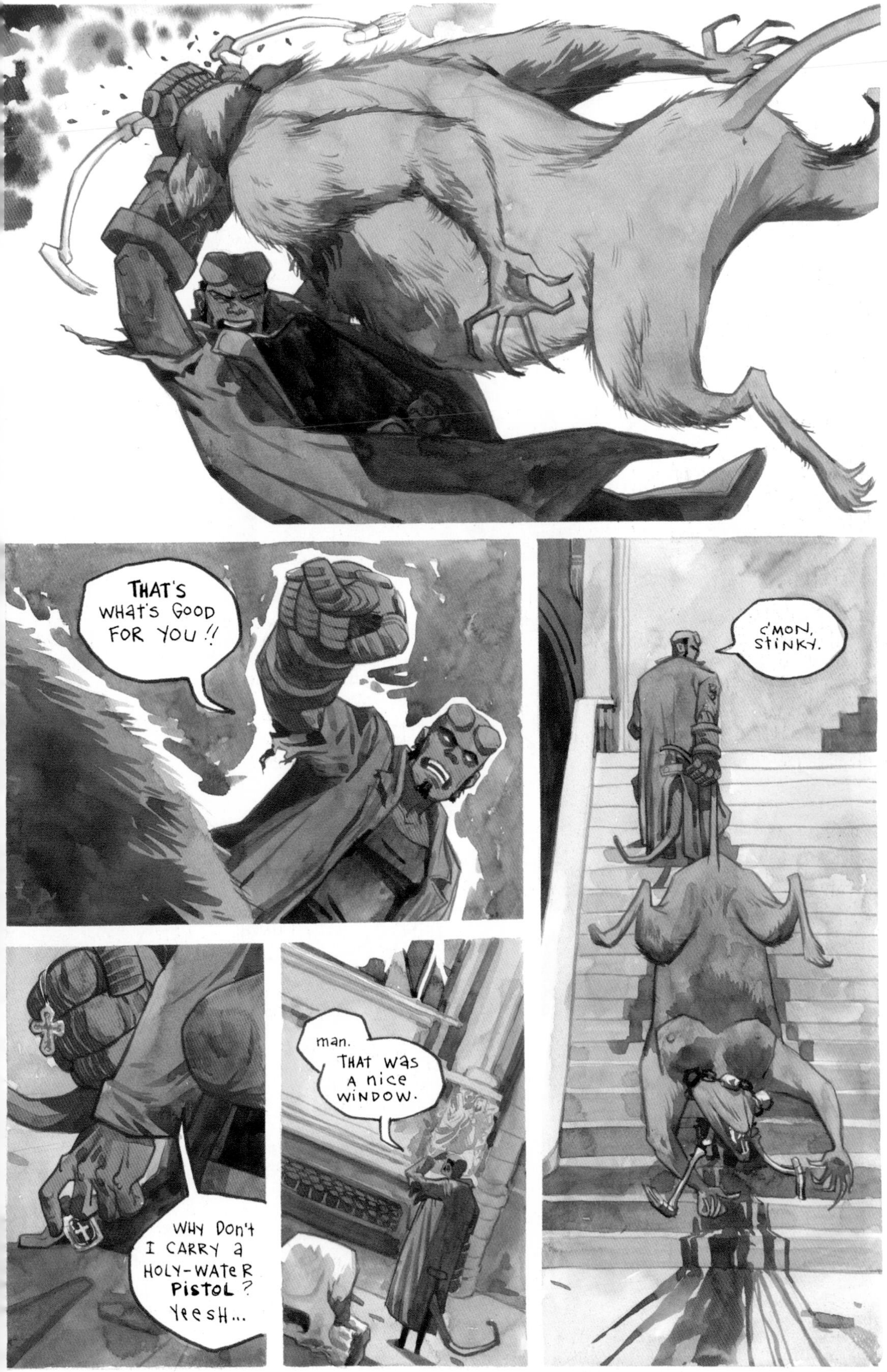
THAT'S WHAT'S GOOD FOR YOU!!
WHY DON'T I CARRY a HOLY-WATER PISTOL? YEESH...
man. THAT WAS A NICE WINDOW.
C'MON, STINKY.

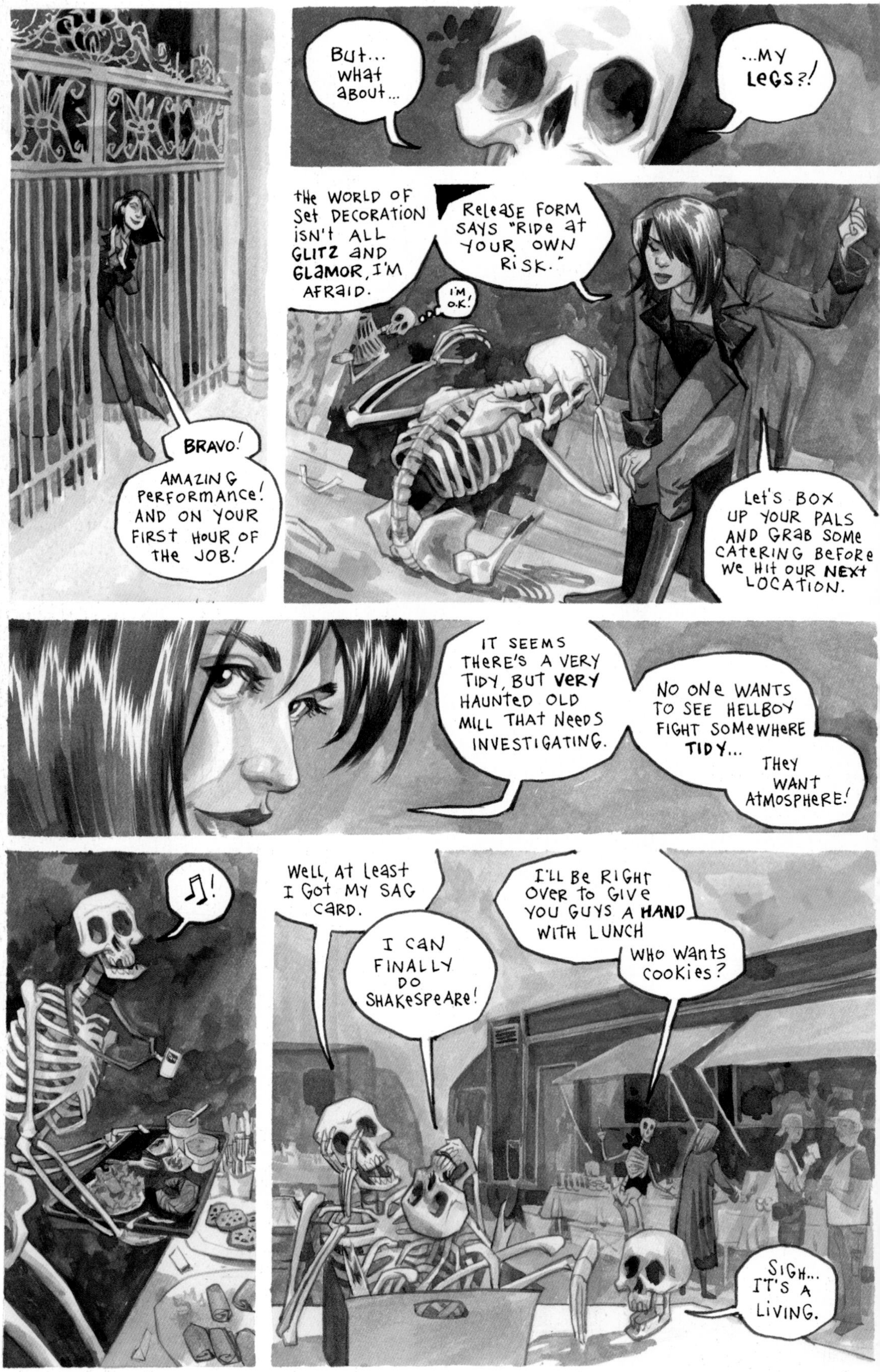
But... what about...
...My LeGs?!
BRAVO! AMAZING PERFORMANCE! AND ON YOUR FIRST HOUR OF THE JOB!
the WORLD OF Set DECORATION isn't ALL GLITZ and GLAMOR, I'M AFRAID.
Release FORM SAYS "Ride at YOUR OWN RiSK."
I'M O.K.!
Let's BOX UP YOUR PALS AND GRAB SOME CATERING BEFORE We Hit OUR NEXT LOCATION.
IT SEEMS THERE'S A VERY TIDY, BUT VERY HAUNTED OLD MILL THAT NEEDS INVESTIGATING.
NO ONE WANTS TO SEE HELLBOY FIGHT SOMEWHERE TIDY...
THEY WANT ATMOSPHERE!
♫!
Well, At least I Got MY SAG CARD.
I CAN FINALLY DO SHAKESPEARE!
I'LL Be RIGHT OVER to GIVE YOU GUYS A HAND WITH LUNCH
WHO Wants COOKIES?
SIGH... IT'S A LIVING.

end.

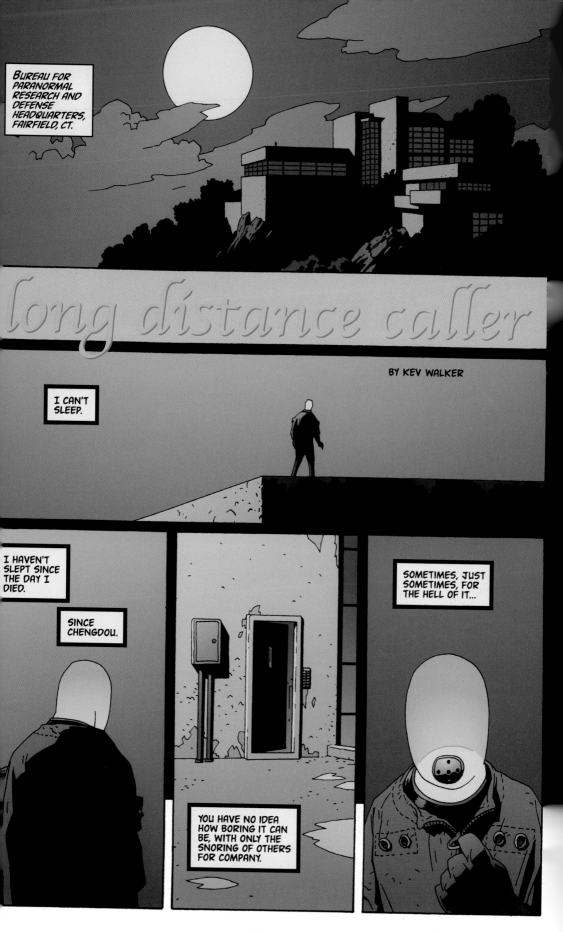

BUREAU FOR PARANORMAL RESEARCH AND DEFENSE HEADQUARTERS, FAIRFIELD, CT.

long distance caller

BY KEV WALKER

I CAN'T SLEEP.

I HAVEN'T SLEPT SINCE THE DAY I DIED.

SINCE CHENGDOU.

SOMETIMES, JUST SOMETIMES, FOR THE HELL OF IT...

YOU HAVE NO IDEA HOW BORING IT CAN BE, WITH ONLY THE SNORING OF OTHERS FOR COMPANY.

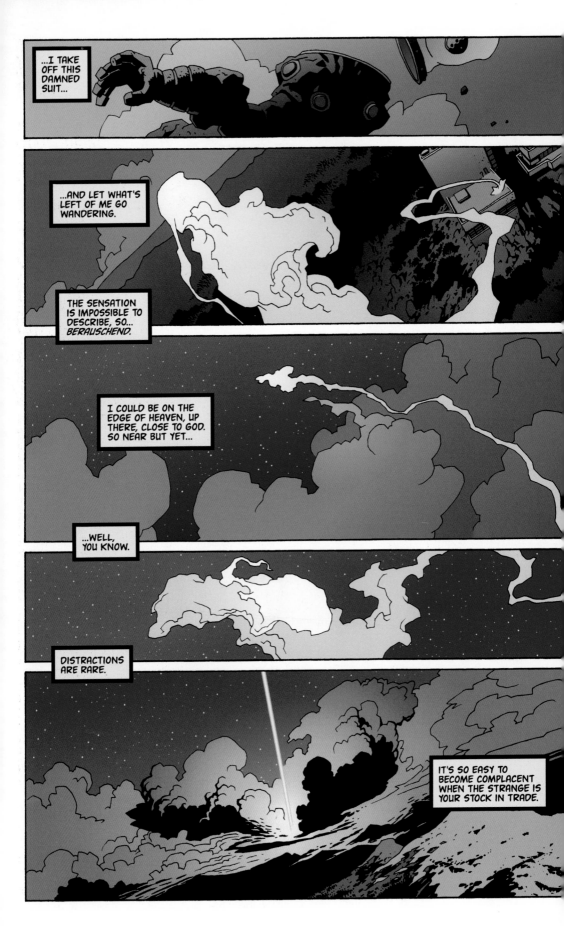

...I TAKE OFF THIS DAMNED SUIT...

...AND LET WHAT'S LEFT OF ME GO WANDERING.

THE SENSATION IS IMPOSSIBLE TO DESCRIBE, SO... *BERAUSCHEND.*

I COULD BE ON THE EDGE OF HEAVEN, UP THERE, CLOSE TO GOD. SO NEAR BUT YET...

...WELL, YOU KNOW.

DISTRACTIONS ARE RARE.

IT'S SO EASY TO BECOME COMPLACENT WHEN THE STRANGE IS YOUR STOCK IN TRADE.

90

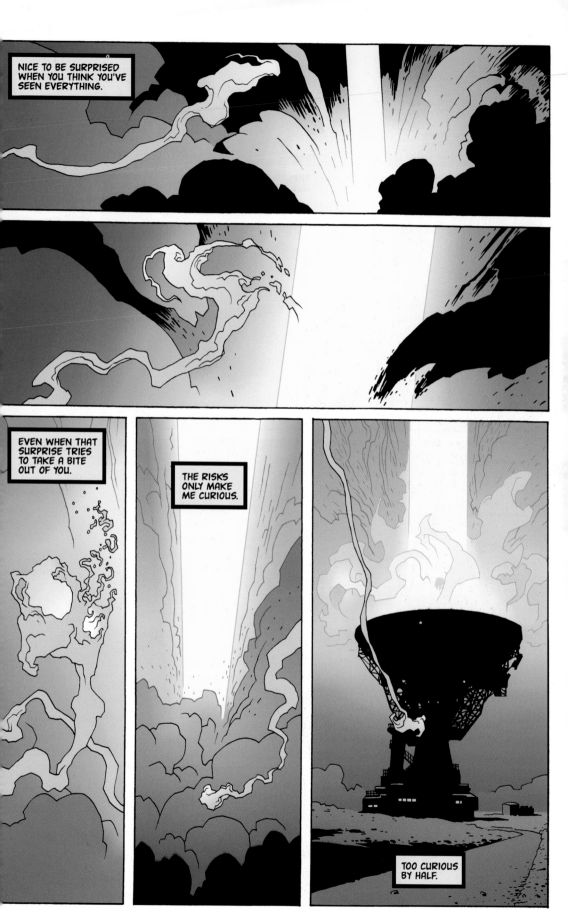

NICE TO BE SURPRISED WHEN YOU THINK YOU'VE SEEN EVERYTHING.

EVEN WHEN THAT SURPRISE TRIES TO TAKE A BITE OUT OF YOU.

THE RISKS ONLY MAKE ME CURIOUS.

TOO CURIOUS BY HALF.

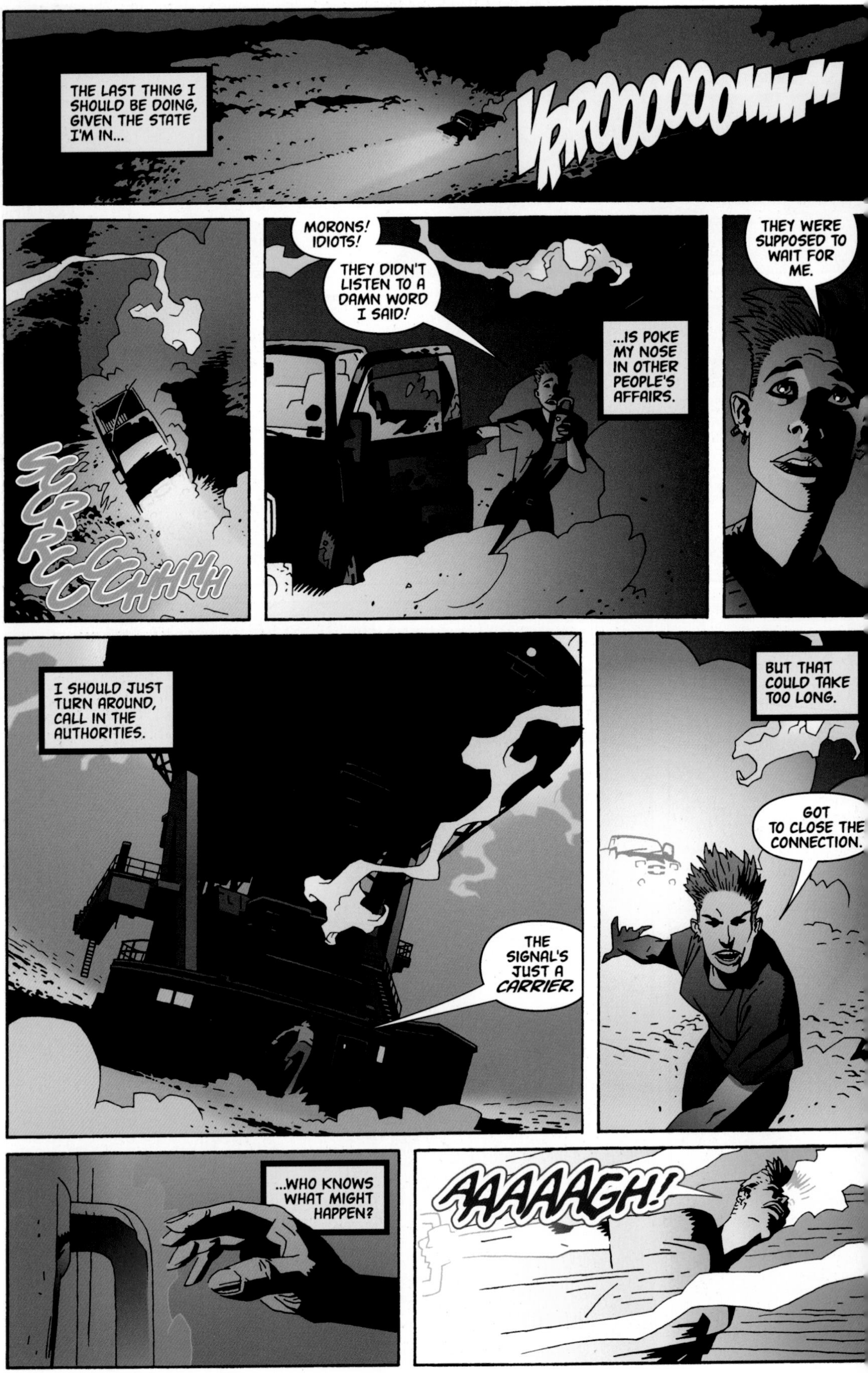

THE LAST THING I SHOULD BE DOING, GIVEN THE STATE I'M IN...
VRROOOOOOMMMM
SCRRCCHHHHH
MORONS! IDIOTS!
THEY DIDN'T LISTEN TO A DAMN WORD I SAID!
...IS POKE MY NOSE IN OTHER PEOPLE'S AFFAIRS.
THEY WERE SUPPOSED TO WAIT FOR ME.
I SHOULD JUST TURN AROUND, CALL IN THE AUTHORITIES.
THE SIGNAL'S JUST A CARRIER.
BUT THAT COULD TAKE TOO LONG.
GOT TO CLOSE THE CONNECTION.
...WHO KNOWS WHAT MIGHT HAPPEN?
AAAAAGH!

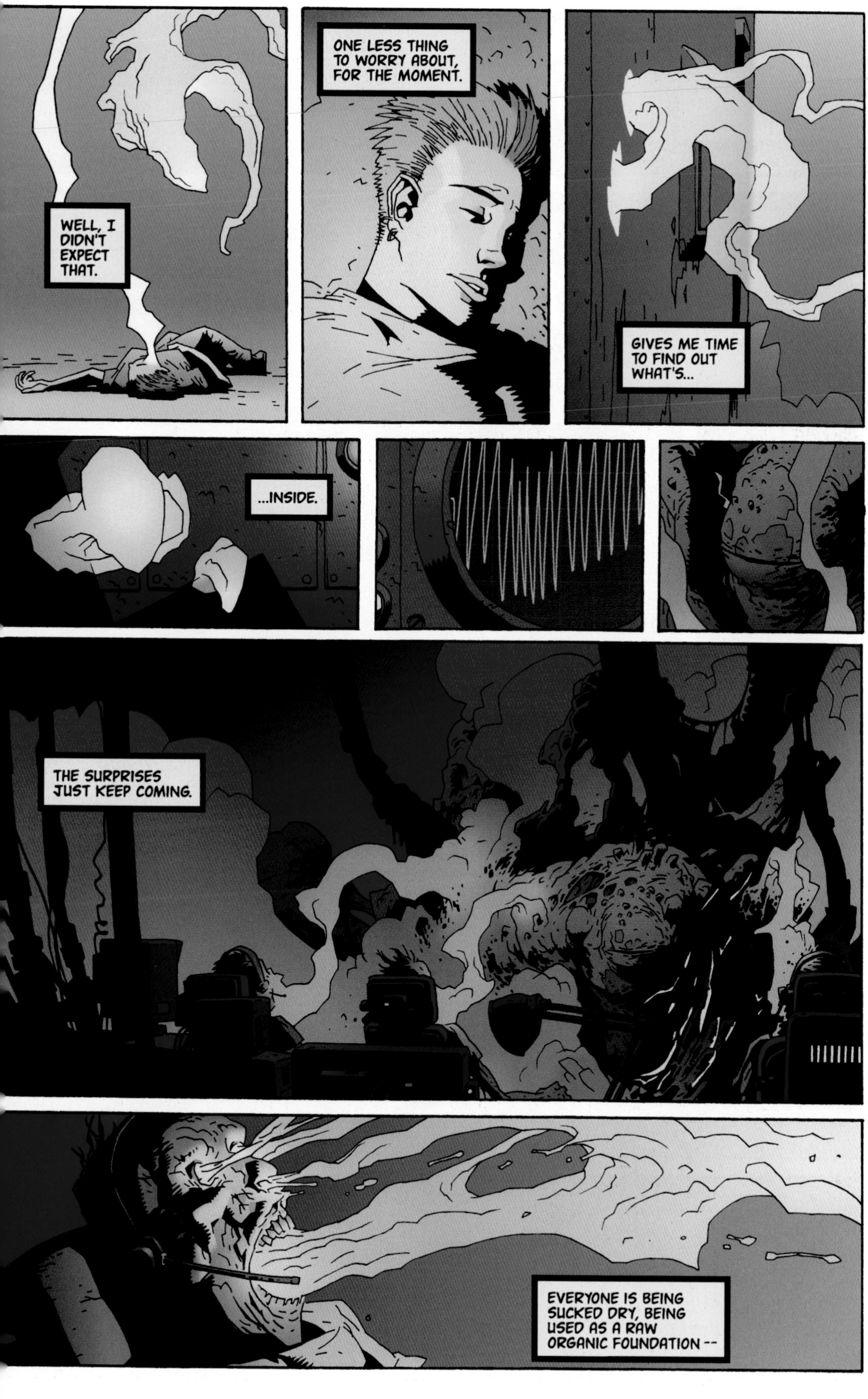
WELL, I DIDN'T EXPECT THAT.
ONE LESS THING TO WORRY ABOUT, FOR THE MOMENT.
GIVES ME TIME TO FIND OUT WHAT'S...
...INSIDE.
THE SURPRISES JUST KEEP COMING.
EVERYONE IS BEING SUCKED DRY, BEING USED AS A RAW ORGANIC FOUNDATION --

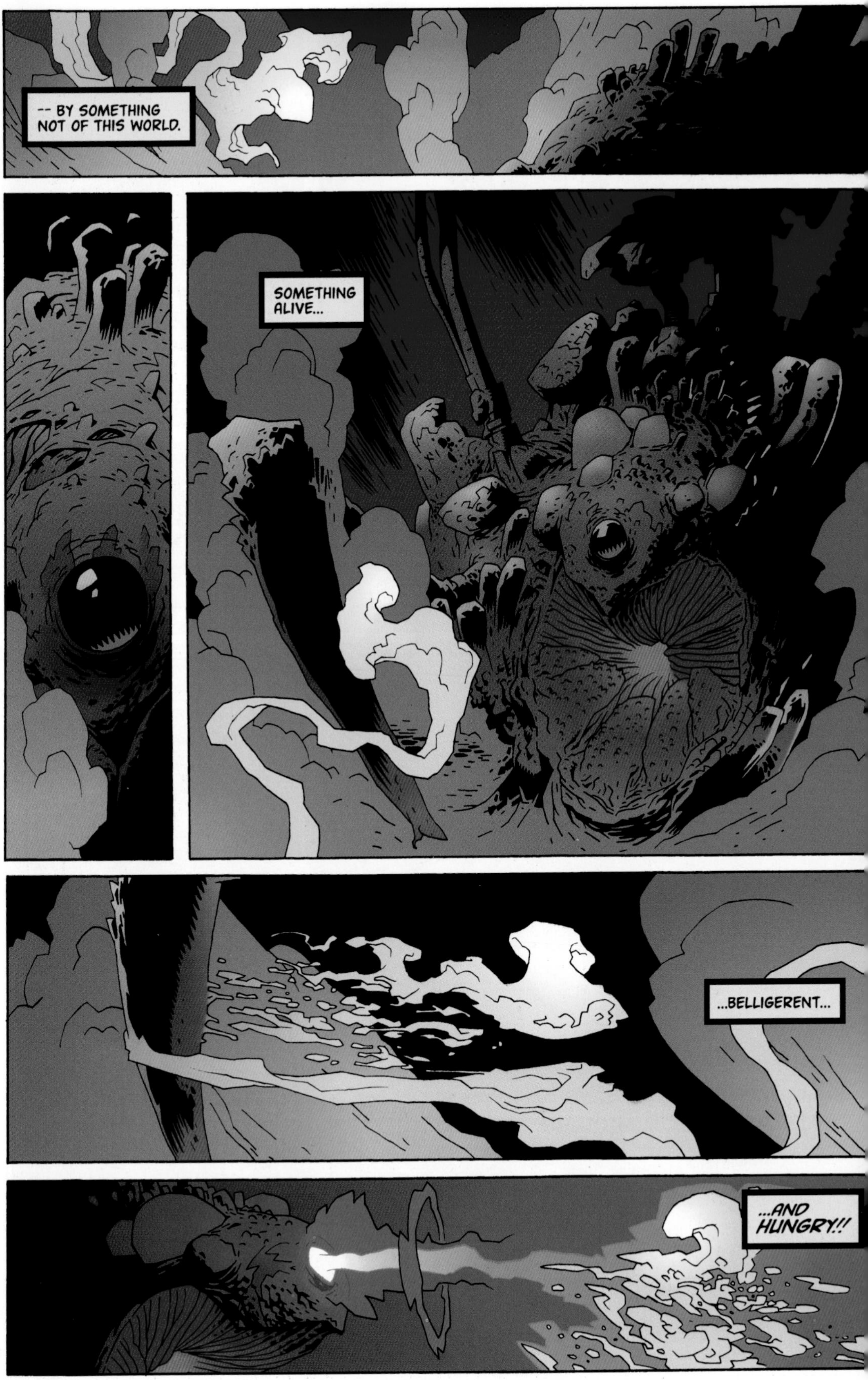
-- BY SOMETHING NOT OF THIS WORLD.
SOMETHING ALIVE...
...BELLIGERENT...
...AND HUNGRY!!

ALL I CAN DO IS DEFEND MYSELF.

BRZZZZSCHIIWKKKK!

STRIKE BACK.

AND HOPE IT WILL BE ENOUGH.

SHE'S COMING 'ROUND.

NNNN NNNNN

PERHAPS NOW SHE MIGHT JUST...

OH MY...

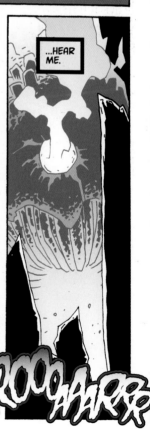

...HEAR ME.

RROOOAAARR

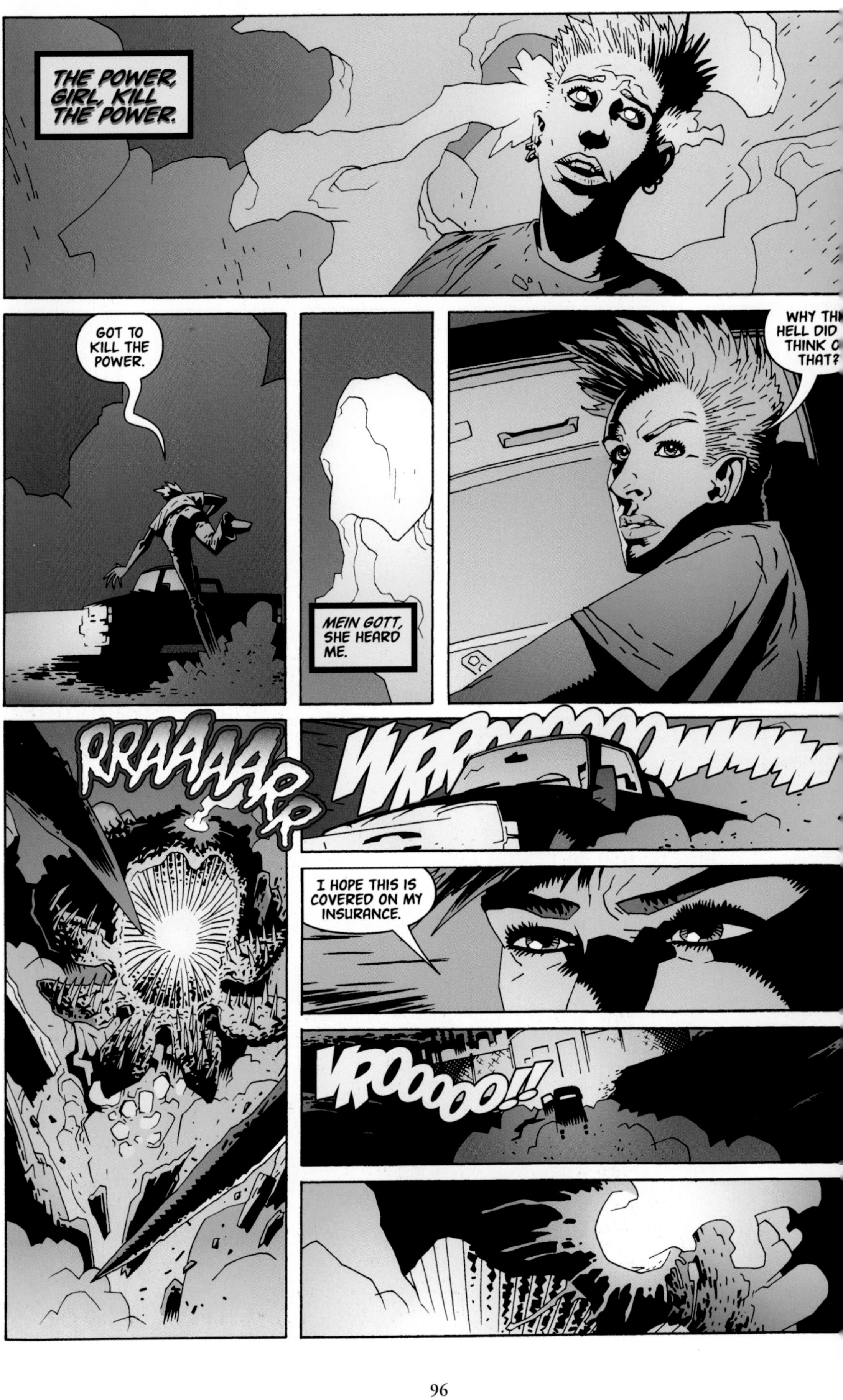
THE POWER, GIRL, KILL THE POWER.
GOT TO KILL THE POWER.
MEIN GOTT, SHE HEARD ME.
WHY THI HELL DID THINK O THAT?
RRAAAARR
WRROOOOOOMMMMM
I HOPE THIS IS COVERED ON MY INSURANCE.
VROOOOOO!!

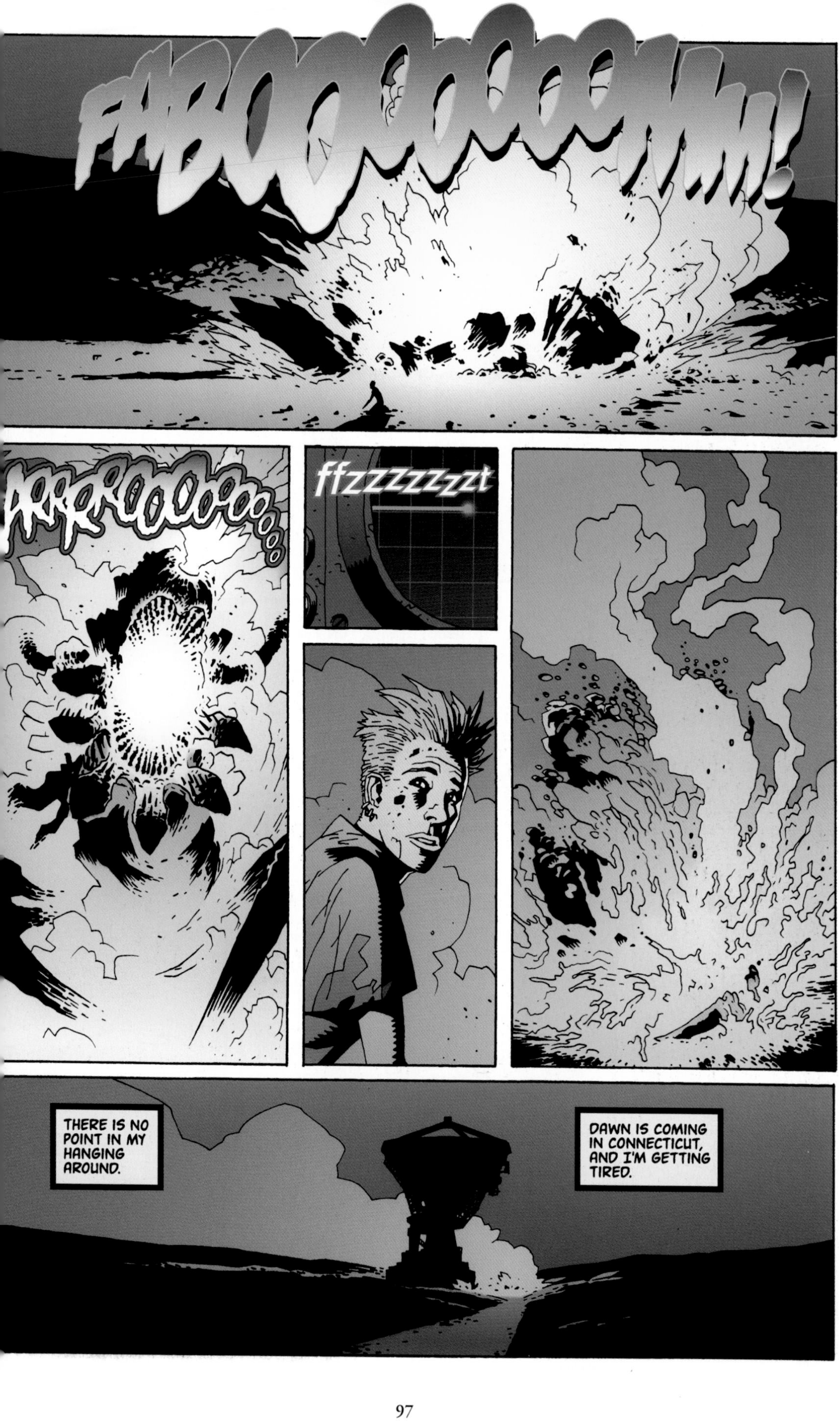
FABOOOOOOOM!
ffzzzzzzzt
THERE IS NO POINT IN MY HANGING AROUND.
DAWN IS COMING IN CONNECTICUT, AND I'M GETTING TIRED.

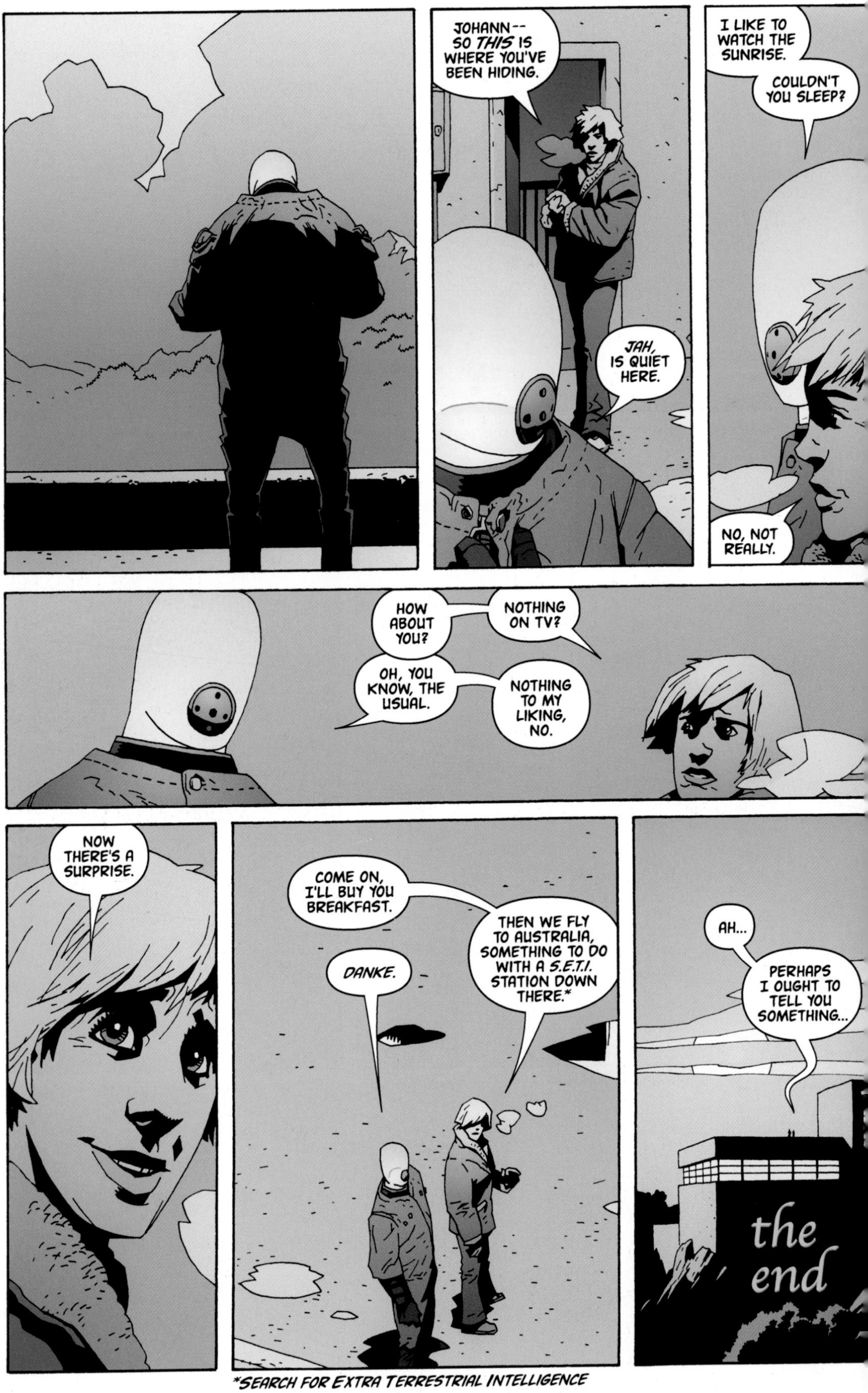
JOHANN-- SO *THIS* IS WHERE YOU'VE BEEN HIDING.
JAH, IS QUIET HERE.
I LIKE TO WATCH THE SUNRISE.
COULDN'T YOU SLEEP?
NO, NOT REALLY.
HOW ABOUT YOU?
NOTHING ON TV?
OH, YOU KNOW, THE USUAL.
NOTHING TO MY LIKING, NO.
NOW THERE'S A SURPRISE.
COME ON, I'LL BUY YOU BREAKFAST.
THEN WE FLY TO AUSTRALIA, SOMETHING TO DO WITH A *S.E.T.I.* STATION DOWN THERE.*
DANKE.
AH...
PERHAPS I OUGHT TO TELL YOU SOMETHING...
the end

*SEARCH FOR EXTRA TERRESTRIAL INTELLIGENCE

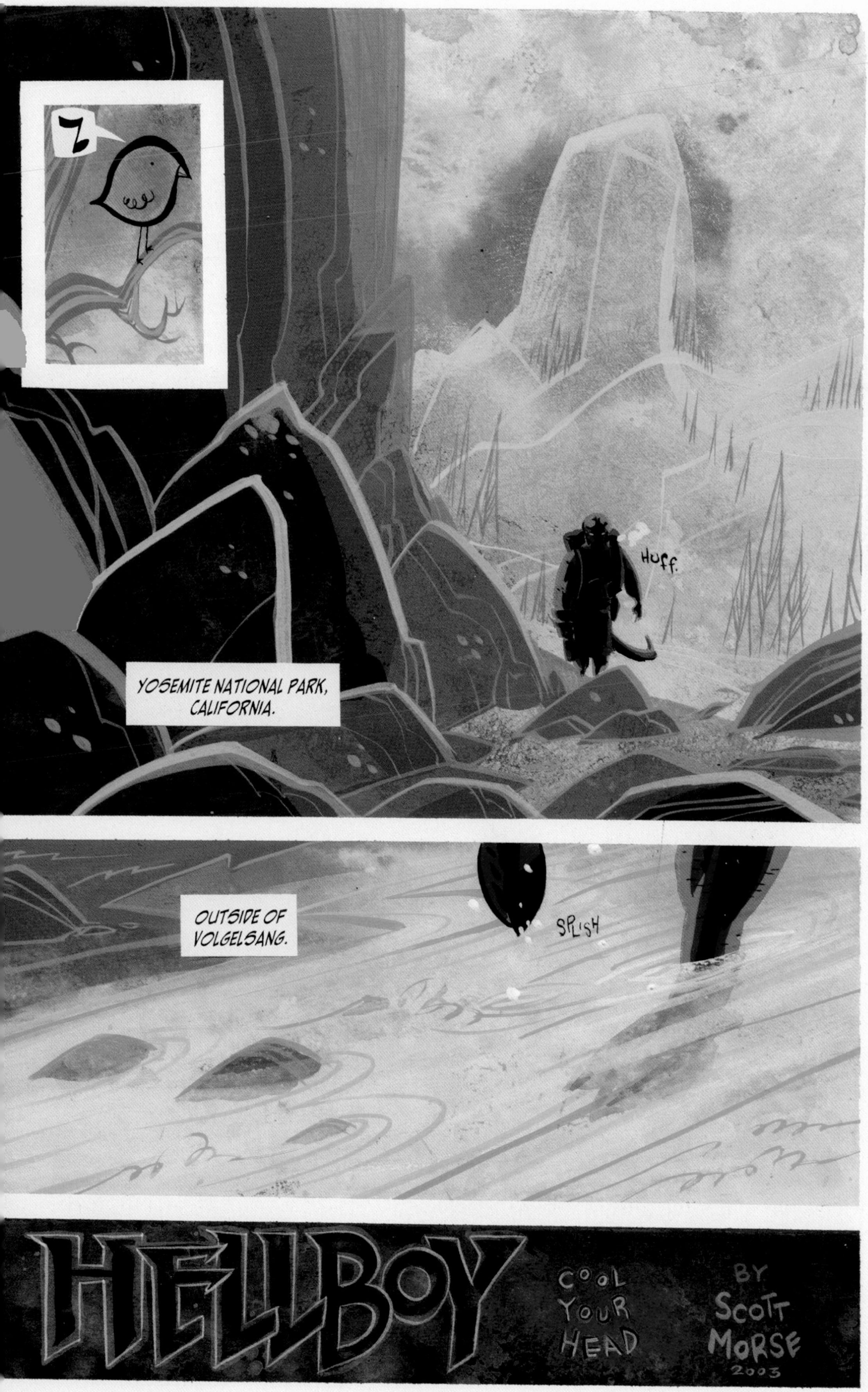

YOSEMITE NATIONAL PARK, CALIFORNIA.
HUFF.
OUTSIDE OF VOLGELSANG.
SPLISH
HELLBOY
COOL YOUR HEAD
BY SCOTT MORSE 2003

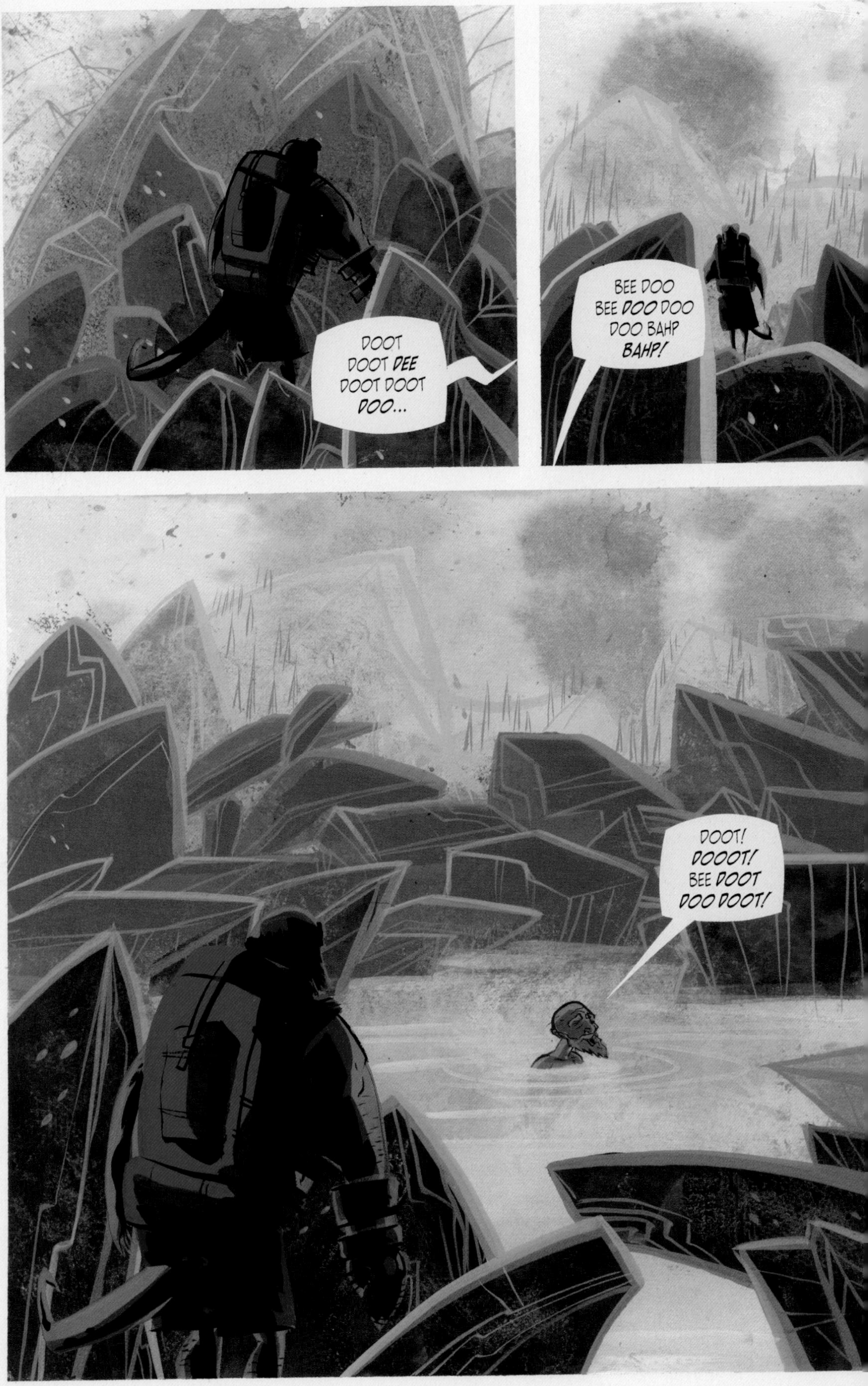
DOOT DOOT DEE DOOT DOOT DOO...
BEE DOO BEE DOO DOO DOO BAHP BAHP!
DOOT! DOOOT! BEE DOOT DOO DOOT!

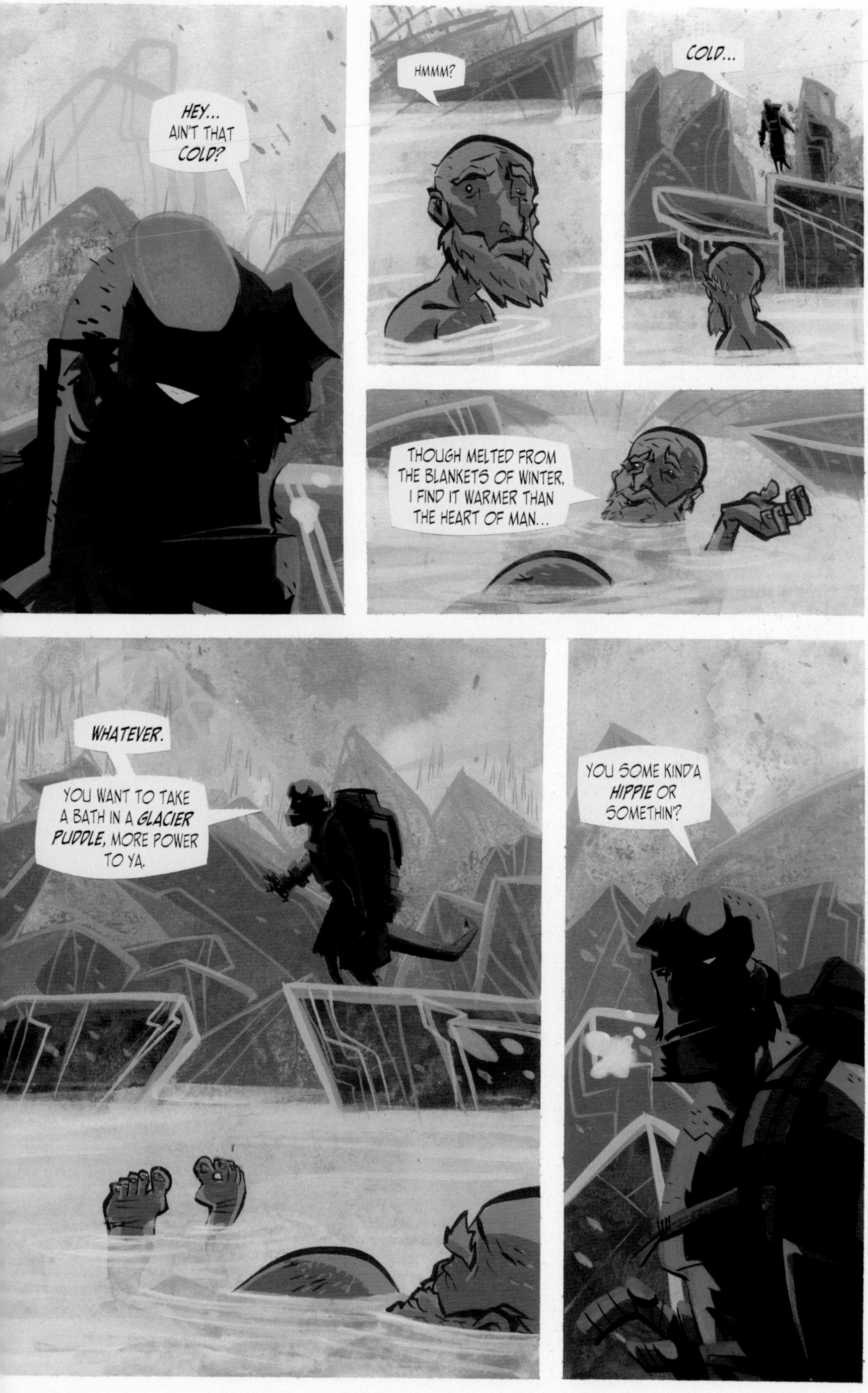
HEY... AIN'T THAT COLD?
HMMM?
COLD...
THOUGH MELTED FROM THE BLANKETS OF WINTER, I FIND IT WARMER THAN THE HEART OF MAN...
WHATEVER.
YOU WANT TO TAKE A BATH IN A GLACIER PUDDLE, MORE POWER TO YA.
YOU SOME KIND'A HIPPIE OR SOMETHIN'?

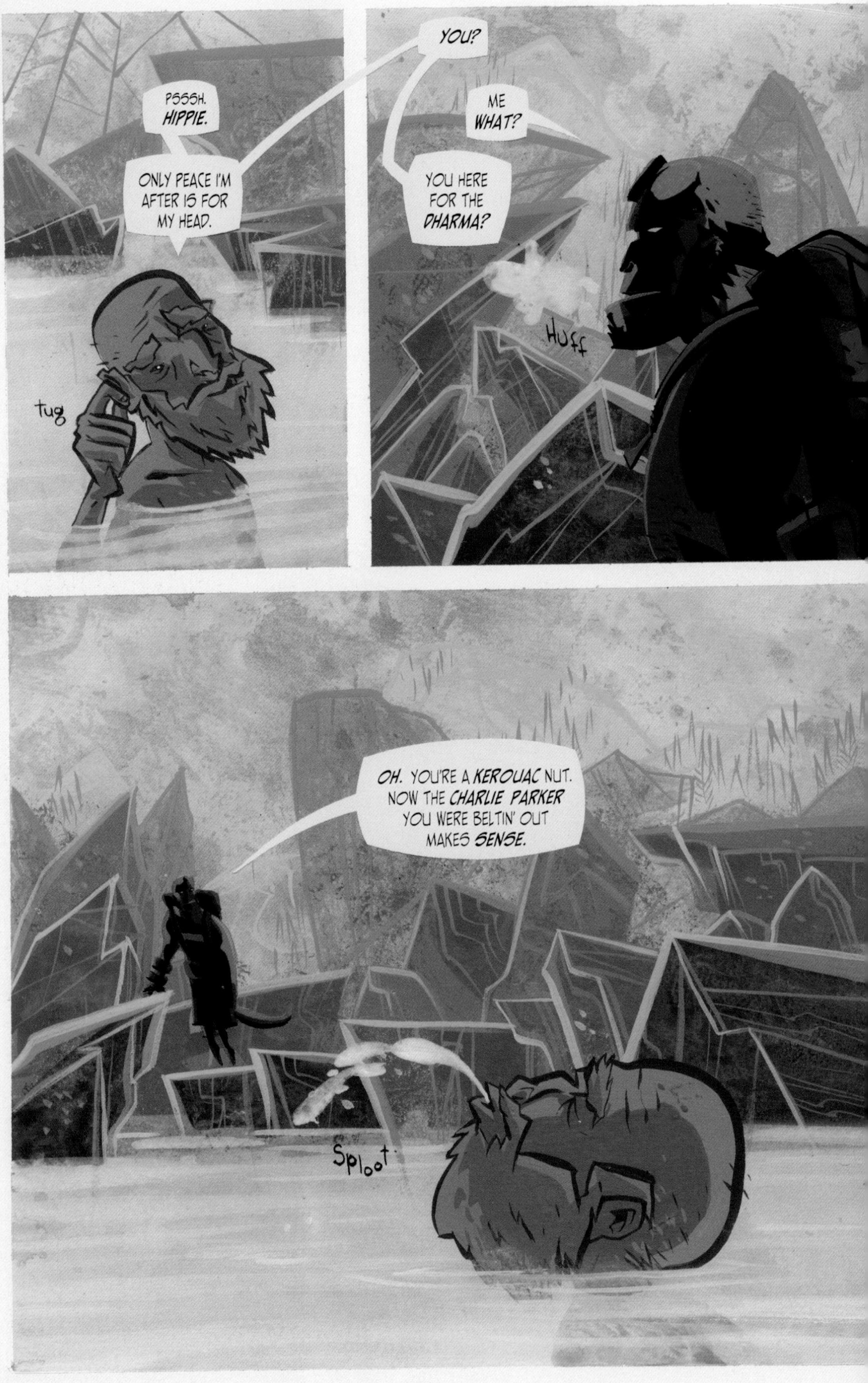
PSSSH. HIPPIE.
ONLY PEACE I'M AFTER IS FOR MY HEAD.
tug
YOU?
ME WHAT?
YOU HERE FOR THE DHARMA?
Huff
OH. YOU'RE A KEROUAC NUT. NOW THE CHARLIE PARKER YOU WERE BELTIN' OUT MAKES SENSE.
Sploot

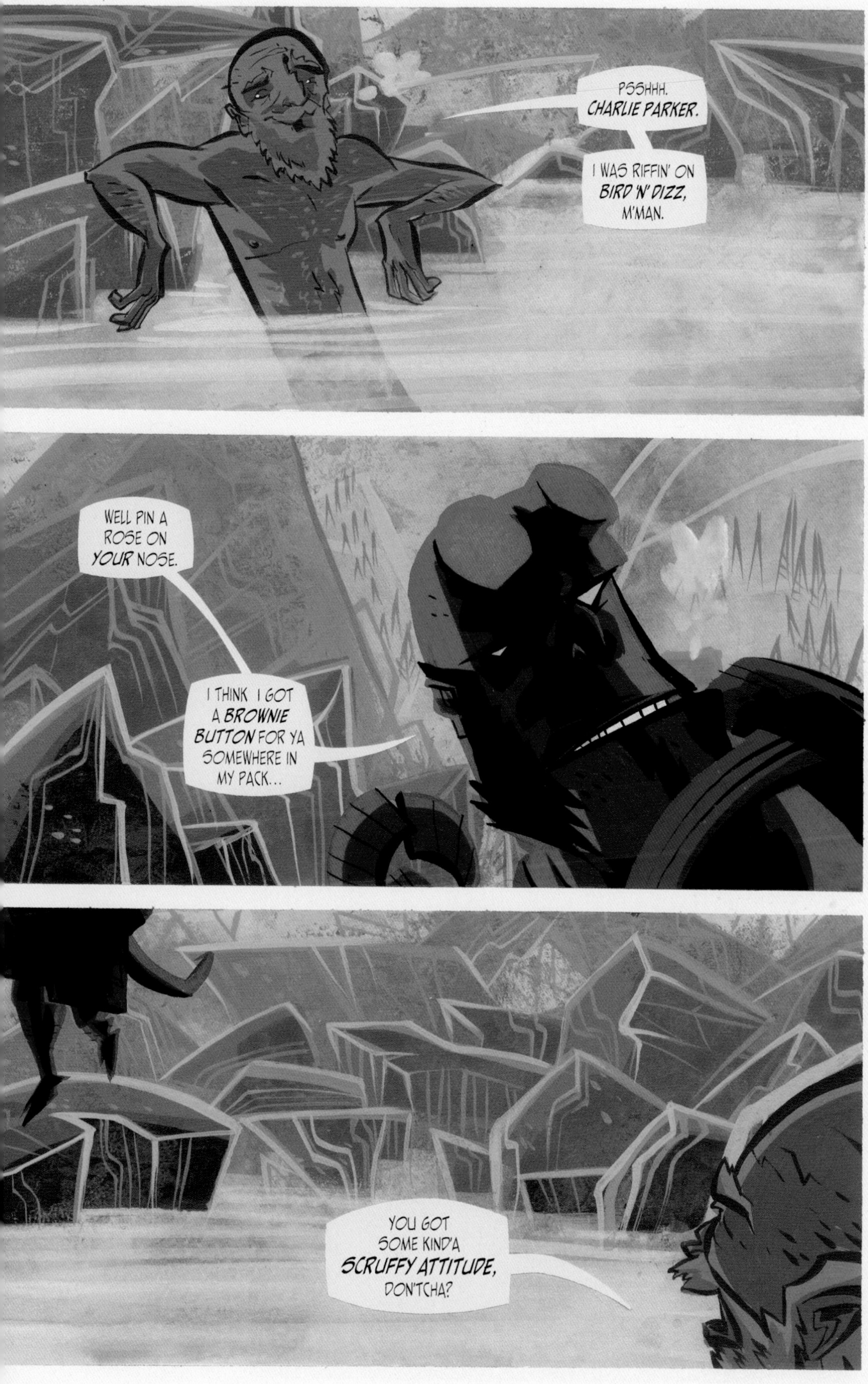
PSSHHH.
CHARLIE PARKER.
I WAS RIFFIN' ON BIRD 'N' DIZZ, M'MAN.
WELL PIN A ROSE ON YOUR NOSE.
I THINK I GOT A BROWNIE BUTTON FOR YA SOMEWHERE IN MY PACK...
YOU GOT SOME KIND'A SCRUFFY ATTITUDE, DON'TCHA?

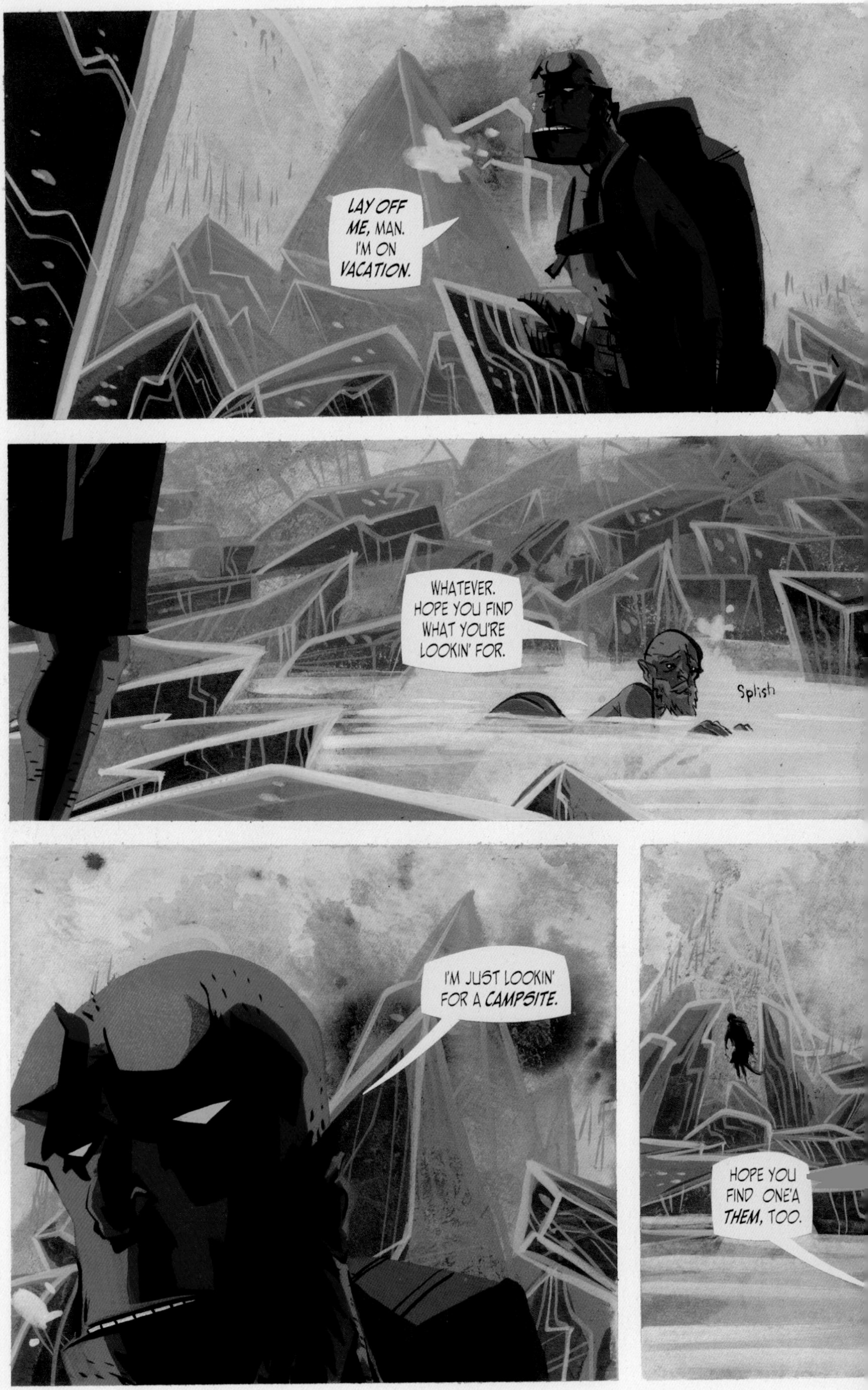
LAY OFF ME, MAN. I'M ON VACATION.
WHATEVER. HOPE YOU FIND WHAT YOU'RE LOOKIN' FOR.
Splish
I'M JUST LOOKIN' FOR A CAMPSITE.
HOPE YOU FIND ONE'A THEM, TOO.

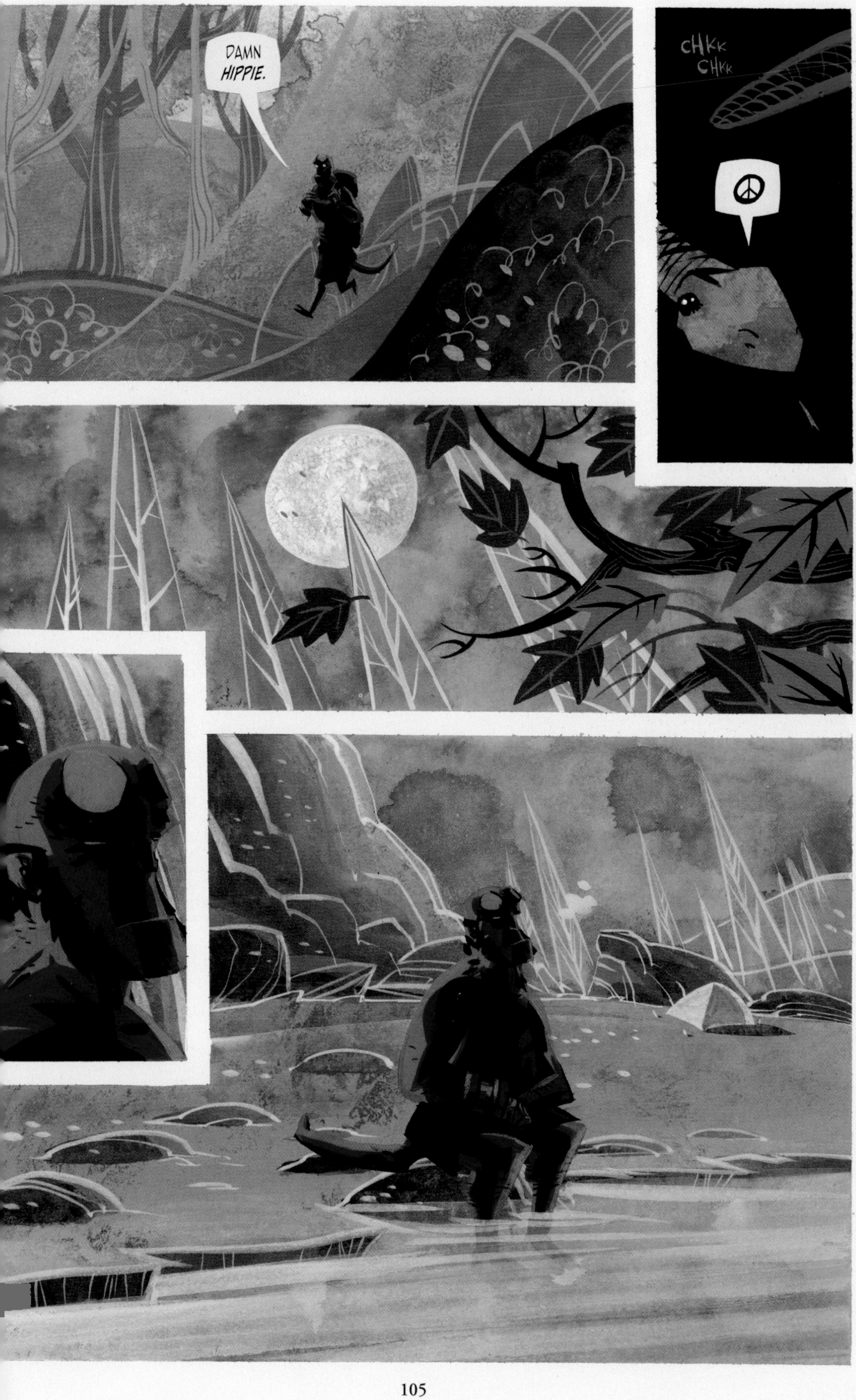
DAMN HIPPIE.
CHKK CHKK
☮

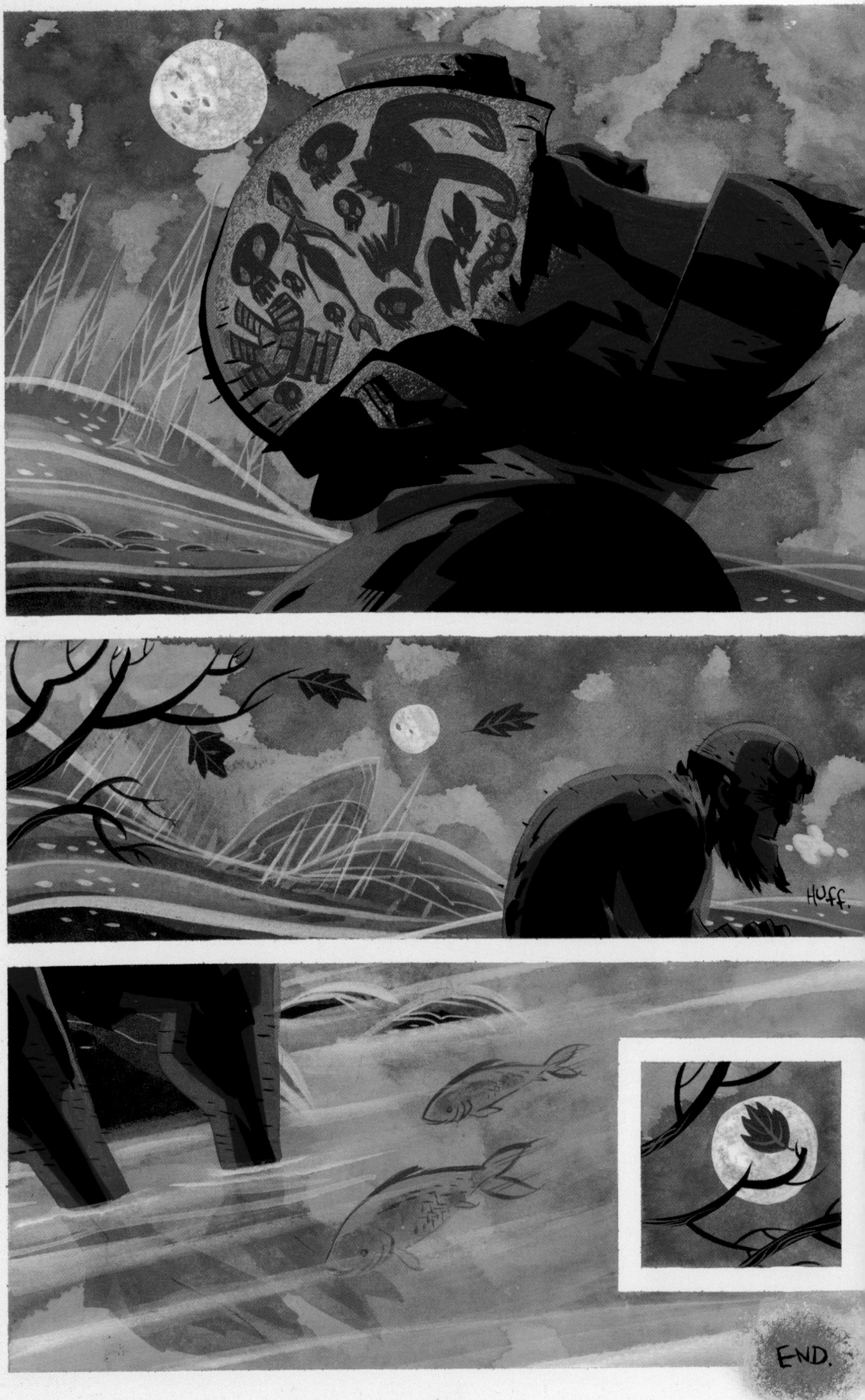
HUFF.
END.

Afterword

IN THE MID 1970s, I was in high school in Oakland, California. I don't remember much about that—not because of drugs or anything, I just have a lousy memory. What I *do* remember from that time was hunting through used bookstores with my brothers. Almost every weekend we took the bus (the 59 or the 76, then the College Avenue 51) into Berkeley and spent long hours looking for stuff. Those were good days. I don't remember exactly what my brothers were buying. Todd (the youngest) was reading a lot of Edgar Rice Burroughs in those days. Scott (the middle) went from Tolkien to "strange but true" stories of UFOs and the Bermuda Triangle. Little by little they spent less time in the bookstores and more time in the used record stores. For me it was always about the books. Ghost- and horror-story anthologies. And the two magic words I was looking for ... *Weird Tales*.

I'm not sure when I first learned that there had been a pulp magazine called *Weird Tales*. There must have been some mention of it in Marvel Comics' *Savage Tales* or *Savage Sword of Conan*. Reading those magazines led me to reading the Conan books, then everything I could get my hands on by Robert E. Howard and his *Weird Tales* contemporaries. The '70s was a horrible time for fashion, but a great time for affordable pulp reprints, especially if you bought them used. For a while there it seemed I was discovering new (old, mostly dead, but new to me) authors every trip in those beautiful, dusty, cluttered, half-lit Berkeley book caves. I could go on and on about those places (Pendragon, Pellucidar, Moe's, Other Change of Hobbit, etc.), but the important thing here is that I was *reading* all that *Weird Tales* stuff. The almost science-fiction cosmic horror of Lovecraft. The weird fantasy of Clark Ashton Smith. The Seabury Quinn occult-detective stories. Henry Whitehead, Frank Bellknap Long, August Derleth, Price, Jacobi, Wellman, Brennan. Vampires, werewolves, lost worlds, mad scientists, giant amoebas, and rampaging fungi. I read a lot of great stuff, and I read a lot of crap. I absorbed it all—and twenty years later, it all came back out as *Hellboy*.

A couple of years ago, Scott Allie and I were racking our brains trying to come up with a title for this *Hellboy* anthology series. I kept saying that it had to be something like *Weird Tales*. Here we had a wide variety of creators producing a wide variety of supernatural stories (like *Weird Tales*), and, through Hellboy, they all owed something to that long-ago pulp-magazine icon. In the end we agreed that no sound-alike title was good enough. My thanks to Scott Allie for doing whatever he needed to secure the *Weird Tales* title, and to the powers that be at Dark Horse for letting him do it. I am thrilled and honored to see the words *Hellboy* and *Weird Tales* linked together, officially, at last.

Mike Mignola
New York City

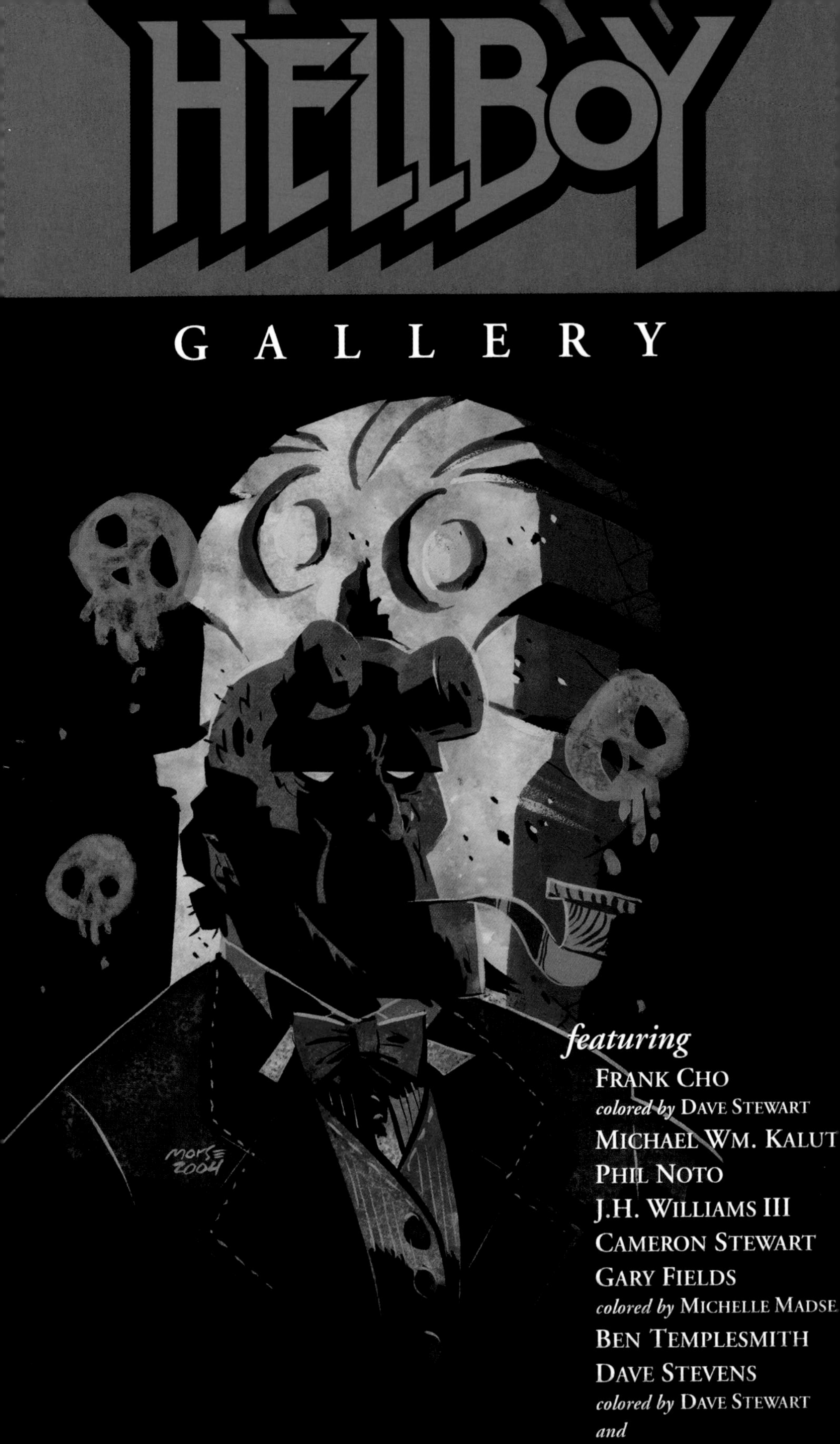
HELLBOY
GALLERY
featuring
FRANK CHO
colored by DAVE STEWART
MICHAEL WM. KALUT
PHIL NOTO
J.H. WILLIAMS III
CAMERON STEWART
GARY FIELDS
colored by MICHELLE MADSE
BEN TEMPLESMITH
DAVE STEVENS
colored by DAVE STEWART
and

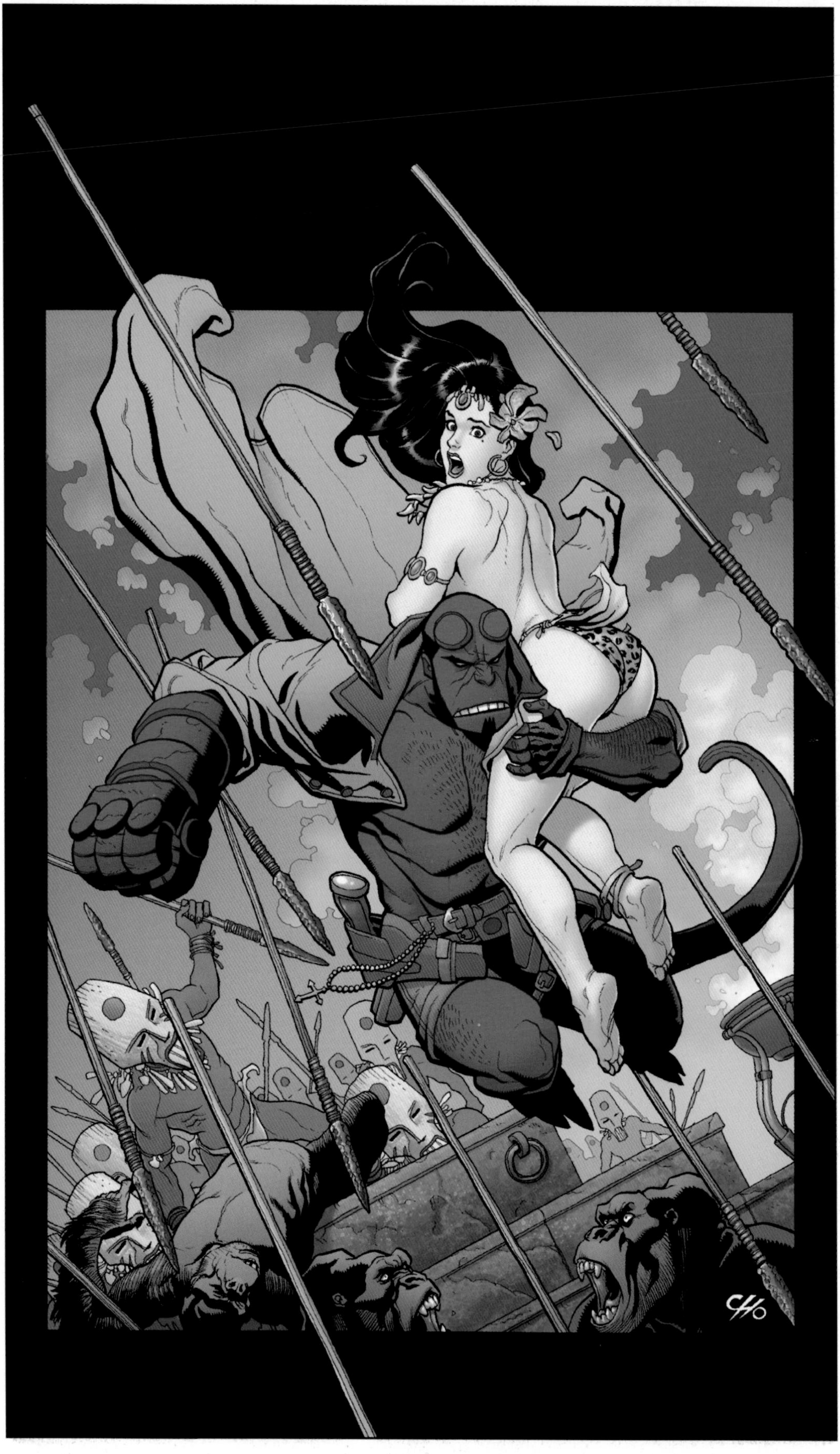
CHO

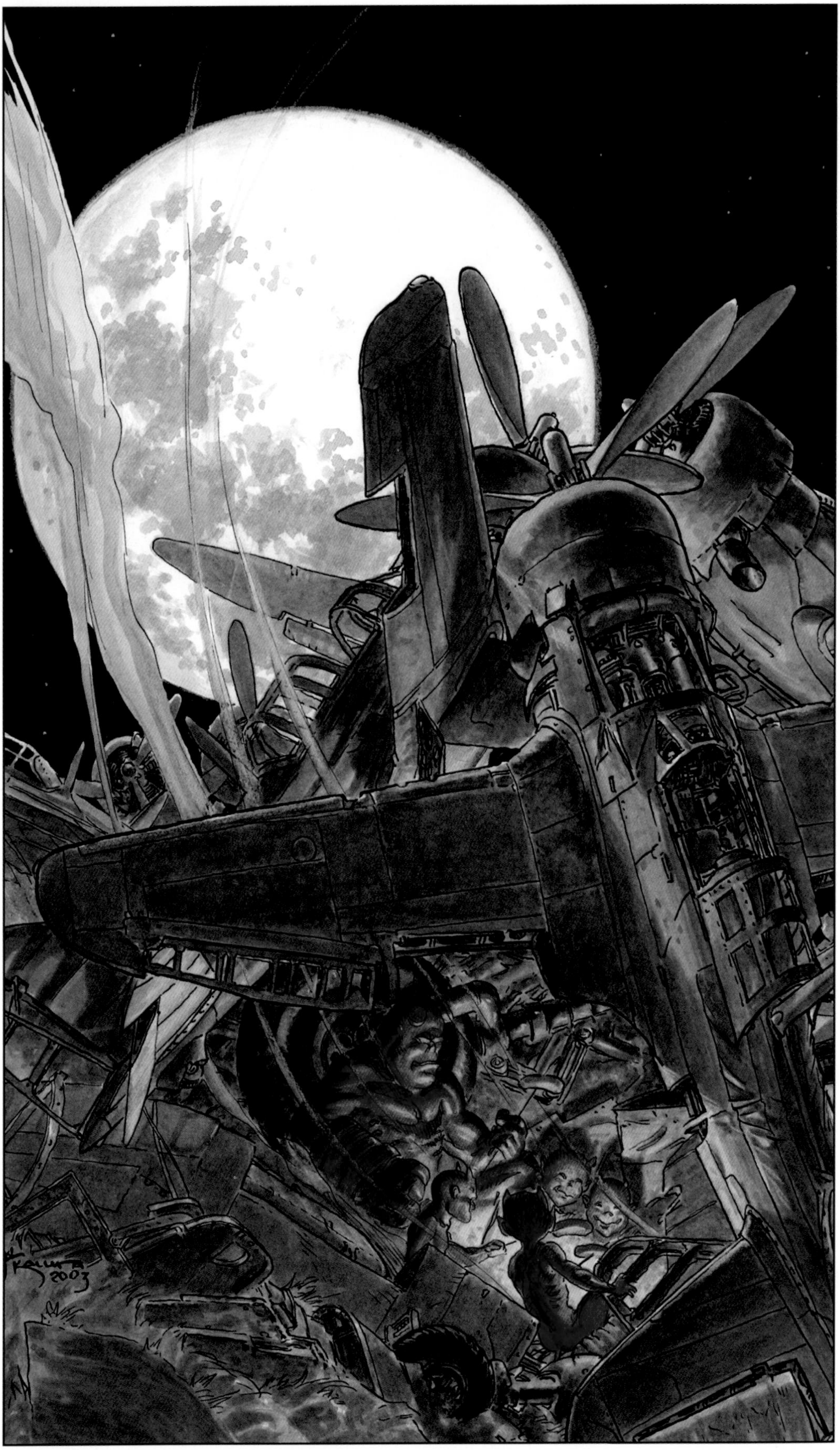

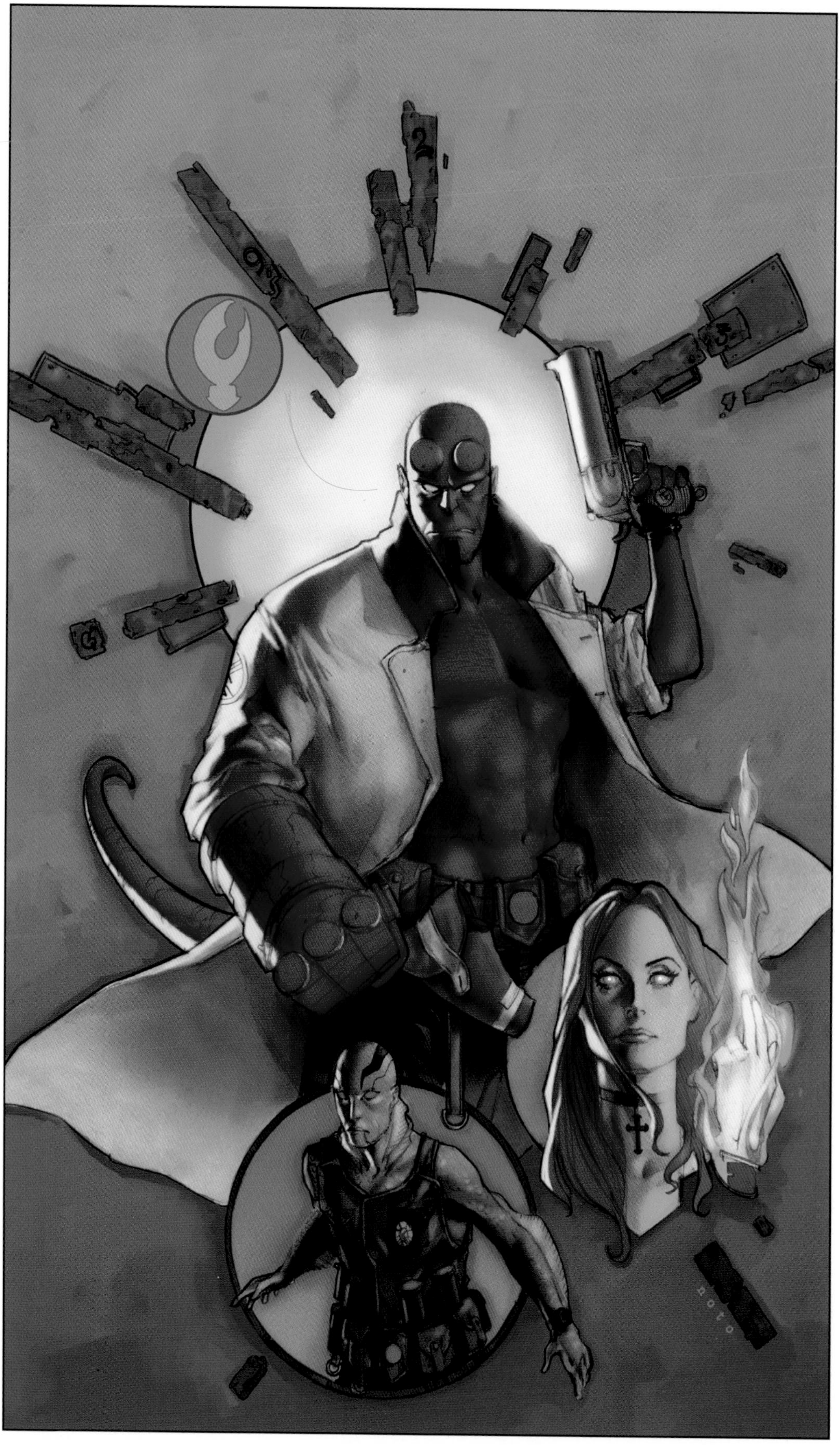

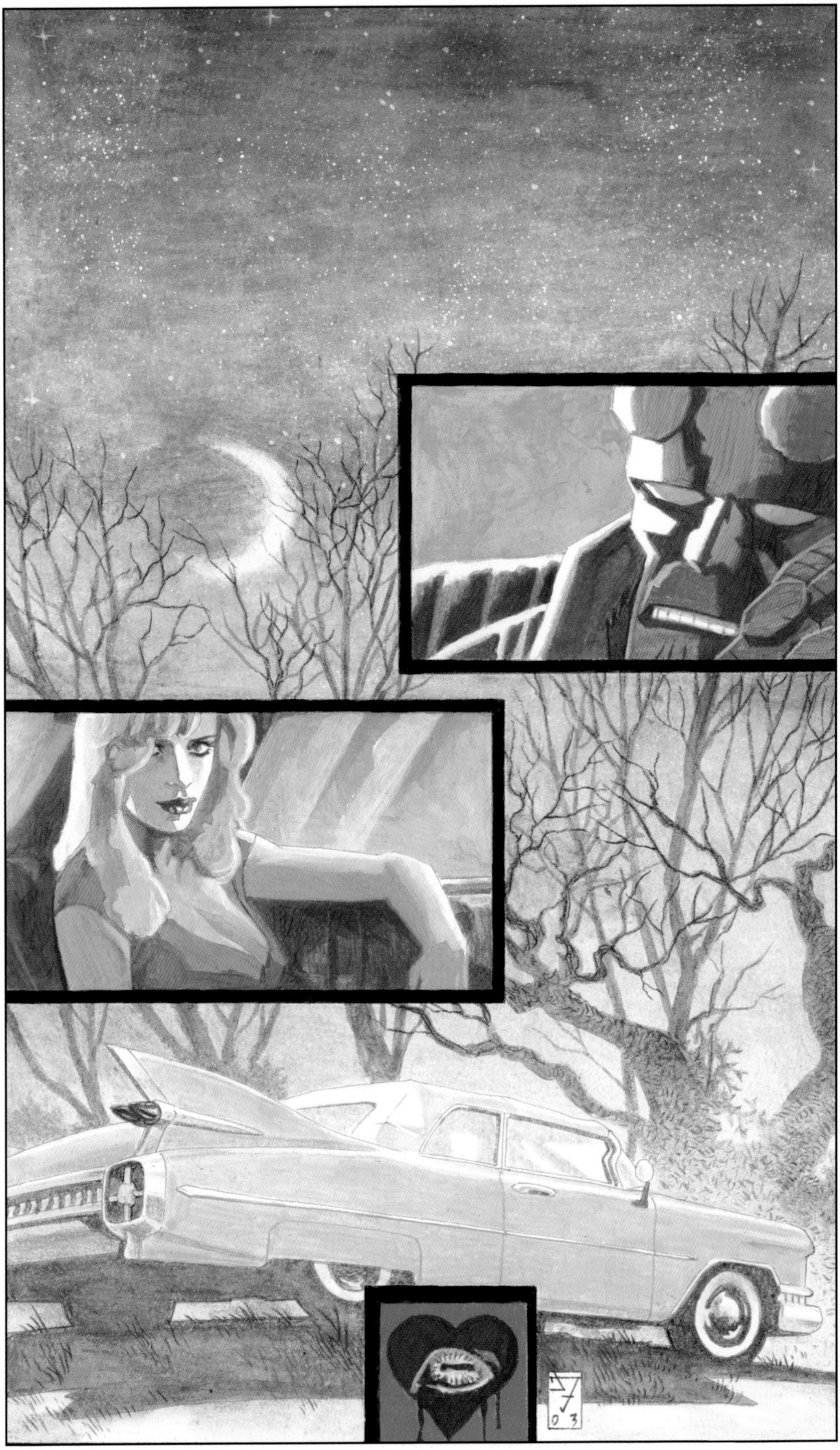

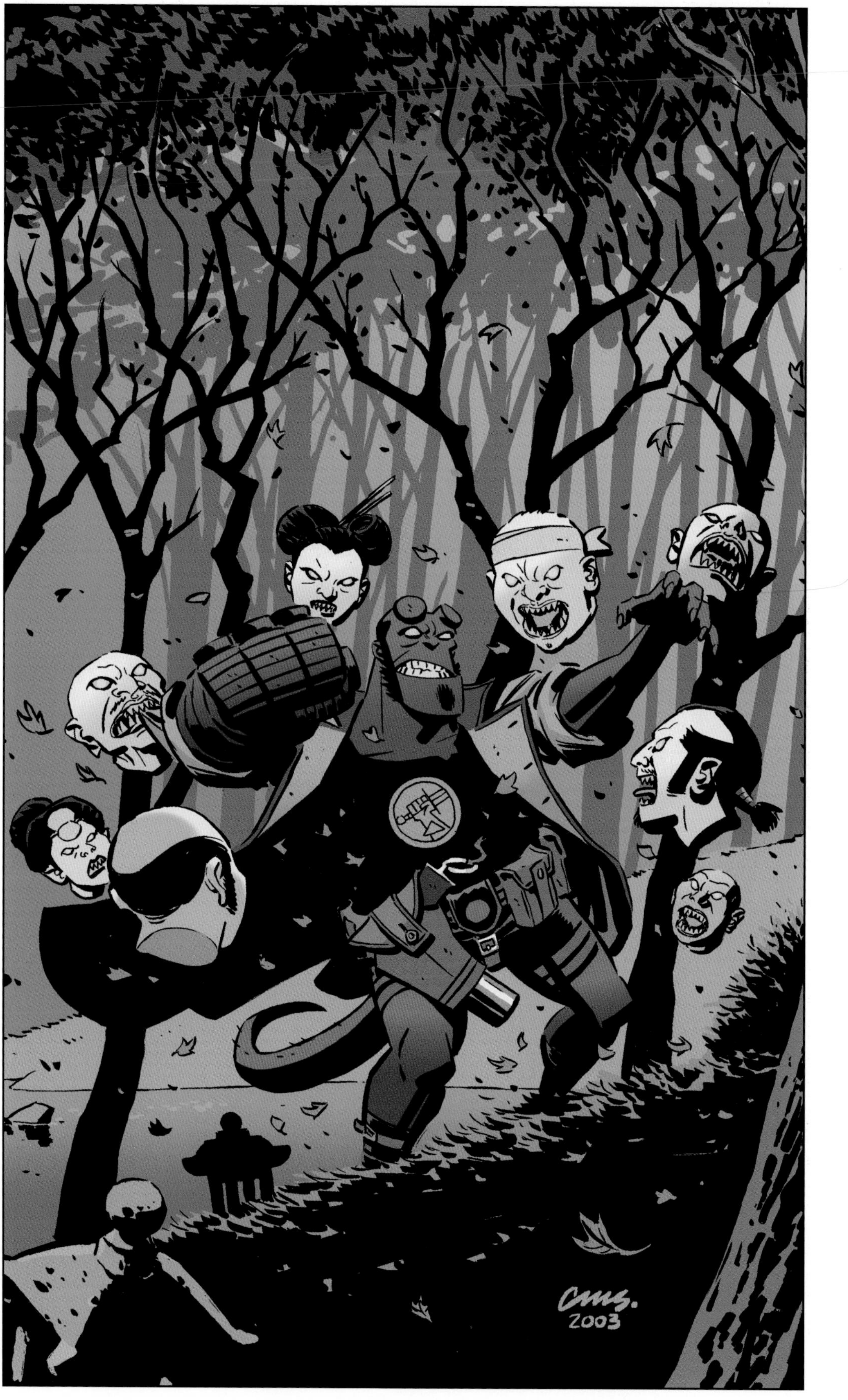

CMG.
2003

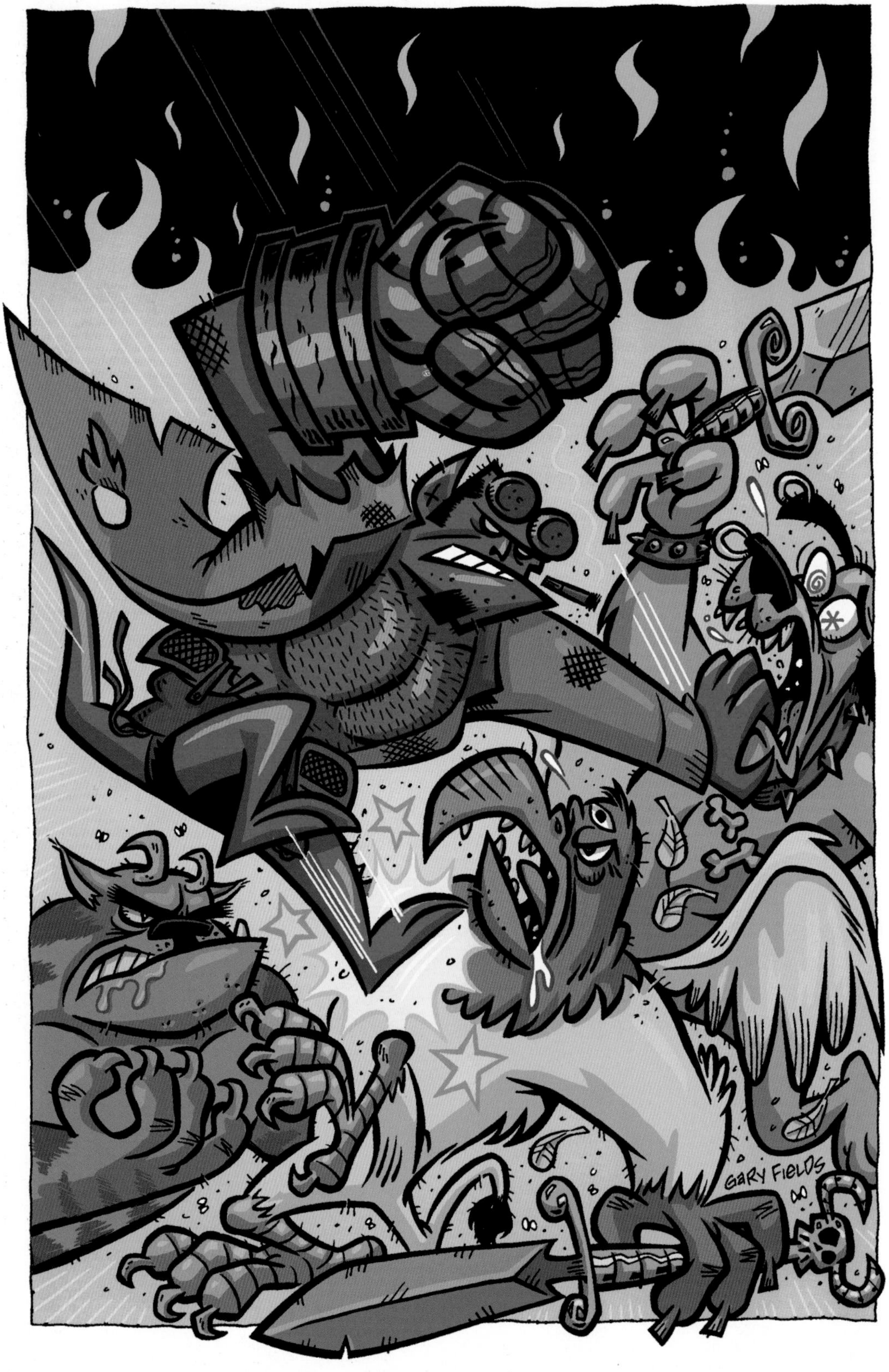
GARY FIELDS

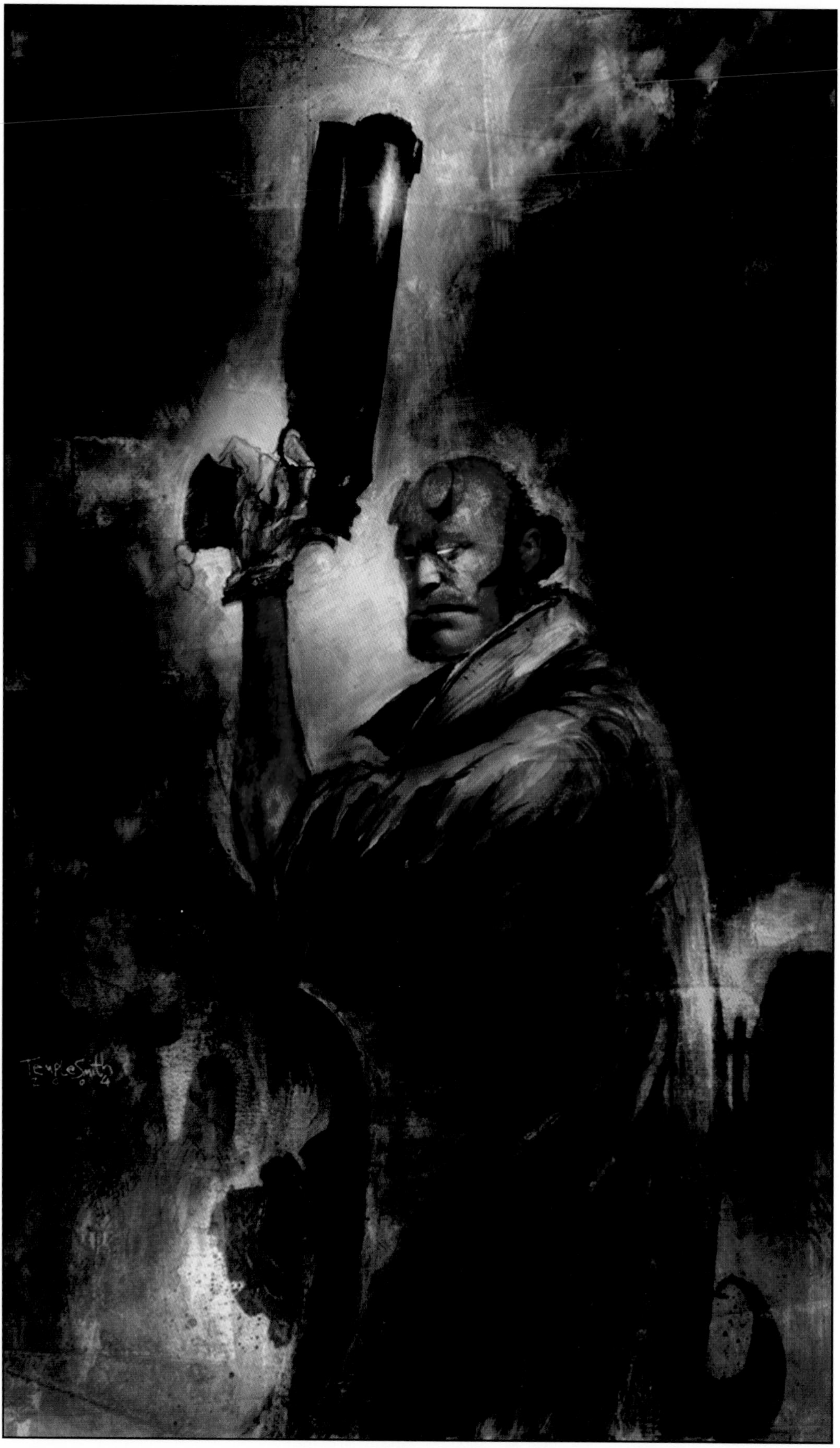

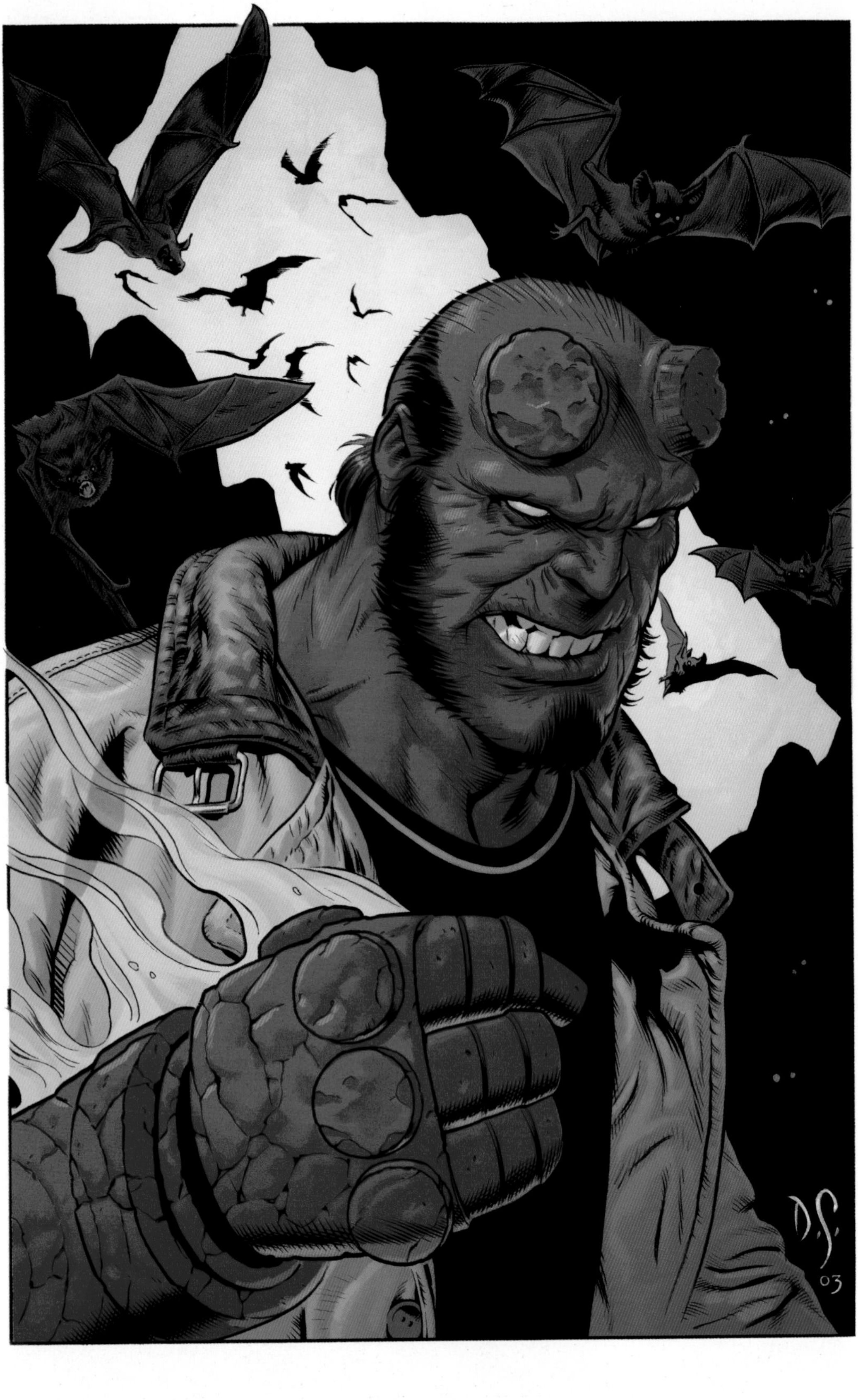

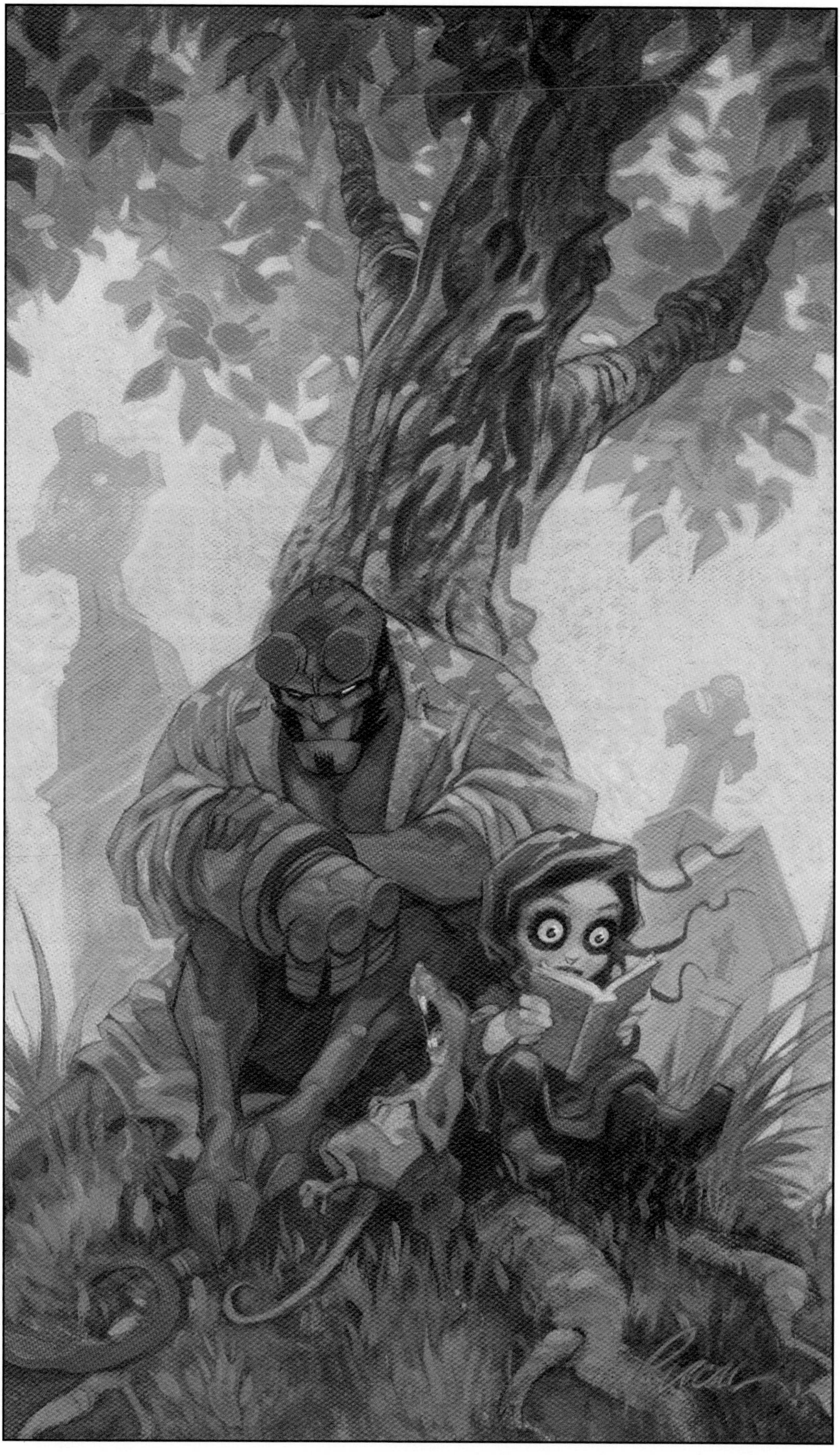

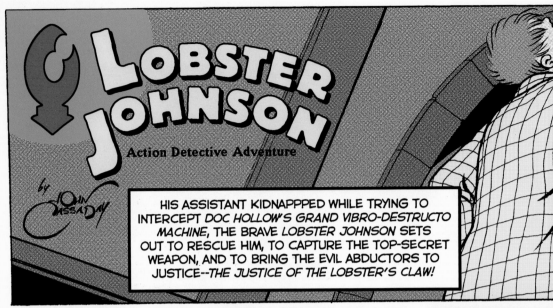

LOBSTER JOHNSON

Action Detective Adventure

by JOHN CASSADAY

HIS ASSISTANT KIDNAPPPED WHILE TRYING TO INTERCEPT *DOC HOLLOW'S GRAND VIBRO-DESTRUCTO MACHINE*, THE BRAVE *LOBSTER JOHNSON* SETS OUT TO RESCUE HIM, TO CAPTURE THE TOP-SECRET WEAPON, AND TO BRING THE EVIL ABDUCTORS TO JUSTICE--*THE JUSTICE OF THE LOBSTER'S CLAW!*

MAKE THINGS MORE DIFFICULT AND YOU'LL GET *WORSE* THAN MERE *JUSTICE,* CRIMSON HOOD!

LET ME SHOW YOU *MY* WARNING, MONSTER!

THE CRIMSON HOOD HITS A SECRET SWITCH ON HIS DESK...

KLIK

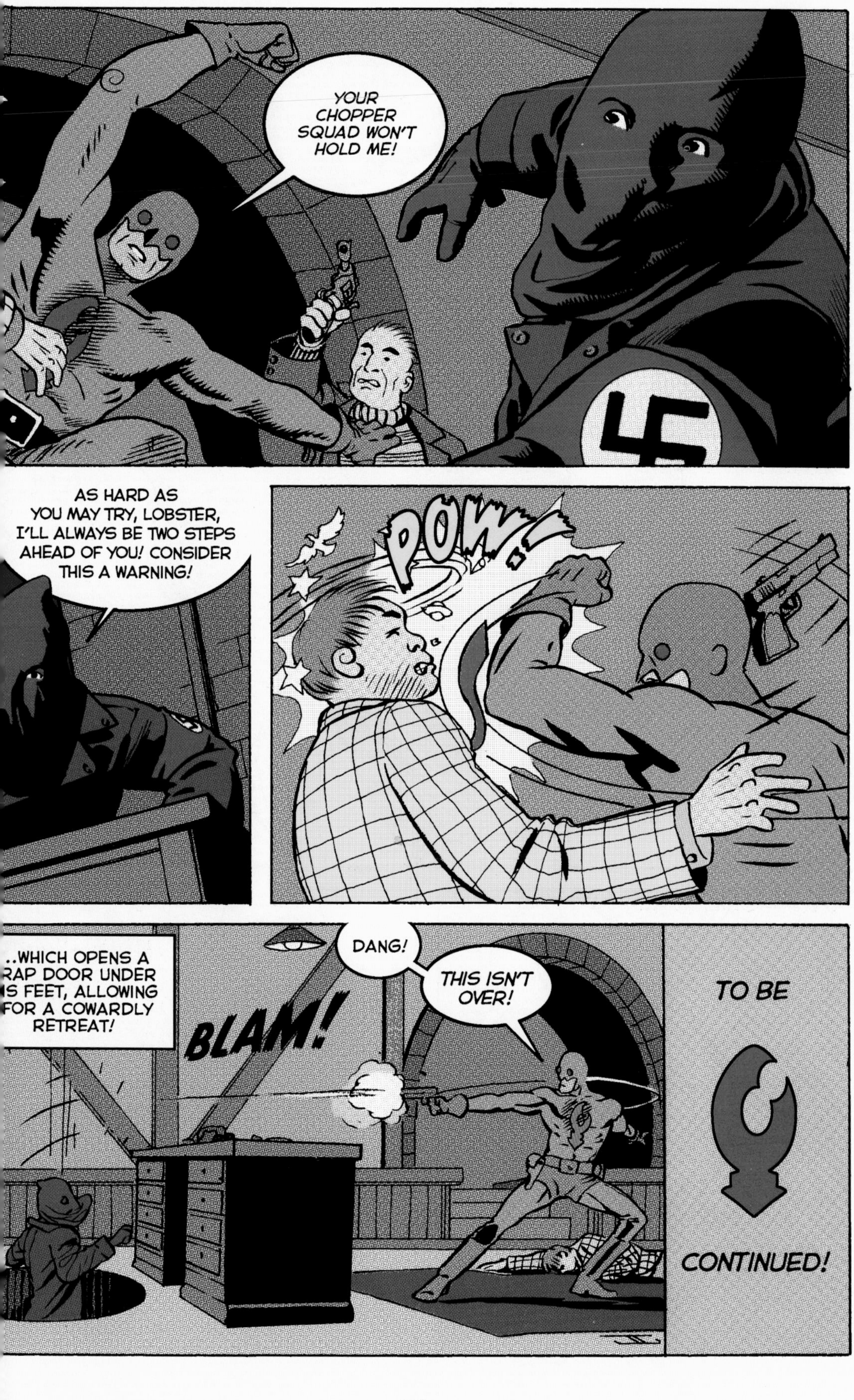
YOUR CHOPPER SQUAD WON'T HOLD ME!
AS HARD AS YOU MAY TRY, LOBSTER, I'LL ALWAYS BE TWO STEPS AHEAD OF YOU! CONSIDER THIS A WARNING!
POW!
..WHICH OPENS A RAP DOOR UNDER S FEET, ALLOWING FOR A COWARDLY RETREAT!
BLAM!
DANG!
THIS ISN'T OVER!
TO BE
CONTINUED!

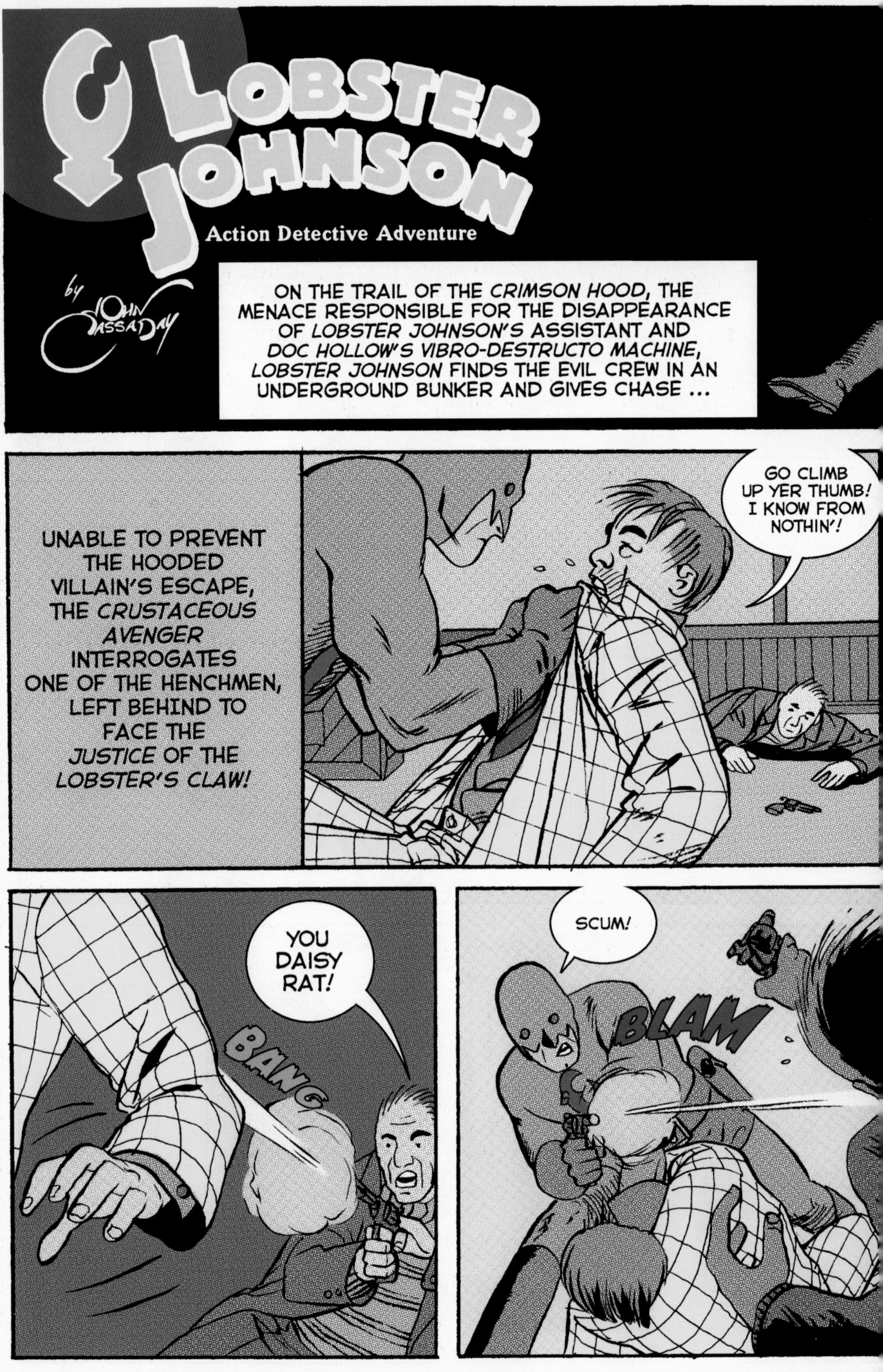
LOBSTER JOHNSON
Action Detective Adventure
by JOHN CASSADAY
ON THE TRAIL OF THE CRIMSON HOOD, THE MENACE RESPONSIBLE FOR THE DISAPPEARANCE OF LOBSTER JOHNSON'S ASSISTANT AND DOC HOLLOW'S VIBRO-DESTRUCTO MACHINE, LOBSTER JOHNSON FINDS THE EVIL CREW IN AN UNDERGROUND BUNKER AND GIVES CHASE ...
UNABLE TO PREVENT THE HOODED VILLAIN'S ESCAPE, THE CRUSTACEOUS AVENGER INTERROGATES ONE OF THE HENCHMEN, LEFT BEHIND TO FACE THE JUSTICE OF THE LOBSTER'S CLAW!
GO CLIMB UP YER THUMB! I KNOW FROM NOTHIN'!
YOU DAISY RAT!
BANG
SCUM!
BLAM

... ONLY TO FIND A *MONSTROUS* BARRICADE!

BIG DOOR.

REVEALED IS THE SCORCHING-HOT BRAND OF THE LOBSTER!

YOUR BOSS LAMBED OFF, PIGEON! TELL ME WHERE HE'S GONE-- OR SUFFER!

ALL RIGHT, ALL RIGHT!! YOU DON'T HAVE TO PUT THE SCREWS ON!

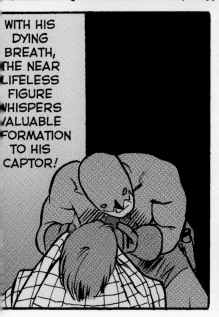

WITH HIS DYING BREATH, THE NEAR LIFELESS FIGURE WHISPERS VALUABLE INFORMATION TO HIS CAPTOR!

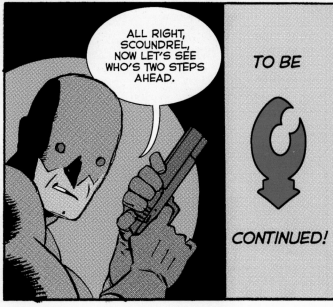

ALL RIGHT, SCOUNDREL, NOW LET'S SEE WHO'S TWO STEPS AHEAD.

TO BE

CONTINUED!

121

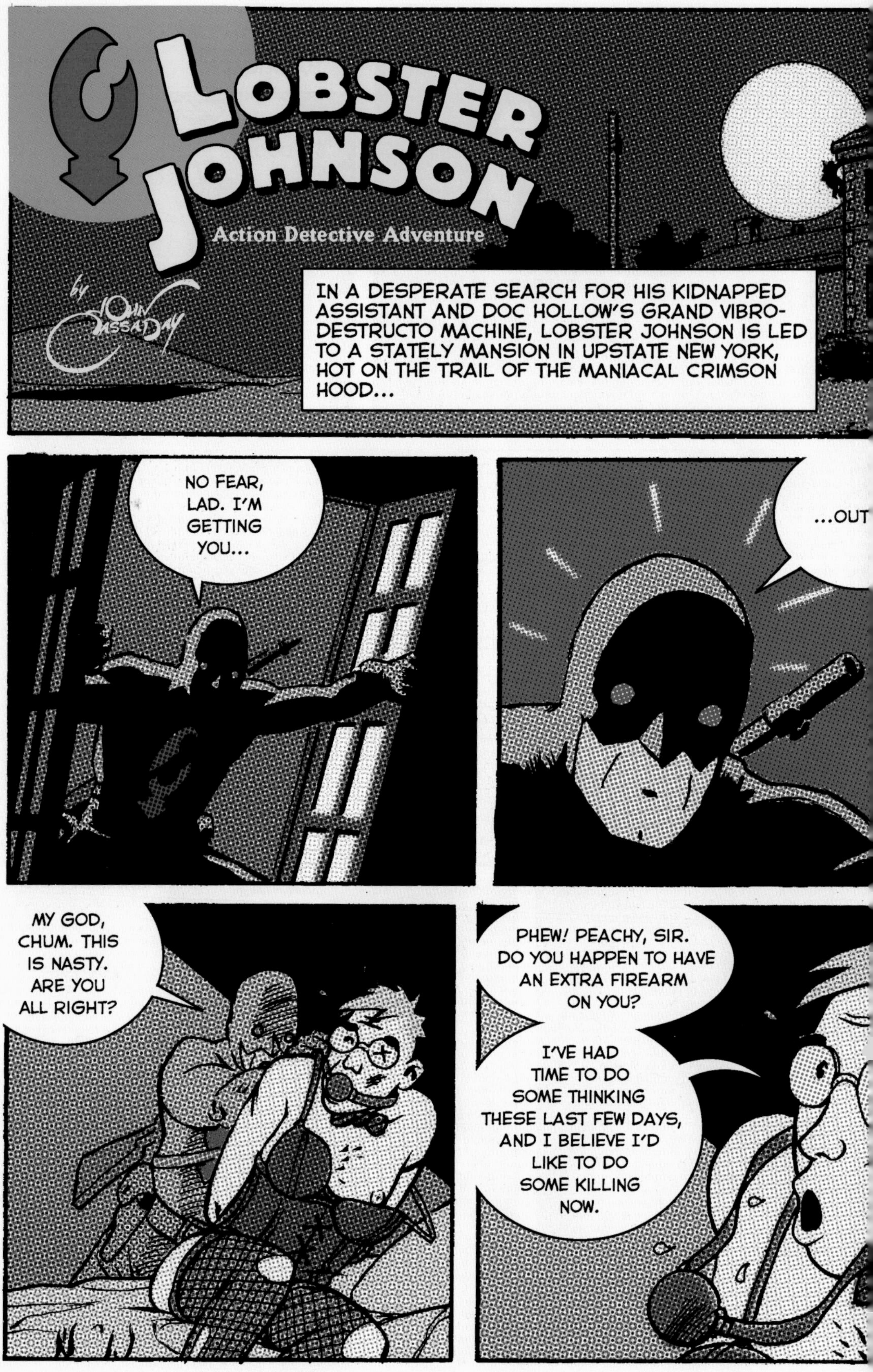
LOBSTER JOHNSON
Action Detective Adventure
by JOHN CASSADAY
IN A DESPERATE SEARCH FOR HIS KIDNAPPED ASSISTANT AND DOC HOLLOW'S GRAND VIBRO-DESTRUCTO MACHINE, LOBSTER JOHNSON IS LED TO A STATELY MANSION IN UPSTATE NEW YORK, HOT ON THE TRAIL OF THE MANIACAL CRIMSON HOOD...
NO FEAR, LAD. I'M GETTING YOU...
...OUT
MY GOD, CHUM. THIS IS NASTY. ARE YOU ALL RIGHT?
PHEW! PEACHY, SIR. DO YOU HAPPEN TO HAVE AN EXTRA FIREARM ON YOU?
I'VE HAD TIME TO DO SOME THINKING THESE LAST FEW DAYS, AND I BELIEVE I'D LIKE TO DO SOME KILLING NOW.

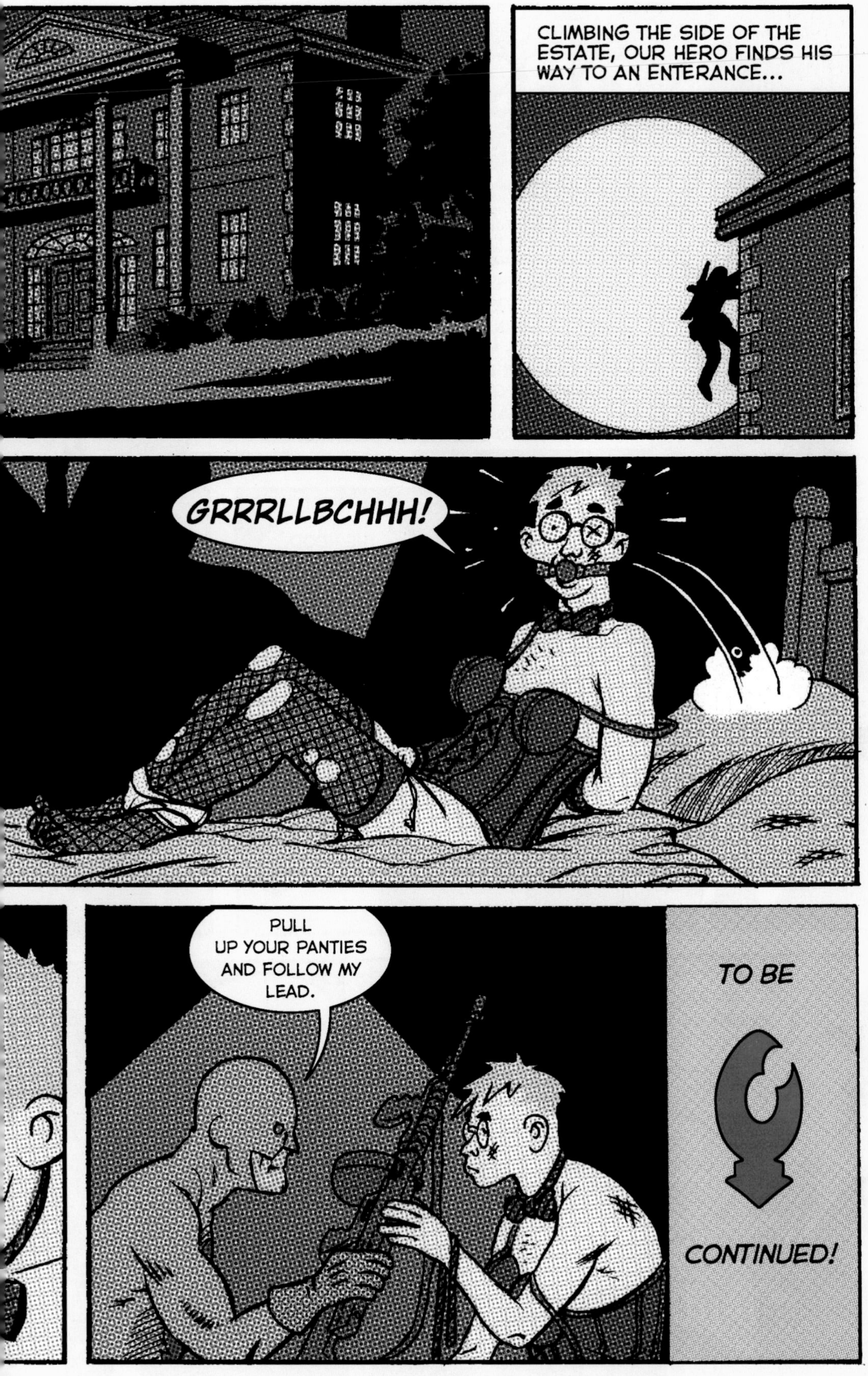
CLIMBING THE SIDE OF THE ESTATE, OUR HERO FINDS HIS WAY TO AN ENTERANCE...
GRRRLLBCHHH!
PULL UP YOUR PANTIES AND FOLLOW MY LEAD.
TO BE
CONTINUED!

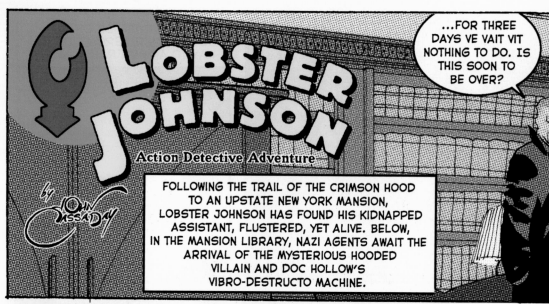

LOBSTER JOHNSON

Action Detective Adventure

by John Cassaday

FOLLOWING THE TRAIL OF THE CRIMSON HOOD TO AN UPSTATE NEW YORK MANSION, LOBSTER JOHNSON HAS FOUND HIS KIDNAPPED ASSISTANT, FLUSTERED, YET ALIVE. BELOW, IN THE MANSION LIBRARY, NAZI AGENTS AWAIT THE ARRIVAL OF THE MYSTERIOUS HOODED VILLAIN AND DOC HOLLOW'S VIBRO-DESTRUCTO MACHINE.

...FOR THREE DAYS VE VAIT VIT NOTHING TO DO. IS THIS SOON TO BE OVER?

EVEN THE TOY UPSTAIRS BORES ME.

THE HOOD SHOULD BE ARRIVING SOON ENOU--

GENTLEMEN.

THIS SHALL MAKE YOUR WAIT WORTHWHILE.

BY ALL MEANS, VE VILL TAKE IT.

EXCELLENT. LET US CELEBRATE. ELMO, BRING US CHAMPAGNE!

...SIR...

...VISITORS...

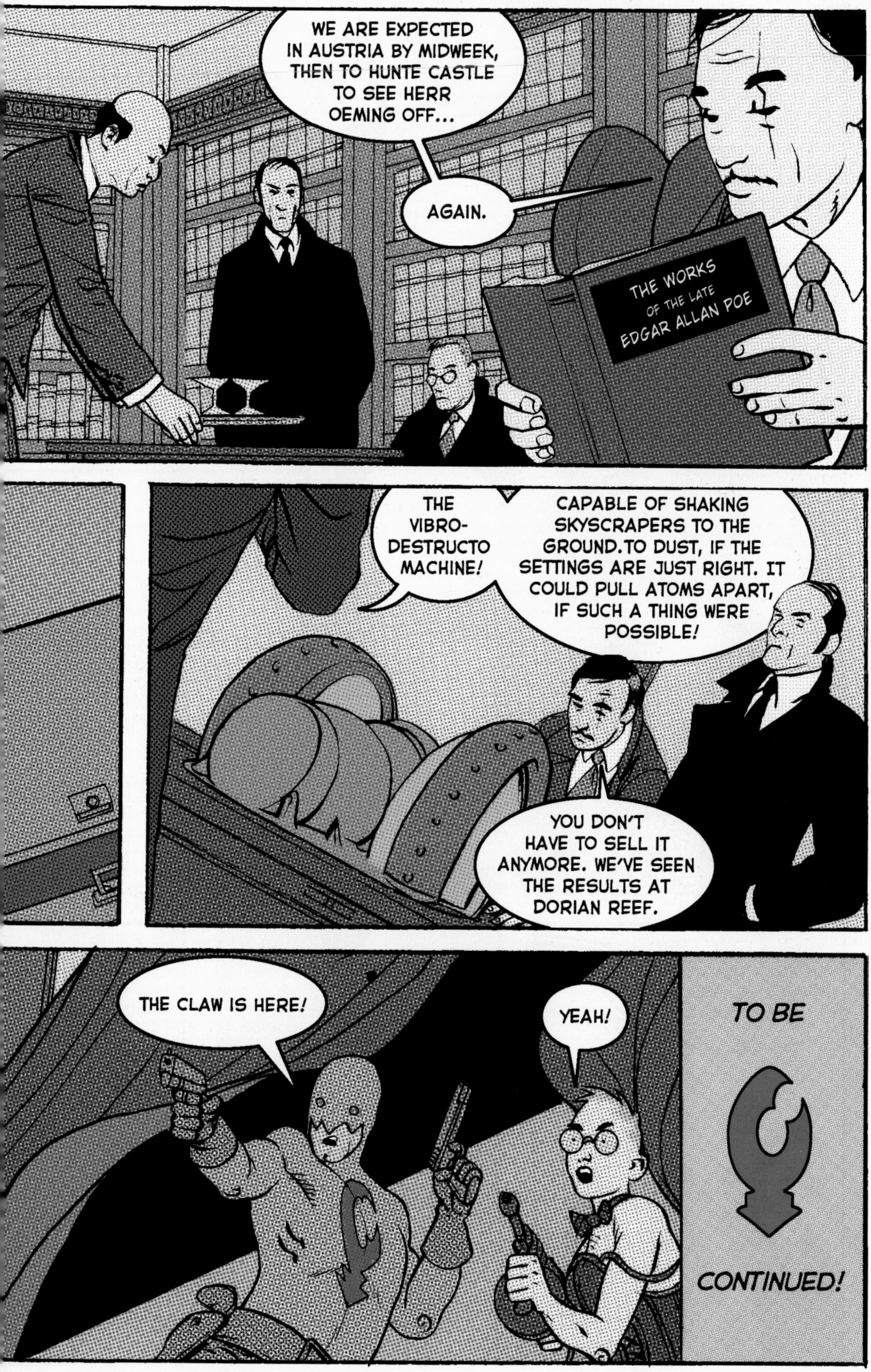
WE ARE EXPECTED IN AUSTRIA BY MIDWEEK, THEN TO HUNTE CASTLE TO SEE HERR OEMING OFF...
AGAIN.
THE WORKS OF THE LATE EDGAR ALLAN POE
THE VIBRO-DESTRUCTO MACHINE!
CAPABLE OF SHAKING SKYSCRAPERS TO THE GROUND.TO DUST, IF THE SETTINGS ARE JUST RIGHT. IT COULD PULL ATOMS APART, IF SUCH A THING WERE POSSIBLE!
YOU DON'T HAVE TO SELL IT ANYMORE. WE'VE SEEN THE RESULTS AT DORIAN REEF.
THE CLAW IS HERE!
YEAH!
TO BE
CONTINUED!

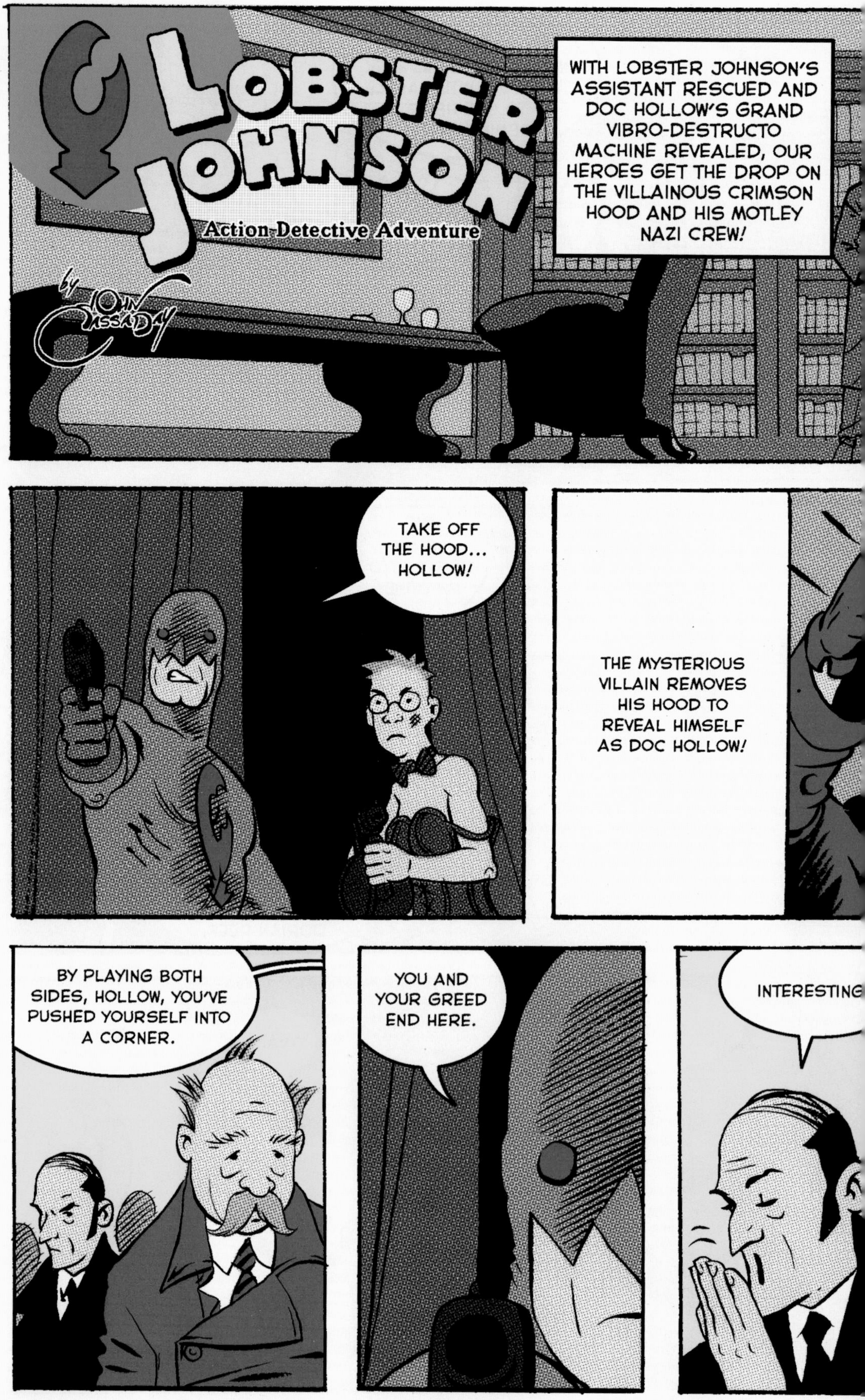
LOBSTER JOHNSON
Action-Detective Adventure
by JOHN CASSADAY
WITH LOBSTER JOHNSON'S ASSISTANT RESCUED AND DOC HOLLOW'S GRAND VIBRO-DESTRUCTO MACHINE REVEALED, OUR HEROES GET THE DROP ON THE VILLAINOUS CRIMSON HOOD AND HIS MOTLEY NAZI CREW!
TAKE OFF THE HOOD... HOLLOW!
THE MYSTERIOUS VILLAIN REMOVES HIS HOOD TO REVEAL HIMSELF AS DOC HOLLOW!
BY PLAYING BOTH SIDES, HOLLOW, YOU'VE PUSHED YOURSELF INTO A CORNER.
YOU AND YOUR GREED END HERE.
INTERESTING

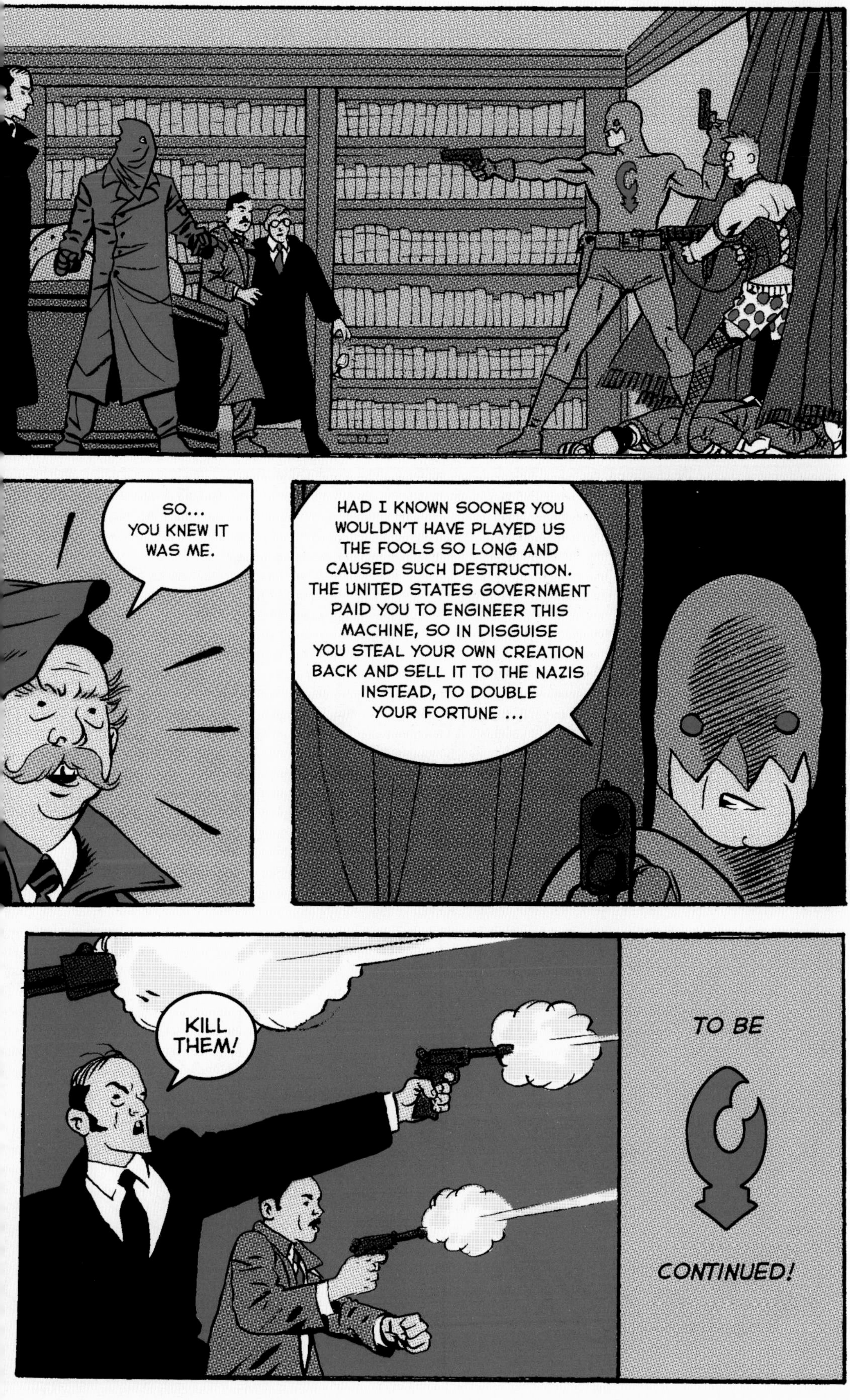
SO... YOU KNEW IT WAS ME.
HAD I KNOWN SOONER YOU WOULDN'T HAVE PLAYED US THE FOOLS SO LONG AND CAUSED SUCH DESTRUCTION. THE UNITED STATES GOVERNMENT PAID YOU TO ENGINEER THIS MACHINE, SO IN DISGUISE YOU STEAL YOUR OWN CREATION BACK AND SELL IT TO THE NAZIS INSTEAD, TO DOUBLE YOUR FORTUNE ...
KILL THEM!
TO BE
CONTINUED!

LOBSTER JOHNSON

Action Detective Adventure

by John Cassaday

BEWARE MY CLAW!

AFTER RESCUING HIS ASSISTANT, LOBSTER JOHNSON NOW TURNS HIS ATTENTION TO RETURNING DOC HOLLOW'S VIBRO-DESTRUCTO MACHINE TO THE AUTHORITIES-- AND BRINGING THE NEFARIOUS RING OF EVILDOERS TO JUSTICE!

WE MUST ESCAPE! WE CANNOT AFFORD TO LOSE!

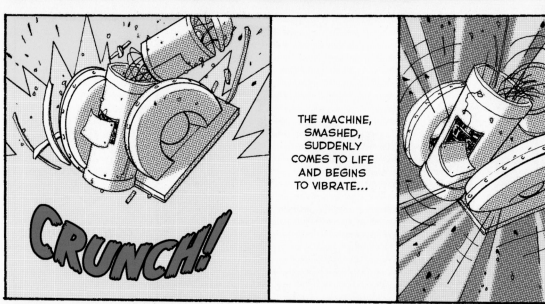

THE MACHINE, SMASHED, SUDDENLY COMES TO LIFE AND BEGINS TO VIBRATE...

CRUNCH!

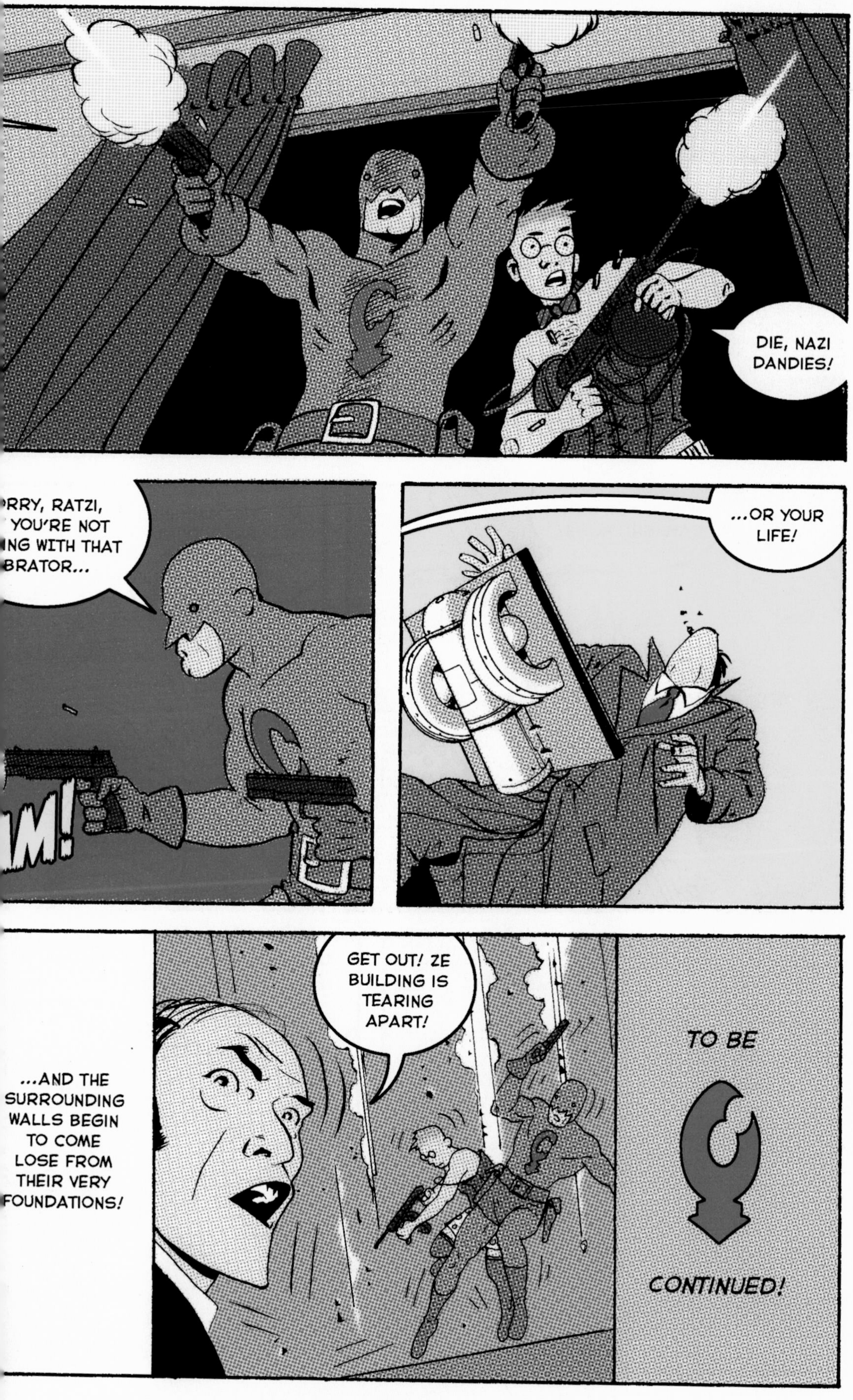
DIE, NAZI DANDIES!
RRY, RATZI, YOU'RE NOT NG WITH THAT BRATOR...
...OR YOUR LIFE!
AM!
...AND THE SURROUNDING WALLS BEGIN TO COME LOSE FROM THEIR VERY FOUNDATIONS!
GET OUT! ZE BUILDING IS TEARING APART!
TO BE
CONTINUED!

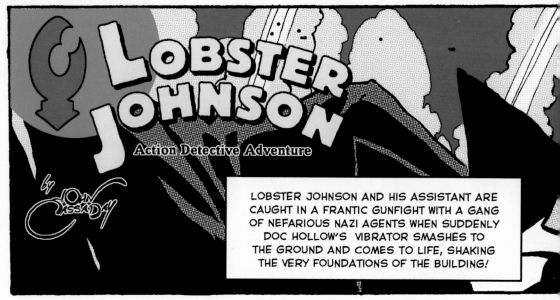

LOBSTER JOHNSON

Action Detective Adventure

by John Cassaday

LOBSTER JOHNSON AND HIS ASSISTANT ARE CAUGHT IN A FRANTIC GUNFIGHT WITH A GANG OF NEFARIOUS NAZI AGENTS WHEN SUDDENLY DOC HOLLOW'S VIBRATOR SMASHES TO THE GROUND AND COMES TO LIFE, SHAKING THE VERY FOUNDATIONS OF THE BUILDING!

FILLIN' 'EM WITH DAYLIGHT, BOSS!

NO!! THE MACHINE IS OVERLOADING! MY WORK! MY LIFE'S WORK!

POP!

JUMPIN' JUNEBUGS! HE... POPPED... LIKE A WATER BALLOON!

DON'T LOSE YOUR MOXY, CHUM. HEAD FOR THE DOOR!

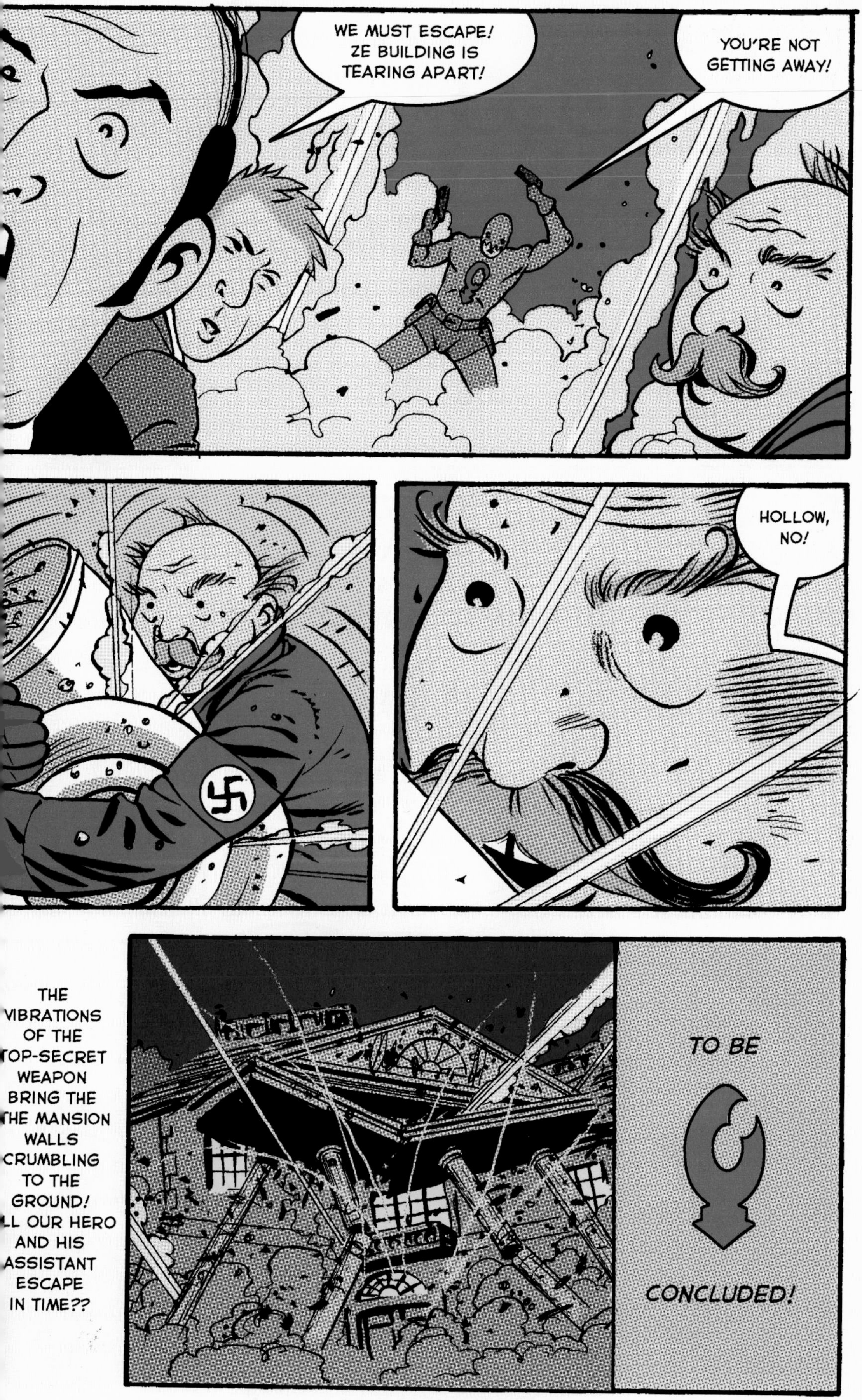
WE MUST ESCAPE! ZE BUILDING IS TEARING APART!
YOU'RE NOT GETTING AWAY!
HOLLOW, NO!
THE VIBRATIONS OF THE OP-SECRET WEAPON BRING THE HE MANSION WALLS CRUMBLING TO THE GROUND! LL OUR HERO AND HIS ASSISTANT ESCAPE IN TIME??
TO BE CONCLUDED!

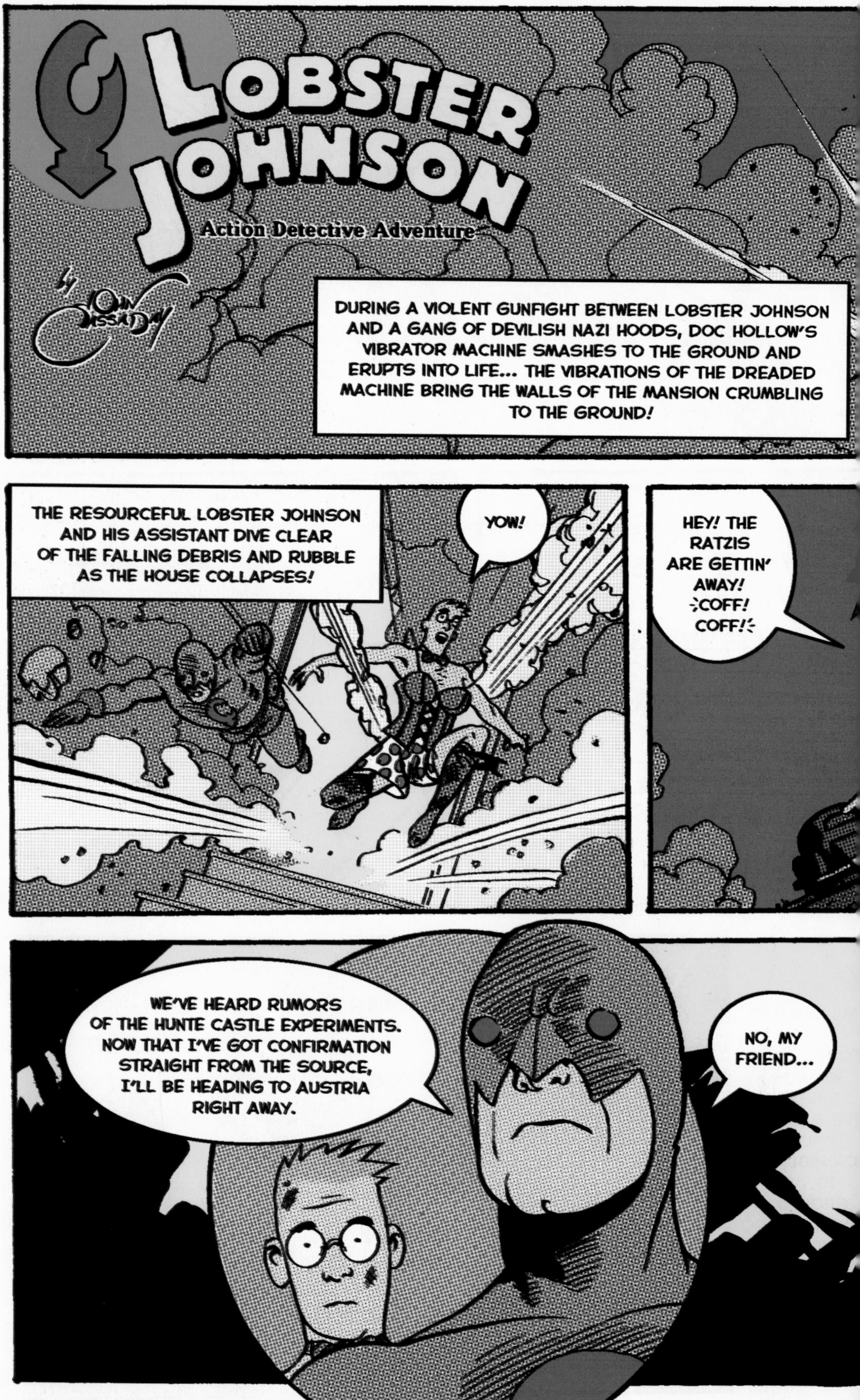
LOBSTER JOHNSON
Action Detective Adventure
by John Cassaday
DURING A VIOLENT GUNFIGHT BETWEEN LOBSTER JOHNSON AND A GANG OF DEVILISH NAZI HOODS, DOC HOLLOW'S VIBRATOR MACHINE SMASHES TO THE GROUND AND ERUPTS INTO LIFE... THE VIBRATIONS OF THE DREADED MACHINE BRING THE WALLS OF THE MANSION CRUMBLING TO THE GROUND!
THE RESOURCEFUL LOBSTER JOHNSON AND HIS ASSISTANT DIVE CLEAR OF THE FALLING DEBRIS AND RUBBLE AS THE HOUSE COLLAPSES!
YOW!
HEY! THE RATZIS ARE GETTIN' AWAY! COFF! COFF!
WE'VE HEARD RUMORS OF THE HUNTE CASTLE EXPERIMENTS. NOW THAT I'VE GOT CONFIRMATION STRAIGHT FROM THE SOURCE, I'LL BE HEADING TO AUSTRIA RIGHT AWAY.
NO, MY FRIEND...

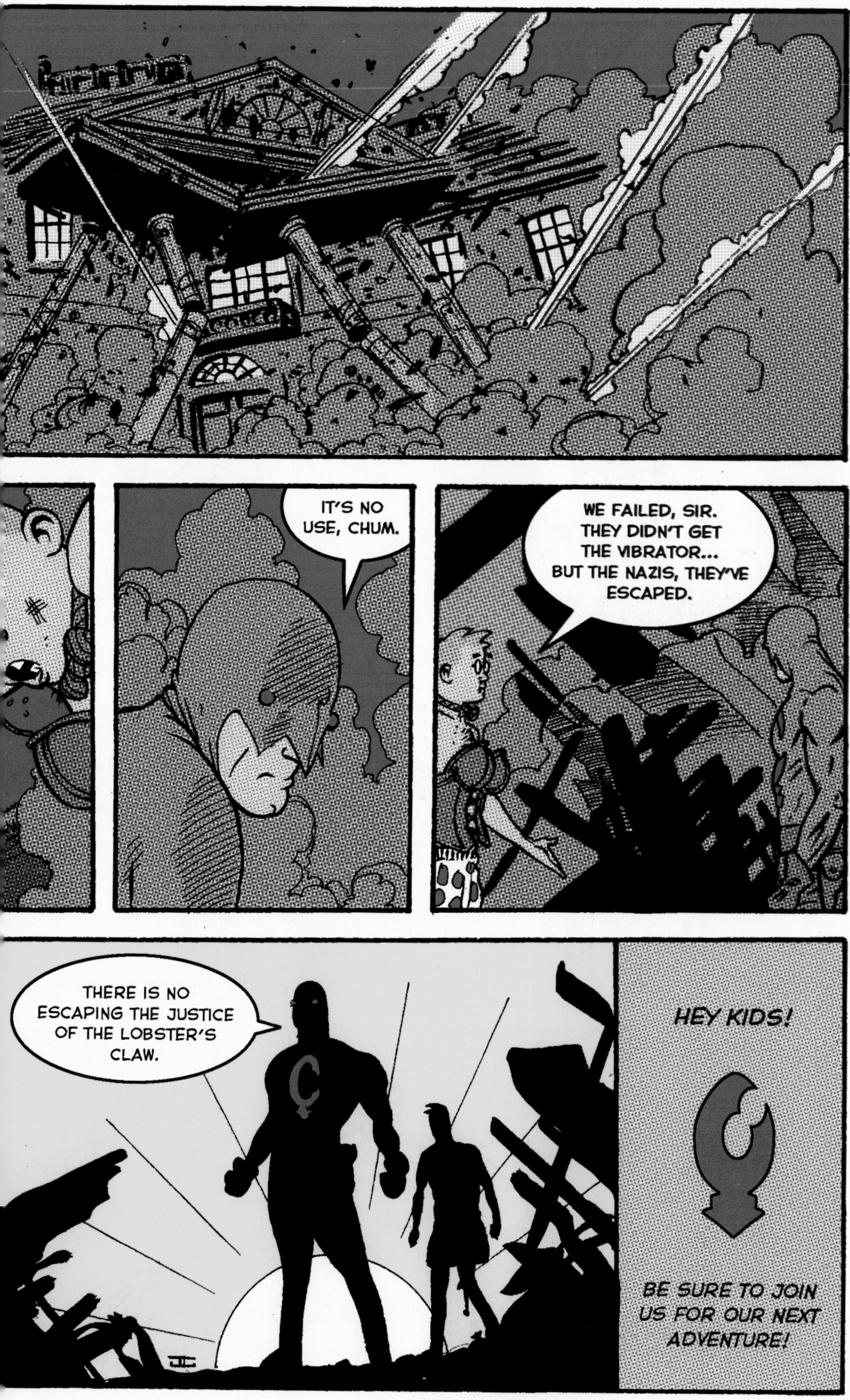
IT'S NO USE, CHUM.
WE FAILED, SIR. THEY DIDN'T GET THE VIBRATOR... BUT THE NAZIS, THEY'VE ESCAPED.
THERE IS NO ESCAPING THE JUSTICE OF THE LOBSTER'S CLAW.
HEY KIDS!
BE SURE TO JOIN US FOR OUR NEXT ADVENTURE!

HELLBOY™

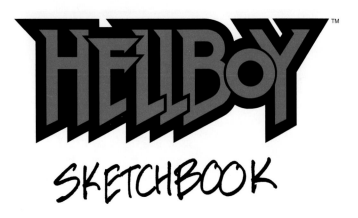

SKETCHBOOK

The following pages feature a special in-depth look at the roughs and studies of two very different *Weird Tales* artists.

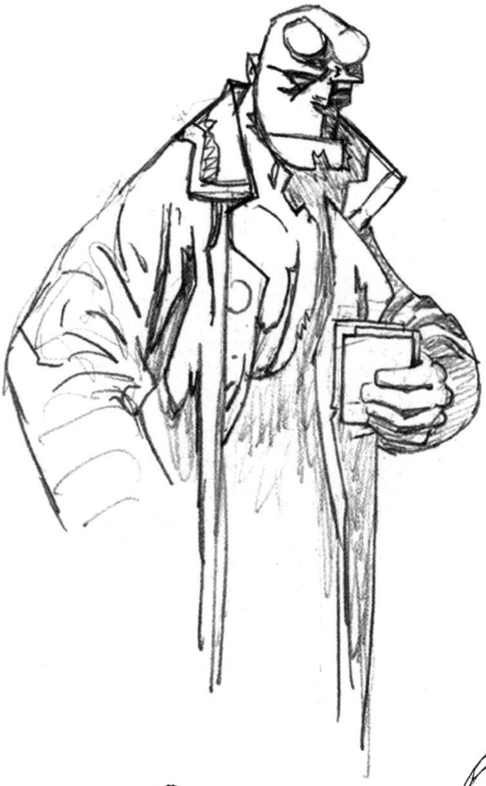

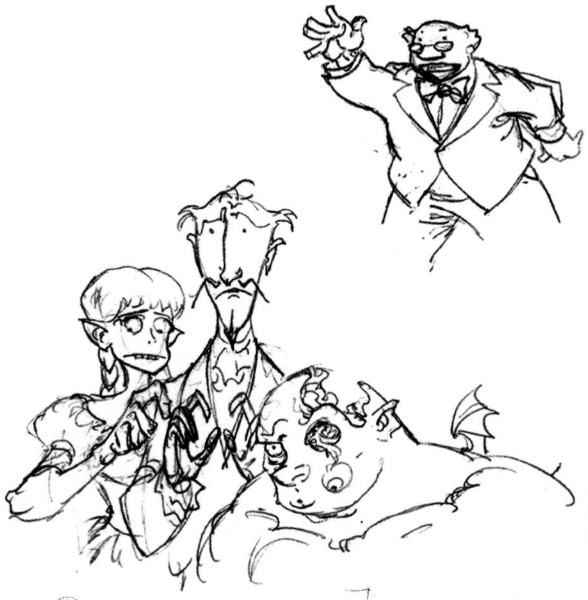

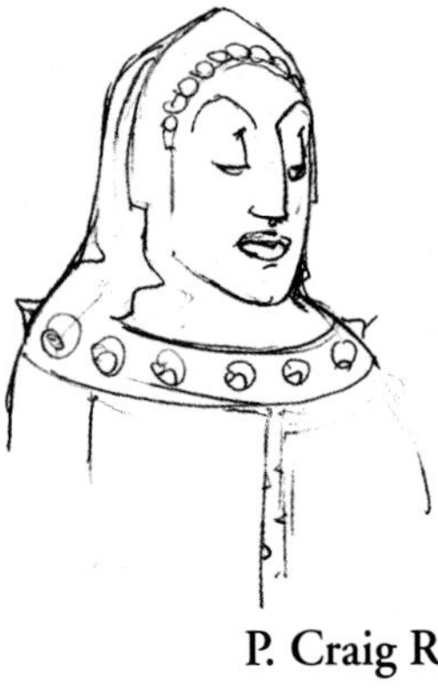

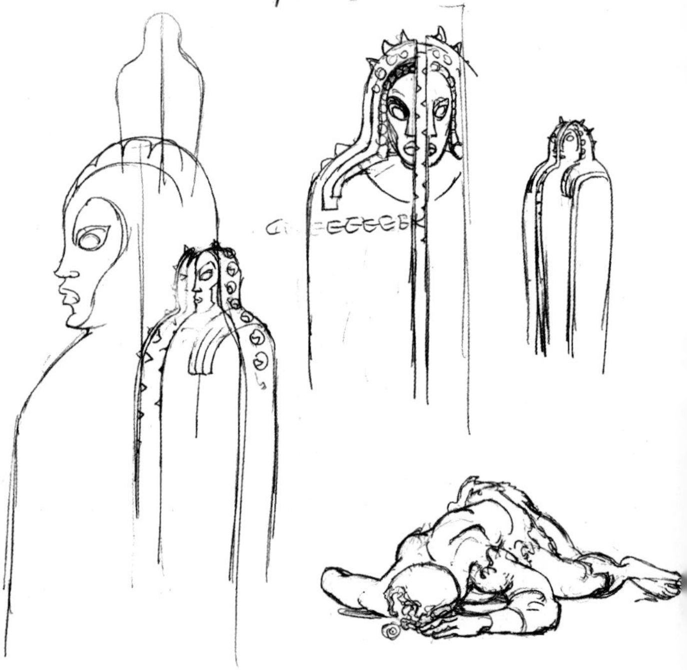

P. Craig Russell

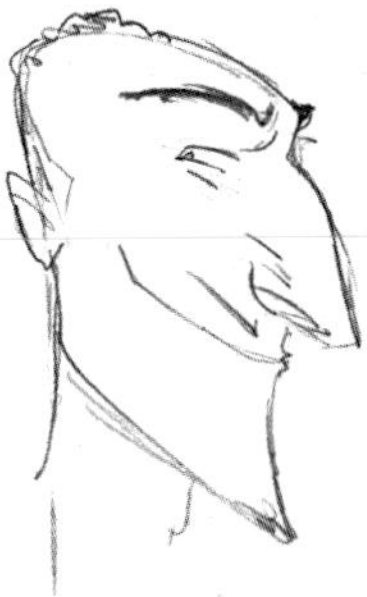

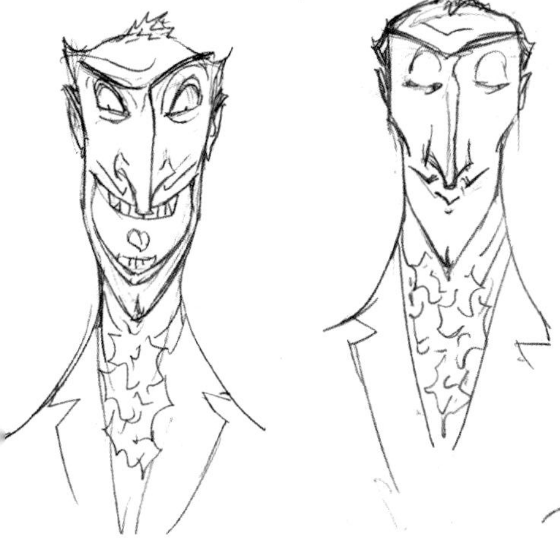

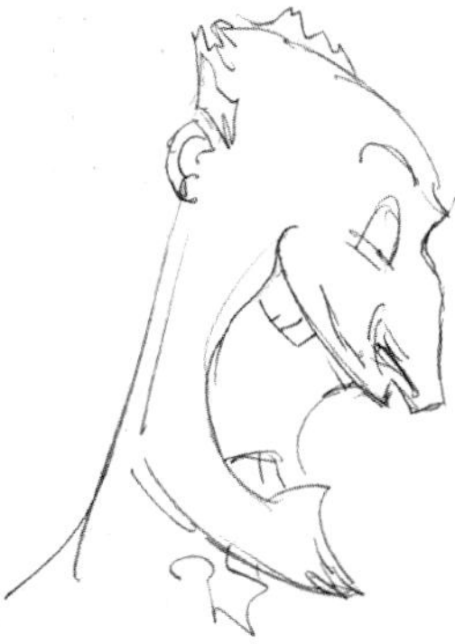

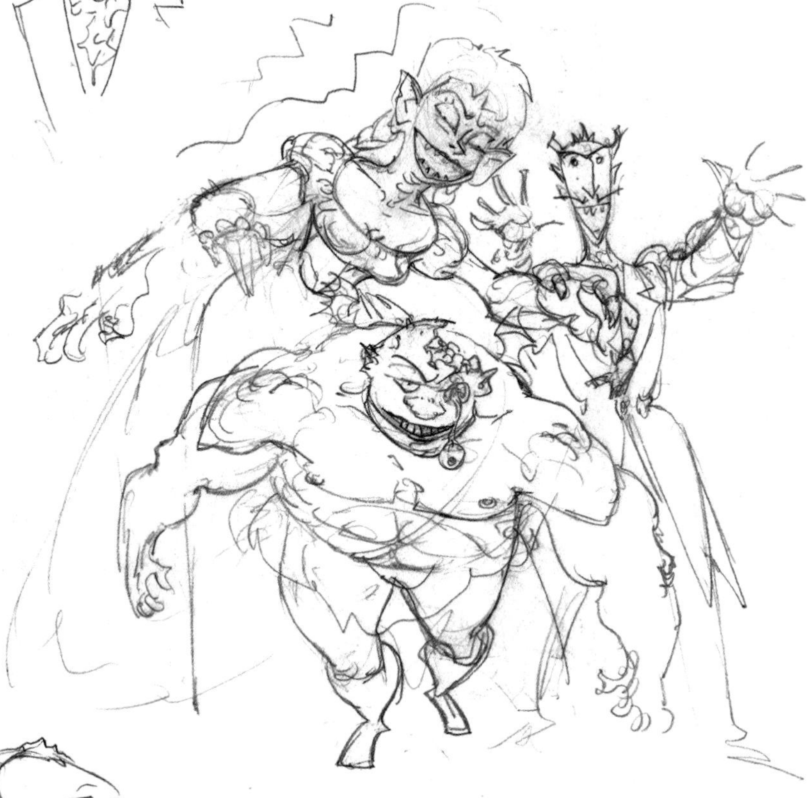

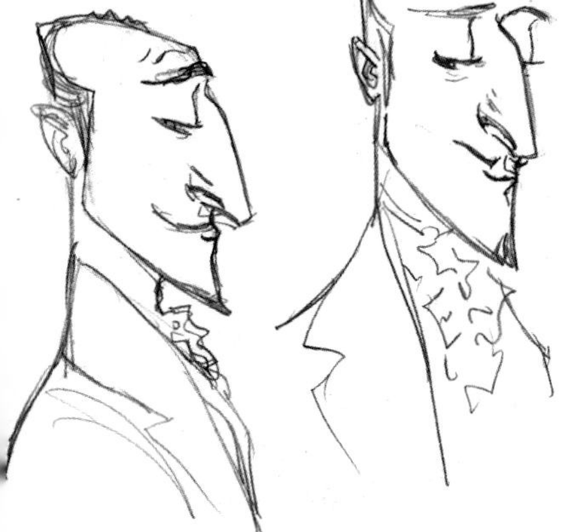

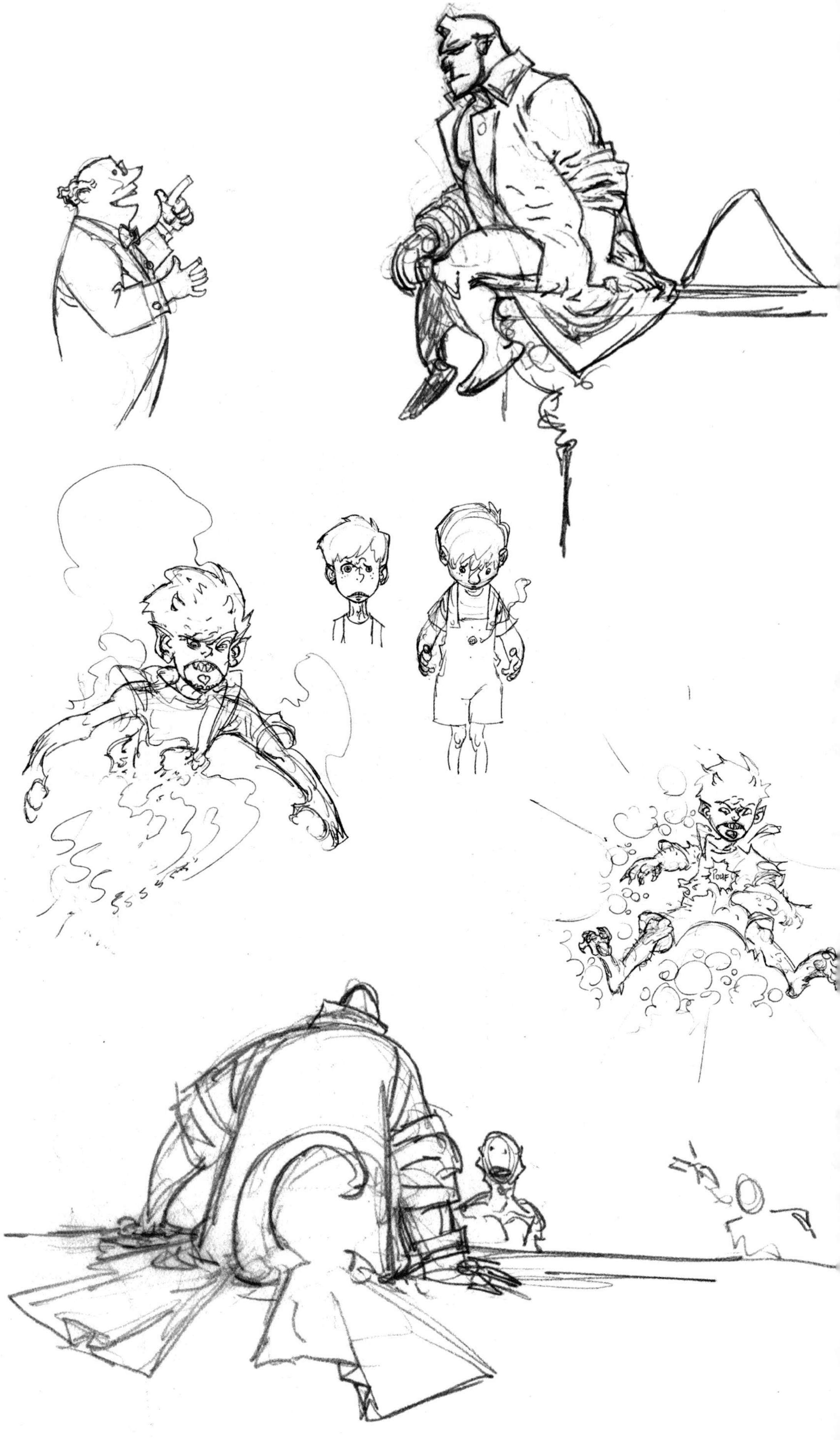
POUF

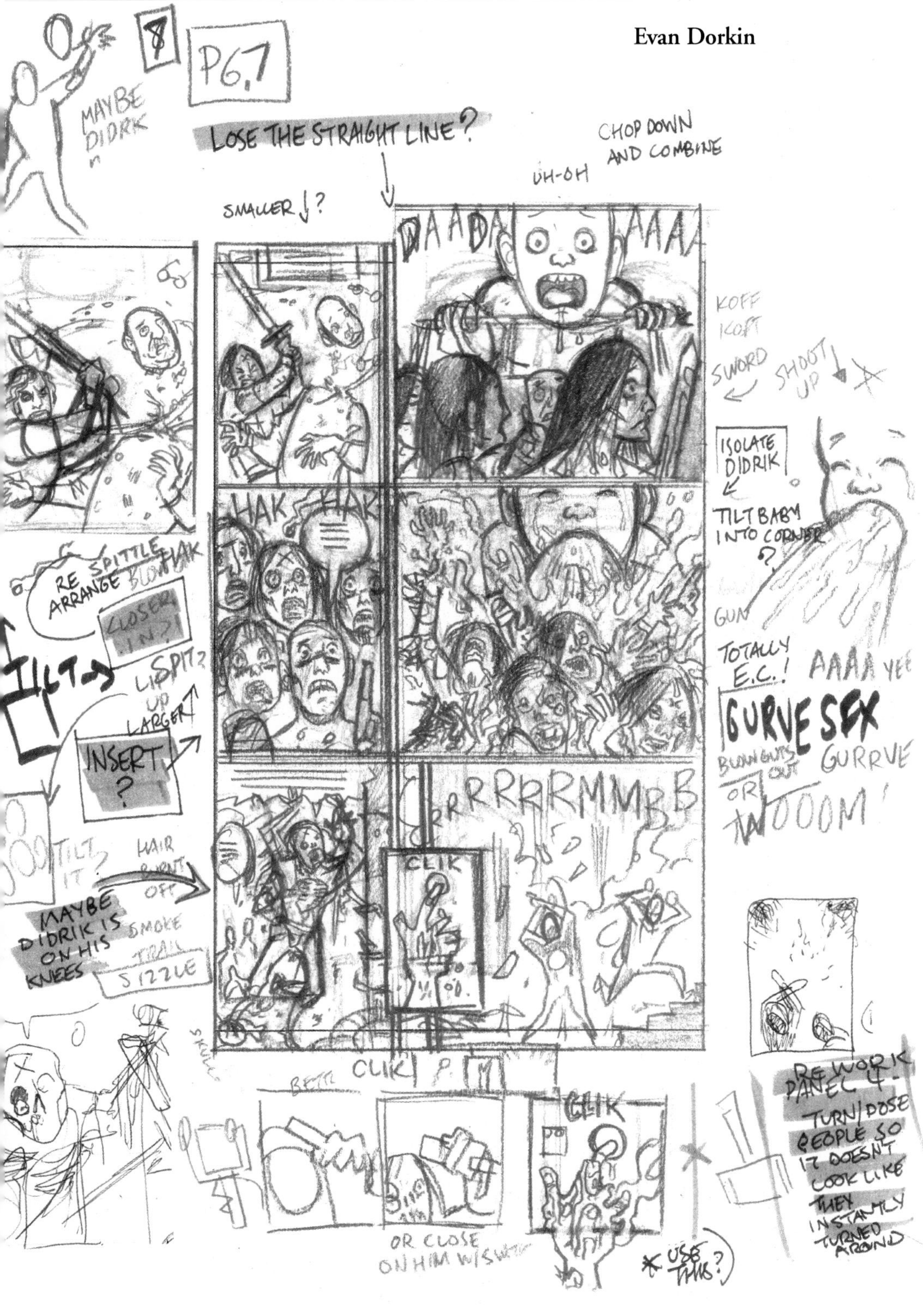
8
P6,7
MAYBE DIDRK
LOSE THE STRAIGHT LINE?
CHOP DOWN AND COMBINE
UH-OH
SMALLER ↓?
KOFF KOFF
SWORD
SHOOT UP
ISOLATE DIDRIK
TILT BABY INTO CORNER ?
GUN
HAK HAK
RE ARRANGE
SPITTLE BLOW
CLOSER IN?
TILT
LIP SPIT? UP LARGER
INSERT ?
TILT IT?
HAIR BURNT OFF
MAYBE DIDRIK IS ON HIS KNEES
SMOKE TRAIL
SIZZLE
TOTALLY E.C.!
AAAA YEE
GURRVE
BURN GUTS OUT
OR WOOOM
RRRRRMMBB
CLIK
CLIK
REWORK PANEL 4 - TURN/POSE PEOPLE SO IT DOESN'T LOOK LIKE THEY INSTANTLY TURNED AROUND
OR CLOSE ON HIM
USE THIS?

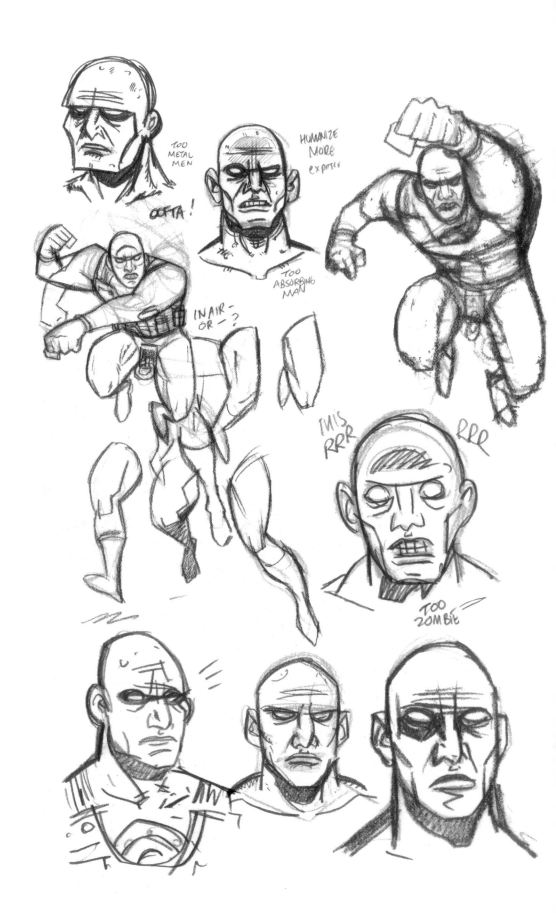

TOO METAL MEN

HUMANIZE MORE exposen

OOFTA!

TOO ABSORBING MAN

IN AIR — OR — ?

THIS RRR

RRR

TOO ZOMBIE

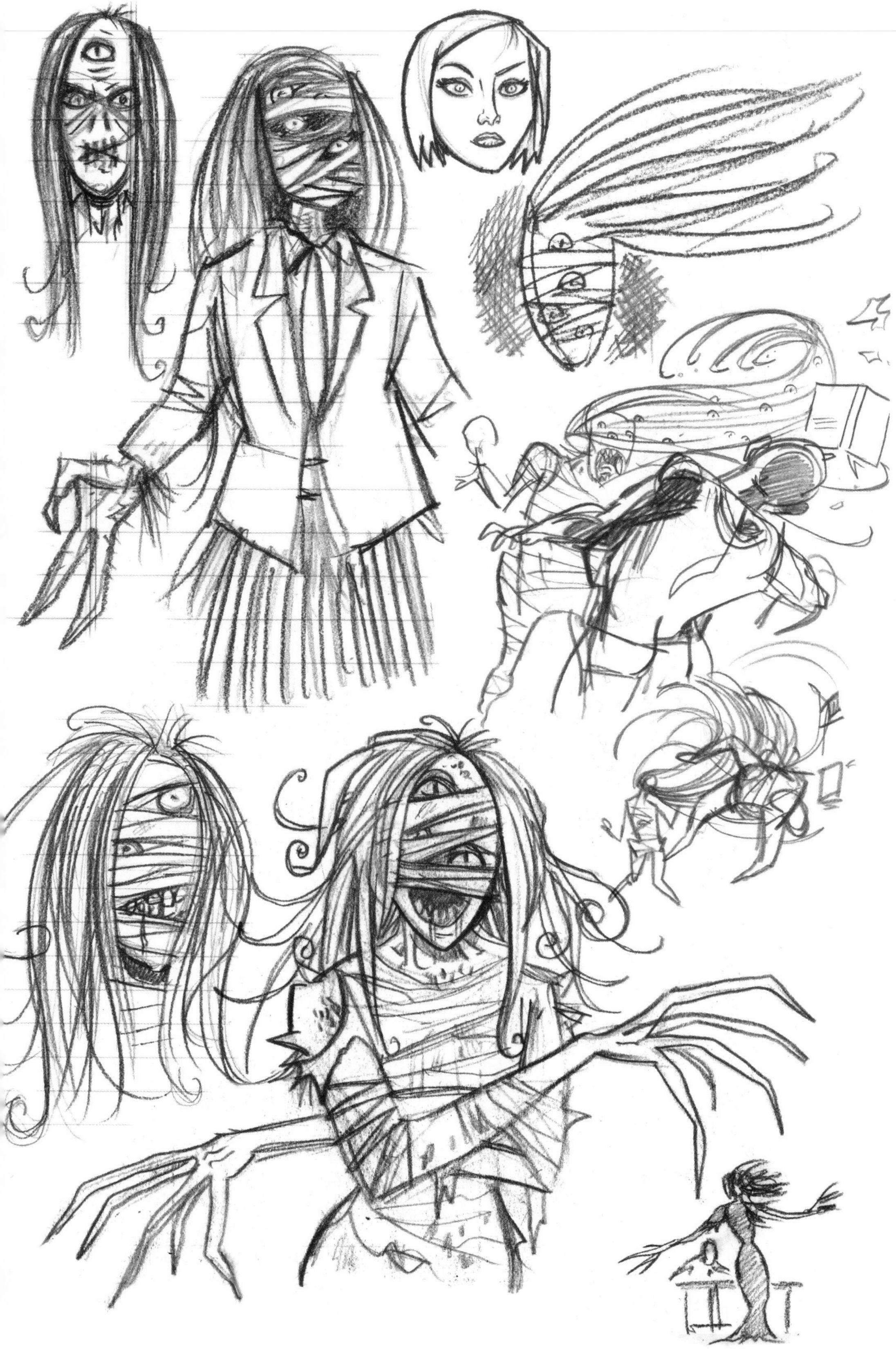

KIA ASAMIYA is one of Japan's foremost manga illustrators. Born in Tokyo in 1963, Mr. Asamiya has written and illustrated literally dozens of novel-length mangas, which are as popular with readers today as they were when they were originally issued. His work includes such classics as *Silent Moebius, Steam Detectives, Martian Successor Nadesico, Compiler, Dark Angel,* and many others. Many of his works have been adapted for animated television series and motion pictures, and his manga are regularly reprinted by publishers the world over.

LEE BERMEJO was born in Athens, Ohio, but spent the majority of his life living in Southern California. After an extended internship at Wildstorm Studios he began working on small miniseries and fill-ins for both Wildstorm and DC, such as *Superman/Gen13, Batman/Deathblow, Hellblazer, and Global Frequency.* Now twenty-six, Lee lives in San Diego and is hard at work on *Lex Luthor: Man of Steel* for DC Comics. He considers the opportunity to work on a Hellboy image to be one of the high points of his short career thus far.

W. HADEN BLACKMAN has been hunting monsters since he was five. He is the author of *The Field Guide to North American Monsters* and *The Field Guide to North American Hauntings,* along with numerous comic-book stories for Dark Horse. He is primarily nocturnal and has yet to be photographed in the wild.

JOHN CASSADAY never got to live his dream of replacing Slayer guitarist Kerry King. Still, he did become a highly respected professional comic-book artist, and that's not so bad for a long-haired kid from Texas. His works to date include acclaimed stints on *Desperadoes, Captain America,* and *Planetary.*

FRANK CHO is a self-taught artist-writer and the creator of the highly successful comic strip *Liberty Meadows.* Cho has won many awards including the prestigious National Cartoonist Society's Awards for Best Comic Book and Book Illustration, the Charles M. Schulz Award for Excellence in Cartooning, Scripps-Howard Award for Best College Cartoonist, College Media Association for Cartooning, and Germany's highest award, the Max & Moritz Medal, for Best International Comic Strip. He has been nominated for the coveted Harvey and Eisner Awards numerous times. Frank Cho currently lives in Elkridge, Maryland with his wife Cari, daughters Emily and Samantha, and their wiener dog Truman.

Bronx native GENE COLAN has been a permanent fixture in the comics industry since 1946, and now his cinematic work is often published directly from pencils. Long associated with such popular characters as Dracula, Daredevil, Batman, Howard the Duck, Captain America, Wonder Woman, Sub-Mariner, Dr. Strange, Silver Surfer, and many others, Colan is comfortable illustrating numerous genres and has taught at both the School of Visual Arts in Manhattan and the Fashion Institute of Technology. Colan currently lives in Florida with his wife Adrienne.

EVAN DORKIN is the Harvey, Eisner, and Ignatz Award-winning creator of *Milk and Cheese* and *Dork* from Slave Labor Graphics, and various Marvel, Dark Horse, and DC comics. His cartooning has appeared in *Esquire, Spin, The Onion, Mad,* and *Nickelodeon* magazine. With Sarah Dyer, he's written for *Space Ghost Coast to Coast, Superman,* and *Batman Beyond,* and created *Welcome to Eltingville,* his very own failed pilot that aired on Cartoon Network's Adult Swim block. He is currently working on his next failed pilot for them.

TOMMY LEE EDWARDS has created art and told stories all his life. He has created promotion and product art for the *Harry Potter, Men in Black,* and *Dinotopia* films, *Star Wars* children's books, conceptual and storyboard work for *Sinbad: Legend of the Seven Seas,* game packaging for Hasbro, and comics such as *ZombieWorld, Batman,* and the upcoming *Question* series from Wildstorm-DC. Currently on Tommy's desk are a series of illustrations for the upcoming film *Batman Begins,* style-guide art for *Star Wars Episode III,* and storyboards and concept art for a sci-fi military game at Electronic Arts.

TOM FASSBENDER is the author of two pulp-fiction novels, a *Buffy the Vampire Slayer* illustrated novel, and a run of *Buffy* comics—all written with Jim Pascoe. Fassbender & Pascoe also own and run UglyTown, the country's premier crime-fiction book publisher.

After graduating from the Kubert School twenty years ago, GARY FIELDS has worked for almost every major comic-book publisher, done comic strips, children's books, *Cracked Magazine,* illustration, character design, gag cartoons, and animation work. He is currently working as a staff illustrator for The Children's Place. He also works for DC Comics on their Cartoon Network books, creates gags and comics for *Nickelodeon Magazine,* and anything else he can get his hands on.

MICHAEL WM. KALUTA took his first professional art assignment in 1969 for Charlton Comics. Within four years, his stunning fantasy/adventure work earned Kaluta what would soon become his signature job—a long run on the DC Comics series *The Shadow.* In the years since, Kaluta has spanned many worlds in both illustration and comics work—from the erotic comedy of *Starstruck,* which ran as a popular feature in *Heavy Metal,* to the art-book adaptation of Thea von Harbou's *Metropolis.*

RON MARZ was dragged into the comics industry fifteen years ago by his pal Jim Starlin. Since then, he's written numerous titles, including *Green Lantern* for DC, *Silver Surfer* for Marvel, and *Star Wars* for Dark Horse. But getting the chance to collaborate with Starlin on a Hellboy story is definitely one of the highlights.

SCOTT MORSE is the author of many graphic novels and short stories, including *Soulwind* (Oni Press), *The Barefoot Serpent* (Top Shelf Productions), *Southpaw* (AdHouse Books), and *Ancient Joe* (Dark Horse). In animation, he's acted as designer, storyboard artist, writer, art director, and producer for Univeral, Cartoon Network, Disney, and Nickelodeon. He lives in Burbank, California, but would rather be backpacking in Yosemite. He knows how to get to Hanging Basket, but it's a secret worth keeping, so don't ask for directions.

PHIL NOTO's comic work includes covers for DC's *Birds of Prey,* artist on Black Bull's *Beautiful Killer,* two *Danger Girl* specials for Wildstorm, and a story for Dark Horse's *Grendel: Black, White, and Red.* Phil previously worked as an assistant animator for Walt Disney Feature Animation for ten years, where his credits included *Lion King, Mulan,* and *Lilo and Stitch.* He currently lives in Orlando, Florida with his wife, Beth.

JIM PASCOE is the author of two pulp-fiction novels, a *Buffy the Vampire Slayer* illustrated novel, and a slew of *Buffy* comics—all written with Tom Fassbender. Fassbender & Pascoe also own and run UglyTown, the country's premier crime-fiction book publisher. On the solo tip, Jim Pascoe's written several *Kim Possible* books for Disney Press.

DOUG PETRIE loves Gene Colan and doesn't care who knows it. Petrie has written and directed episodes of *Buffy the Vampire Slayer* and written screenplays for *The Fantastic Four* and *Harriet the Spy*. He lives in Los Angeles with his wife Alexa and son Henry.

After honing his skills with the small-press satire *Violent Man*, WILL PFEIFER got his big break with the Vertigo mini-series *Finals*. Other credits include *Bizarro Comics, H-E-R-O, X-Men Unlimited, Space Ghost*, and *Batman: Black and White*. He lives in Illinois with his lovely and understanding wife, Amy. And, by day, he works for a great metropolitan newspaper (really!).

STEVE PURCELL is best known as the creator of *Sam and Max*, the dog and rabbit crime-fighting duo who debuted in comic-book form in 1987, and went on to appear in a video game and an animated TV series. Steve has worked with LucasArts on video games including *Indiana Jones, The Dig, the Monkey Island series*, and *Sam and Max Hit the Road*, and currently works at Pixar.

PHILIP CRAIG RUSSELL, a graduate of the University of Cincinnati with a degree in painting, has run the gamut in comics. After establishing a name for himself at Marvel, he went on to become one of the pioneers in opening new vistas for this underestimated field. His award-winning opera adaptations include a five-hundred page, two-volume *Ring of the Nibelung* from Dark Horse, with many others, including *The Magic Flute*, currently being collected in a three-volume set from NBM, where he also continues his ongoing project retelling the fairy tales of Oscar Wilde. Russell has done several projects with Neil Gaiman, including *The Sandman* and *Murder Mysteries*, and along the way has become a highly respected artist's artist with his fine-lined, realistic style, and revolutionary storytelling.

JIM STARLIN was born in Detroit, Michigan in 1949. He served in the U.S. Navy, 1968 to 1971, as a photographer's mate. In 1972, he started his comics career at Marvel, and has been working on and off with comics ever since. Comics work includes *Breed, Captain Marvel, Cosmic Odyssey, Dreadstar, Master of Kung Fu, Thanos Quest, The End of the Marvel Universe*, and stints on almost every major character in mainstream comics.He co-wrote four novels with Diana Graziunas, and is the co-founder of Electric Prism, a software design and new-media company in Woodstock, New York.

DAVE STEVENS was born and raised in Portland, Oregon, but he still turned out okay. In the nearly thirty years since his big break inking the legendary Russ Manning on *Tarzan*, he has won extraordinary acclaim of his own for his paintings and illustrations. In 1991, Disney made his comic series *The Rocketeer* into a major motion picture.

CAMERON STEWART is one of four founding members of The Royal Academy of Illustration and Design, a comics collective in Toronto. He has drawn stories for Dark Horse in *B.P.R.D.: Soul of Venice* and *Tales of the Vampires*, written by series creators Mike Mignola and JossWhedon, respectively. He has worked extensively for DC Comics, including an acclaimed run on *Catwoman* with Ed Brubaker, and as artist and co-creator of *Seaguy* with Grant Morrison. He is indestructible when exposed to sunlight.

DAVE STEWART started out as a design intern at Dark Horse, and is now the award-winning colorist of *Hellboy* and many, many other books. In addition to coloring some of the best artists in comics, he practices kung fu, speaks

Cherokee, and raises chihuahuas, which makes him a cross-cultural triple threat in his native state of Idaho, and keeps him up most nights.

BEN TEMPLESMITH is a semi-living legend on the comic-book convention circuit. Contrary to popular mythology, Ben was not raised by dingoes and he doesn't drink *that* much tequila. He does, however, draw a great deal of comic books, which to-date include *Criminal Macabre, 30 Days of Night, Hellspawn, Singularity 7, Dark Days,* and *Return to Barrow.*

CRAIG THOMPSON was born in Traverse City, Michigan in 1975 and raised outside a small town in central Wisconsin. His first graphic novel, *Good-Bye, Chunky Rice,* won him the 1999 Harvey Award for Best New Talent along with nominations for Eisner, Ignatz, Firecracker, and Eagle awards. While working on his second graphic novel, *Blankets,* Craig paid the bills writing, drawing, and designing comics and illustrations for Dark Horse, Nickelodeon, DC Comics, Marvel, OWL, National Geographic Kids, and a myriad of other publications. He currently resides in Portland, Oregon.

JILL THOMPSON is a renowned illustrator and the creator of the award-winning, all-ages cartoon book series *Scary Godmother.* Her work has been seen in books ranging from *Classics Illustrated* and *Wonder Woman* to *Sandman.* Jill is a longtime resident of Chicago, where she lives with her husband, comic-book writer Brian Azzarello.

Before going freelance, KEVIN WALKER designed confectionery packaging for people with no imagination. His career in comics began with England's *2000 AD,* and was interrupted by a stint as Concept Artist on the *Judge Dredd* film. Other credits include designs for Game Workshops, cards for *Magic the Gathering,* several computer games, and comics written and illustrated for DC Comics, Dark Horse, and Marvel. He lives and works in Yorkshire, England, where he struggles with his first novel and the fading dreams of becoming the British Olympic sprint champion.

After receiving an MFA in Printmaking from Penn State, SIMEON WILKINS thought Hollywood the next logical step. He met Guillermo del Toro while slinging DVDs to celebrities in Los Angeles, and got his first big break storyboarding the *Hellboy* movie. Now busy boarding a CG feature for Sony Pictures, Simeon still finds time to work on comics and teach his ten-month-old son, Evan, all about giant monster movies.

J.H. WILLIAMS III is an Eisner Award-winning artist who has worked in the comics industry since 1991. He has done projects for DC, Marvel, Dark Horse, and Humanoids, among others, but his most noted work thus far is *Promethea,* co-created with Alan Moore, for Wildstorm. J.H. currently resides in California's central valley with his wife and business manager Wendy who tolerates his toy/music/comic/monster movie/Adriana Lima and Bettie Page obsessions.

AKIRA YOSHIDA has been writing and creating in the Japanese manga and anime industries for years. A long-time fan of American comic books, he prayed for the day when he would be able to break down international borders and write in the United States. With this *Hellboy* story, he sees that wish fulfilled. He credits the anime *Akira* for his success as it is the only reason

HELLBOY™

by MIKE MIGNOLA

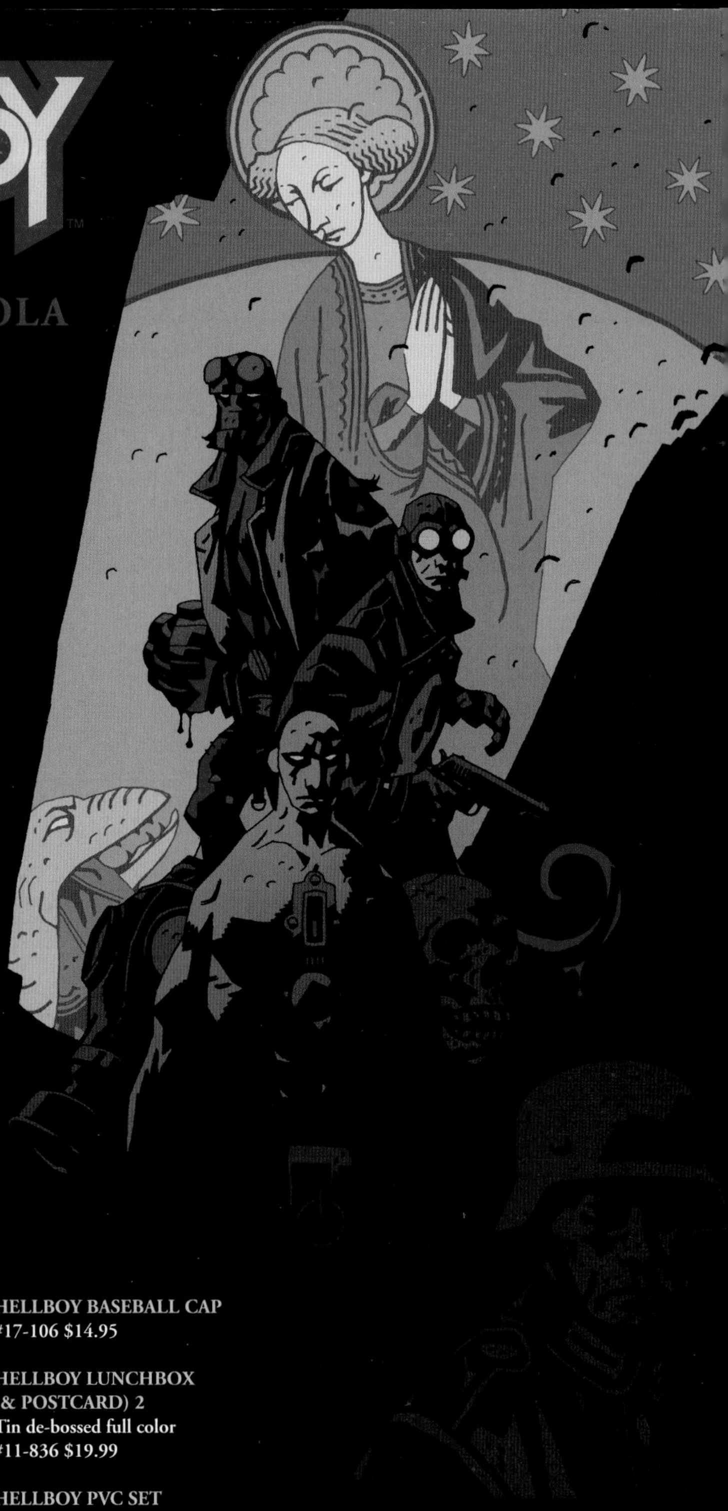

SEED OF DESTRUCTION
with John Byrne
ISBN: 1-59307-094-2 $17.95

WAKE THE DEVIL
ISBN: 1-59307-095-0 $17.95

THE CHAINED COFFIN AND OTHERS
ISBN: 1-59307-091-8 $17.95

THE RIGHT HAND OF DOOM
ISBN: 1-59307-093-4 $17.95

CONQUEROR WORM
ISBN: 1-59307-092-6 $17.95

THE ART OF HELLBOY
ISBN: 1-59307-089-6 $29.95

HELLBOY WEIRD TALES
Volume 1
By John Cassaday, Jason Pearson, Eric Powell, Alex Maleev, Bob Fingerman and others
ISBN: 1-56971-622-6 $17.95

HELLBOY WEIRD TALES
Volume 2
By John Cassaday, JH Williams III, P. Craig Russell, Jim Starlin, Frank Cho, Evan Dorkin and others
ISBN: 1-56971-953-5 $17.95

B.P.R.D. HOLLOW EARTH AND OTHERS
By Mike Mignola, Chris Golden, Ryan Sook and others
ISBN: 1-56971-862-8 $17.95

B.P.R.D. THE SOUL OF VENICE AND OTHERS
By Mike Oeming, Guy Davis, Scott Kolins, Geoff Johns and others
ISBN: 1-59307-132-9 $17.95

ODD JOBS
Short stories by Mike Mignola, Poppy Z. Brite, Chris Golden and others
Illustrations by Mike Mignola
ISBN: 1-56971-440-1 $14.95

ODDER JOBS
Short stories by Frank Darabont, Guillermo del Toro and others
Illustrations by Mike Mignola
ISBN: 1-59307-226-0 $14.95

HELLBOY BASEBALL CAP
#17-106 $14.95

HELLBOY LUNCHBOX (& POSTCARD) 2
Tin de-bossed full color
#11-836 $19.99

HELLBOY PVC SET
#10-666 $39.99

HELLBOY JOURNAL
#12-309 $9.99

HELLBOY TALKING BOARD
Pressed paper playing board with wooden planchette
#10-248 $24.99

HELLBOY ZIPPO LIGHTER
#17-101 $29.95

HELLBOY BOOKS AND MERCHANDISE CAN BE VIEWED AT www.darkhorse.com

To find a comics shop in your area, call 1-888-266-4226
For more information or to order direct:
•On the web: www.darkhorse.com
•E-mail: mailorder@darkhorse.com
•Phone: 1-800-862-0052 or (503) 652-9701
Mon.-Sat. 9 A.M. to 5 P.M. Pacific Time

DARK HORSE COMICS™ drawing on your nightmares